StoryCraft

STORYCRAFT

50 Theme-Based Programs Combining Storytelling, Activities and Crafts for Children in Grades 1–3

by Martha Seif Simpson
and Lynne Perrigo

ILLUSTRATED BY LYNNE PERRIGO

McFarland & Company, Inc., Publishers
Jefferson, North Carolina, and London

ALSO BY MARTHA SEIF SIMPSON

Reading Programs for Young Adults:
Complete Plans for 50 Theme-Related Units for
Public, Middle School and High School Libraries
(McFarland, 1997)

Environmental Awareness Activities for Librarians and Teachers:
20 Interdisciplinary Units for Use in Grades 2–8
(McFarland, 1995)

Summer Reading Clubs:
Complete Plans for 50 Theme-Based Library Programs
(McFarland, 1992)

Library of Congress Cataloguing-in-Publication Data

Simpson, Martha Seif.
StoryCraft : 50 theme-based programs combining storytelling,
activities and crafts for children in grades 1–3
p.   cm.
Includes bibliographical references and index.
ISBN 0-7864-0891-X (softcover : 50# alkaline paper) ∞
1. Storytelling.   2. Handicraft—Study and teaching (Primary)
3. Children's libraries—Activity programs.   4. Children—
Books and reading.   I. Perrigo, Lynne, 1962–   .   II. Title.
LB1042.S56   2001   372.67'7—dc21   00-67653

British Library cataloguing data are available

Manufactured in the United States of America

Cover illustrations by Lynne Perrigo.

McFarland & Company, Inc., Publishers
Box 611, Jefferson, North Carolina 28640
www.mcfarlandpub.com

To Connie Rockman and Bina Williams,
StoryCraft alumni and treasured friends.

—M.S.S. & L.P.

Acknowledgments

We would like to thank our professional colleagues and the support staff of the Stratford Library Association's Children's Department, our many teen volunteers who help us with StoryCraft sessions, and all the first, second and third graders—past, present, and future—who join us for StoryCraft each month.

We also want to thank the members of the ALSC/Econo-Clad Committee, who recognized the significance of StoryCraft and selected it for the Outstanding Literature Program Award in 1999.

Contents

Introduction:
The Origin of StoryCraft

Most libraries conduct weekly storytimes for preschool children. But once these youngsters move on to elementary school, libraries do not usually offer regularly scheduled programs for them during the school year. As children outgrew our preschool storytimes, the need for a program at Stratford Library specifically targeted to children in grades 1–3 was evident. Previously, our department had offered a monthly craft for children in grades 1–6. Although it was popular, the program was discontinued for several reasons. It was difficult to find a craft that was simple enough for a 6 year old, yet interesting to a 12 year old. Because the program was conducted by one librarian and the project was often complicated, attendance was limited to 12 patrons. We also questioned the validity of offering a library program that did not promote literacy.

After months of considering which skills we wanted these newly independent readers to achieve, we created StoryCraft, with these objectives in mind:

(a) To offer an age-appropriate program to children in grades 1–3 who have "graduated" from our preschool storytimes.

(b) To attract children to a program of storytelling and booktalking by including music, activities, and a craft.

(c) To introduce children to quality fiction and nonfiction books relating to a different theme each month via storytelling and booktalking.

(d) To train children to carefully select books that suit their own needs, interests, and reading abilities.

(e) To reinforce in children the habit of checking out library books on a regular basis.

StoryCraft, as the name implies, combines storytelling and a craft, as well as activities, music, and booktalking. It meets one Wednesday per month for one hour in the Stratford Library's program room, and can accommodate up to 40 participants. Each session revolves around a theme. The first half hour consists of a warm-up activity, a story, a participation activity, and booktalks. During the second half hour, children work on a craft that corresponds with the monthly theme. We always play an audiocassette or CD of theme-related music while the children enter the room at the beginning of the session and during the craft. Several fiction and nonfiction books on the theme are available for children to check out. More books also go on display during the month in the Children's Department beside the Story-Craft bulletin board. Two librarians conduct StoryCraft, with the help of several young adult volunteers. The program is free to the public, but preregistration is required to ensure we have enough craft materials.

Convincing children (and their parents) to rush to the library for an after-school program is not always easy. Parents' lives are hectic, and most children would rather watch TV after school than do anything remotely educational, like listening to booktalks. That is the reason for including the craft element. Kids love to create things, and parents love the things their kids create. Patrons will always flock to the library to participate in an arts and crafts program. The craft is the enticement, the honey, the dangling carrot. But before they are allowed to have "dessert," the children must attend the first half hour—the "meat and pota-toes" of stories and booktalks, interspersed with fun activities to hold their inter-est. The craft also reinforces the monthly theme, since it is a tangible reminder of the stories told and books discussed at the program.

When we started StoryCraft in February 1997, many of the children signed up because of the craft, which we had expected. Only a small number of children checked out books at the first few sessions. After we developed a core group of children and they came to expect a selection of interesting books at each meeting, more books were taken. Now children go immediately to the book display upon entering the room, before we start the opening activity. When the children finish the craft, they browse through the books again and make their selections. The titles that are booktalked are especially popular. Our Circulation Department comments that they are always swamped when StoryCraft lets out. It is gratify-ing to know that we are succeeding in our goals of training children to carefully select and check out books on a regular basis.

StoryCraft has proven to be a success at Stratford Library for several rea-sons. It is valuable to our young patrons because it connects children and books. Children are learning to recognize quality fiction and nonfiction literature and to choose books that interest them. They are developing a habit of lifelong reading. They are also discovering that listening to stories, reading books, and going to the library is fun.

StoryCraft offers opportunities for our teenage patrons. The Children's Depart-ment has a large group of young adult volunteers. Teens aid us in preparing the craft materials, pulling books, and putting up displays. During the sessions, they help us manage the children, especially during the activities. Most importantly, they provide several extra pairs of hands to assist the children with their craft pro-jects. They also help us clean up afterwards. Our library has several well-trained teens who look forward to participating in StoryCraft each month.

StoryCraft benefits the library by filling our need for a storytime-type program for children who are beginning readers. It enables us to retain the patronage of our former preschoolers and their parents. It provides an interactive and entertaining outlet for children who are developing interests in art, music, drama, and of course, reading. The program also generates good publicity in the community.

StoryCraft is one of Stratford Library's most popular programs. Although each session requires a good deal of preparation, the rewards are great for the patrons and the library alike. We think that you will have lots of fun creating your own StoryCraft sessions.

Helpful Hints

Although we schedule one hour-long StoryCraft session per month, feel free to adapt the frequency and length of the program to suit your needs. Here are several tips to keep the sessions running smoothly:

- Since the program has so many elements, it is best to have two librarians plan and conduct the sessions. Also recruit some trustworthy teen volunteers to assist with setup, crowd control, the activities, the craft project, and cleanup. With experience, you will be able to estimate how many helpers you will need for a particular session.

- Create an attractive flyer to advertise each StoryCraft theme. Keep a sign-up sheet in the Children's Department so children can preregister for the session. Limit the number of children you accept to a set number, depending upon the size of the program facility and the amount of help you have. If you offer the program once a month, or less frequently, call the children a couple of days in advance to remind them to come.

- We use lots of recycled materials to create our crafts. One of our staff members has become quite adept at storing all our collected materials. We try to plan our projects a few months in advance, so we will know what materials to gather. It is helpful to email staff about upcoming craft needs and to keep a box in the staff lounge to collect these items. We sometimes display item(s) we need for the following month's craft next to the sign-up sheet, and ask parents to donate their recyclables.

- Make a name tag (first name) ahead of time for each child. It doesn't have to be fancy; recycled paper and masking tape are fine.

- Depending on your situation, you may want to conduct the opening and participation activities, story, and booktalks in a different order from that presented here. However, always (unless otherwise instructed) save the craft for last, so the children will not be distracted from the first half of the program. Allow approximately 20 to 30 minutes for the craft, depending upon its complexity, and gauge the stories and activities to fill the rest of the time.

- If the craft is to be done in the same room as the first half of the program, do not set the craft materials on the tables before the children arrive. If you do, they will want to do the craft immediately and you will never get them to settle down for the other activities. We keep our craft materials and several plastic trays on a cart. When one librarian has the children engaged in a story or activity, the other librarian and teen volunteers quietly distribute the small decorative items into trays, and then place all the craft materials on the tables. By the time the first half of the program is done, everything is set and ready to go.

- Always take a camera to capture some exciting moments during the program. When the children have completed their craft projects, take a group picture of them holding their creations.

- Some activities suggest ideas for sing-alongs or creating songs with the children. It is a good idea to print out lyrics (in large type) and hold them up so children can see the words. You may also want to set up an audiocassette player and record their singing. Children love it when you play the song back to them.

Each StoryCraft unit includes suggestions for:

1. Bulletin Board. An attention-grabbing bulletin board will entice your young patrons to sign up for the upcoming StoryCraft session. Display several theme-related books nearby for patrons to check out.

2. Background Music. Music adds a whole new dimension to the StoryCraft experience. It draws in the participants and gives them something to listen to while they browse the books before the session begins. During the craft, it adds to the fun. And when the program is over and you have to clean up, music makes the job go by much faster. You will need about 45 minutes worth, along with a CD or audiocassette player. Music suggestions include a mix of classical selections, popular music (lots of "golden oldies"), and show tunes. We often create our own tapes of theme-related music, choosing various songs from different sources. The young adult volunteers appreciate the background music, too.

3. Opening Activity. Often, this is a song to set the mood for the session. Sometimes, we start with a dance or a discussion of the current topic to explain the event. This warm-up activity is generally simpler than the participation activity, to allow for patrons who arrive late. Text and music sources are listed for each unit under Other Resources.

4. Story. Some stories involve interaction with the children. Others require the use of simple props. And some stories are simply told without any gimmicks at all. There is at least one story suggested for each unit, and additional selections may be listed in Other Resources.

5. Participation Activity. This longer activity may take several forms. Children may be asked to make up the words to a song or story, read a play, participate in a race or group activity, play a guessing game, join in a dance, or pretend to act out a situation. Any required materials are listed. Depending on what you have planned for the session, you may want to use this activity as your warm-up, instead of the one suggested for the opening activity.

6. Craft. A list of the materials needed to complete one craft item is given. The craft instructions are divided into two parts. *Ahead of time* explains how to prepare the materials prior to the program—teen volunteers are often willing to help with this. *At the program* tells what children have to do to make the item. If assembling the craft is tricky, the directions will point out where children may need extra help. For the more involved projects, you will want to recruit more teen volunteers than usual. Many units include patterns or pictures showing how the craft item should look. Don't forget to take a photo of the children with their completed crafts (and broad smiles).

7. Suggested Booktalks. You will probably give three to six short booktalks per session, but several books are suggested. If possible, choose an assortment of different types of literature: picture books, easy readers, chapter books, nonfiction, folklore, poetry, biographies, and fun books. This last group includes collections of jokes or riddles, and drawing or craft instructions. Balance your selection of titles to expose children to a wide variety of books. Be sure to tell them that all books are available for them to check out after the session.

8. Other Resources. All stories, poems and songs mentioned in the unit are listed in this section, along with several alternate selections. Craft ideas we found in other books and magazines are cited. Suggested sound recordings to use as background music or during an activity are also included.

9. Patterns. Patterns for craft projects accompany many of the units. In some cases, they may be drawn to a smaller scale to fit on the pages of this book. Enlarge or alter the patterns as you see fit.

At the back of the book, you will find two appendices. "Recipes" includes instructions for making modeling dough, dyeing pasta, and stiffening string, which may be needed for some of the craft projects. "Resources" cites some publications we have found useful in finding crafts to make, stories to tell, and songs to record as background music.

Because each StoryCraft session requires extensive preparation, we have devised the following checklist to help you organize your program:

Before the program

- Reserve the library's program room.
- Print flyers and sign-up sheets for the upcoming session and display them in the Children's Department. You may also want to make flyers available elsewhere in the library.
- Gather fiction and nonfiction books relating to the theme.

- Set up a bulletin board and book display.
- One librarian prepares a story to tell and acquires props, if necessary.
- The other librarian prepares several booktalks.
- Gather and prepare all necessary materials for the craft. Many young adult volunteers like to cut out patterns and otherwise help in craft preparation.
- Make a sample of the craft.
- Prepare the activities to be used. Gather all necessary props, learn songs, etc.
- Find or record music to play during the program.
- Recruit several young adult volunteers (the number will change depending on the difficulty of the craft and the number of participants expected) to set up before the program, work during it, and clean up afterward.
- Two days before the program, telephone all the children who have registered and remind them to come.

On the day of the program
- Set up tables (covered with plastic tablecloths) and chairs in the program room. Make sure to leave an open area where you and the children can do the activities and sit for the stories and booktalks during the first half hour.
- Write name tags for the children.
- On a table near the entrance to the program room, place the flyer and sign-up sheet for next month's StoryCraft, along with the name tags for this day's session.
- Bring in and display theme-related books that children will be able to check out.
- Set up music equipment and other materials such as story props and a camera.
- Carry in the craft materials but do not put them on the tables yet.

During the program
- While one librarian does the opening activity and tells a story, the other librarian and the volunteers distribute the craft materials at the tables.
- Take photos of children looking at books, listening to the story, participating in the activities, making the craft project, and holding up their finished items.

After the program
- Clean up time.
- We like to keep a scrapbook of our StoryCraft sessions. Include a copy of the flyer, your program plan, craft instructions, a list of books gathered, and photos of the StoryCraft bulletin board and session.

Balloons and Bubbles

Balloons and Bubbles

Bulletin Board

Make a colorful hot air balloon of construction paper with a real basket hanging beneath it. On either side of the hot air balloon, use tape to attach bunches of real balloons to the board. Tie a piece of colorful yarn onto each balloon and gather the hanging pieces of yarn together with a ribbon tied in a bow. Add a border of bubbles cut from pale blue construction paper. Caption this bulletin board "Up, Up and Away!"

Background Music

Record popular songs such as "Up, Up and Away" (5th Dimension), "Tiny Bubbles" (Don Ho), "I'm Forever Blowing Bubbles" (Lawrence Welk), or play some light and airy waltzes.

Opening Activity

Sing "Bubblegum Blues" by Marcia Louis.
Materials: Bubble gum.
Invite the children to watch a bubble gum blowing contest and to guess who the winner will be. This activity works particularly well if you have a few teen volunteers who are willing to perform. The teen who blows the biggest bubble without popping it will be named Supreme Bubble Blower and all the contestants should get a big round of applause.

Story

Read *A Balloon for Grandad*, by Nigel Gray, *Harvey Potter's Balloon Farm*, by Jerdine Nolen, or *I'm Flying!* by Alan Wade.
Materials: Balloons.

You will be using the balloon props differently depending on which story you choose. Be creative.

Participation Activity

Explore bubbles or balloons together.

Materials: Bubble soap; bubble wand; plastic margarine containers with lids; plastic straws.

Blow some bubbles using a classic wand with a loop at the end. Let the children chase or try to pop the bubbles you blow. Give each child a pre-made "Bubbling Bubble Machine" using directions from *Better Homes and Gardens Water Wonders* so that they can blow their own bubbles. Have the children pretend to float like soap bubbles. Pretend to blow up like balloons. Let the air out fast. Blow up again and let the air out slowly. Blow up like balloons a final time and then pop.

Craft—Balloon Creatures

Materials: Large and small party balloons; markers; colored tape; colored poster board; lightweight, colored paper; self-adhesive stickers in various generic shapes such as stars and hearts; blank, self-adhesive mailing labels and self-adhesive dots in various sizes and colors; scissors; colored tape.

Procedure: Ahead of time inflate the balloons and knot them closed. Cut out feet (see pattern) from colored poster board.

At the program children should use a cutout of feet as a base for a balloon creature. Tape one or more balloons to the base or to each other to design a creature. The children can use stickers, dots, mailing labels, colored tape, and colored paper to give the creatures facial features, horns, tails, wings, etc. (or use photocopies of patterns from the "Fantastic Creatures" unit). The paper may be attached using either colored tape or stickers.

Suggested Booktalk Titles

Picture Books

Appelt, Kathi. *Elephants Aloft*. Harcourt, 1993.
Brunhoff, Jean de. *The Travels of Babar*. Random, 1934.
Calhoun, Mary. *Hot-Air Henry*. Morrow, 1981.
Duke, Kate. *Aunt Isabel Makes Trouble*. Dutton, 1996.
Lamorisse, Albert. *The Red Balloon*. Delacorte, 1956.
McGrory, Anik. *Mouton's Impossible Dream*. Harcourt, 2000.
Mahy, Margaret. *Beaten by a Balloon*. Viking, 1997.
Wade, Alan. *I'm Flying!* Knopf, 1994.
Wegan, Ron. *The Balloon Trip*. Houghton, 1981.

FEET

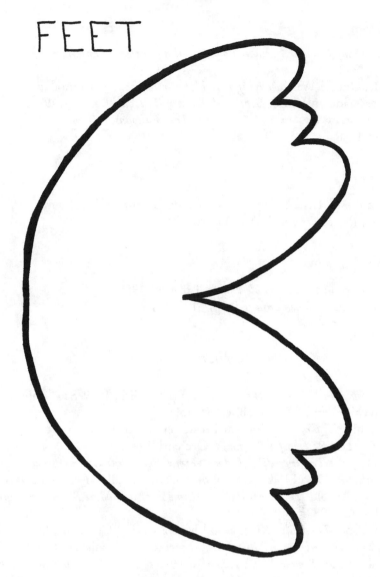

Easy Readers

Bonsall, Crosby Newall. *Mine's the Best*. HarperCollins, 1996.
Coerr, Eleanor. *The Big Balloon Race*. Harper & Row, 1981.
Edwards, Frank B. *Troubles with Bubbles*. Bungolo, 1998.
Lorimer, Janet. *The Biggest Bubble in the World*. Watts, 1982.
Woodruff, Elvira. *Show-and-Tell*. Holiday, 1991.

Chapter Books

Appelton, Victor, II. *Tom Swift and His Dyna-4 Capsule*. Grossett & Dunlap, 1969.

Nonfiction

Bell, J.L. *Soap Science: A Science Book Bubbling with 36 Experiments*. Addison-Wesley, 1993.
Bellville, Cheryl Walsh. *Flying in a Hot Air Balloon*. Carolrhoda, 1993.
Carlisle, Madelyn Wood. *Beautiful, Bouncy Balloons*. Barron's, 1992.
Hayman, Leroy. *Up, Up, and Away! All About Balloons, Blimps and Dirigibles*. Messner, 1980.

Biography

de Grummond, Lena Young, and Lynne de Grummond DeLaune. *Jean Felix Piccard, Boy Balloonist*. Bobbs-Merrill, 1968.

Just for Fun

Simon, Seymour. *Soap Bubble Magic*. Lothrop, 1985.
Wardlaw, Lee. *Bubblemania*. Alladin, 1997.

Other Resources

Better Homes and Gardens Water Wonders. Meredith, 1989. See "Bubbling Bubble Machine" and "The Bubbliest Bubblers."
"Bubble-ology." *Copycat*. Copycat Press, Sept./Oct. 1994.
Gray, Nigel. *A Balloon for Grandad*. Orchard, 1988.
Gregson, Bob. *The Incredible Indoor Games Book: 160 Group Projects, Games, and Activities*. David Lake, 1982. Contains some balloon-related activities.
Grummer, Arnold. *The Great Balloon Game Book and More Balloon Activities*. Greg Markim, 1987.
King, Wayne. *The Waltz King*. Good Music Record Company, 1985.
Louis, Marcia. *Bubblegum Blues* (sound recording). Louis Louis, 1991.
Mandell, Muriel. *Simple Science Experiments with Everyday Materials*. Sterling, 1989. Contains instructions for "Blowing Up a Balloon with a Lemon."
Nolen, Jerdine. *Harvey Potter's Balloon Farm*. Lothrop, 1994.
Paxton, Tom. *Balloon-alloon-alloon* (sound recording). Pax Records, 1987.
Sitarz, Paula Gaj. *More Picture Book Story Hours*. Libraries Unlimited, 1990. See "Balloons: Large and Small."
Sitarz, Paula Gaj. *Story Time Sampler*. Libraries Unlimited, 1997. See the "Wind, Kites and Balloons" section.
Sparks, Karen Unger, and others. *Brownie Girl Scout Handbook*. Girl Scouts, 1993. "Blow Up a Balloon" using vinegar and baking soda.
Strauss, Johann. *Waltzes* (sound recording).
Wade, Alan. *I'm Flying!* Knopf, 1994.

Beat It!

Drums

Bulletin Board

In the center of the area, put up a huge white circle ringed in yellow to symbolize a bass drum. Print the words "Beat It!" on the white space, with a mallet striking the drum beneath the caption. On either side, post pictures of various drums, including marching band and orchestra types, as well as drums from various cultures and countries.

Background Music

Play a recording of drum music (see suggestions under Other Resources).

Opening Activity

Tell the children they are going to use their bodies as drums by clapping their hands, stomping their feet, and slapping their thighs. Then play a call-and-response game with them. You play a rhythm, such as clap clap slap slap stomp, and the children have to repeat the rhythm back to you. Invent different patterns for them to imitate, making the beats progressively faster or more complex.

Story

Tell *The Cat's Purr* by Ashley Bryan, or one of the folklore selections listed below.

Craft—Coffee Can Drums

Make the drums before the participation activity, so the children can use them during that part of the program.

Materials: 12 oz. or 16 oz. coffee cans (empty) with the plastic lids; construction paper; paper strips and cutouts for decoration; feathers; markers and crayons; yarn; glue sticks; scissors.

Procedure: Ahead of time cover the outside of the coffee cans with construction paper, but not the tops or bottoms. Cut out paper decorations.

At the program let the children decorate their coffee can drums with the cut paper, feathers, markers, and crayons. Use yarn for tie-on fringe and drum harnesses.

Participation Activity

Tell the children that they will be participating in a drum circle.

Materials: Drums, assorted percussive instruments, alarm clock.

Provide an assortment of percussive items, such as bells, rattles, pots and pans to bang on, etc. The children can beat on the drums they made or play another instrument, changing items if desired. Show the children an alarm clock and set it for the exact amount of time you want the drumming to go on. Make it clear that they must stop banging their instruments when the alarm goes off (or you may never get them to stop).

Suggested Booktalk Titles

Picture Books

Coleman, Evelyn. *To Be a Drum*. Whitman, 1998.
Emberley, Barbara. *Drummer Hoff*. Simon & Schuster, 1987.
Hooper, Maureen Brett. *The Christmas Drum*. Boyds Mills, 1994.
Keats, Ezra Jack. *The Little Drummer Boy*. Aladdin, 1987.
Millman, Isaac. *Moses Goes to a Concert*. Farrar, 1998.
Pinkney, Brian. *Max Found Two Sticks*. Simon & Schuster, 1994.
Pinkwater, Daniel Manus. *Bongo Larry*. Marshall Cavendish, 1998.
Rubel, Nicole. *Conga Crocodile*. Houghton, 1993.
Siegelson, Kim L. *In the Time of the Drums*. Hyperion, 1999.
Waddell, Martin. *The Happy Hedgehog Band*. Candlewick, 1992.
Walter, Mildred. *Ty's One Man Band*. Scholastic, 1984.
Wundrow, Deanna. *Jungle Drum*. Millbrook, 1999.

Easy Readers

Benchley, Nathaniel. *George the Drummer Boy*. Harper & Row, 1987.
Diller, Harriet. *Big Band Sound*. Boyds Mills, 1996.

Chapter Books

Brill, Marlene Targ. *Diary of a Drummer Boy*. Millbrook, 1998.
Giff, Patricia Reilly. *Yankee Doodle Drumsticks*. Dell, 1992.
Price, Susan. *The Ghost Drum*. Farrar, 1987.

Folklore

Courlander, Harold. *The King's Drum and Other African Stories*. Harcourt, 1962.
  See "The King's Drum."
Lake, Mary Dixon. *The Royal Drum: An Ashanti Tale*. Mondo, 1996.
Souhami, Jessica. *The Leopard's Drum: An Asante Tale from West Africa*. Little,
  Brown, 1995.

Nonfiction

Leanza, Frank. *How to Get Started with Drums*. Crystal, 1991.
Price, Christine. *Talking Drums of Africa*. Scribner, 1973.

Other Resources

African Drums & Afro-Caribbean Grooves (sound recording). Laserlight, 1998.
Bring in 'Da Noise, Bring in 'Da Funk (sound recording). BMG, 1996. Track: "The
  Pan Handlers."
Bryan, Ashley. *The Cat's Purr*. Atheneum, 1987.
Caribbean Island Steel Drum Favorites (sound recording). Laserlight, 1996.
Jazz Club: Drums (sound recording). PolyGram, 1989.
Lark in the Morning web site, www.larkinam.com/MenComNet/Business/Retail/
  Larknet/Catalog, has lots of African drums for sale.
Orozco, Jose Luis. *De Colores: And Other Latin-American Folk Songs for Children*.
  Dutton, 1994. See "The Drum Song."

Best Buddies

Friendship

Bulletin Board

Make a border of paper dolls in brightly colored paper all holding hands.
On large pieces of construction paper mount pictures of different friends from popular children's book series such as George and Martha, Frog and Toad or Henry and Mudge. Caption this display "Best Buddies."

Background Music

Here are a few of the many songs about friendship that would work well in a recording of background music: "We Go Together" (from *Grease*), "You're My Best Friend" (Queen), "Getting to Know You" (from *The King and I*), "With a Little Help from My Friends" (The Beatles or Richie Havens), "Bridge Over Troubled Water" (Simon and Garfunkel), "Stand by Me" (The Drifters and others), and "You've Got a Friend" (Carole King or James Taylor).

Opening Activity

Sing "Glad to Have a Friend Like You" from *Free to Be ... You and Me.*

Story

Tell "The Whispering Bear" from *Aesop's Fables*, retold in verse by Tom Paxton. **Materials:** Bear puppet.

Participation Activity

Have children stand in a circle, fold their arms across their fronts and then hold hands with the two children on either side. Tell the children that they are going to pass a secret friendship squeeze from person to person all the way around the circle. The leader starts by squeezing the hand of the child to his or her right. That child then squeezes the hand of the next child who then squeezes the hand of the next child and so on. Make sure to tell children that they have to stand quietly and concentrate, squeezing should be firm and definite and no one should squeeze before it is his or her turn. The last child in the circle should announce when he or she has received the friendship squeeze. If you are working with a large group, you may wish to break up into smaller groups to make this activity easier.

Craft—Friendship Bracelets

Materials: Yarn cut into seven-inch lengths; pony beads or some other kind of large-holed beads; masking tape; liquid glue.

Procedure: Ahead of time dip the ends of the yarn into liquid glue and let dry or wrap the ends in pieces of masking tape, making sure that the result is small enough to go through holes in the beads being used. This will make it easier for the children to thread the beads.

At the program have the children tape a two-inch tail of yarn to their work surface, preferably a table. Talk about color patterns if you wish before having the children string their beads onto their yarn. Mention that a Friendship Bracelet is usually meant to be given to a friend, so the children may want to think of a friend and choose colors that they know their friend likes. Each child may string as many or as few beads as he or she likes, leaving enough free yarn at the end so that the bracelet can be tied comfortably around the child's wrist and can be slipped off over the hand. You will need to help the children with fitting their bracelets and tying them closed with two or three overhand knots. Cut off any extra yarn. If there is time, each child may make a second bracelet for themselves.

Suggested Booktalk Titles

Picture Books

Ada, Alma Flor. *Dear Peter Rabbit*. Atheneum, 1994.
Aliki. *Best Friends Together Again*. Greenwillow, 1995.
Bottner, Barbara. *Bootsie Barker Bites*. Putnam, 1992.
Cohen, Miriam. *Will I Have a Friend?* Macmillan, 1967.
Fern, Eugene. *Pepito's Story*. Yarrow, 1991.
Howe, James. *Pinky and Rex*. Atheneum, 1990. Also others in the series.
Marshall, James. *George and Martha*. Houghton, 1972. Also others in the series.
Rathman, Peggy. *Officer Buckle and Gloria*. Putnam, 1995.
Stevenson, James. *The Worst Person in the World*. Greenwillow, 1978.
Vincent, Gabrielle. *Ernest and Celestine*. Greenwillow, 1982. Also others in the series.

Easy Readers

Brandenberg, Franz. *Leo and Emily*. Greenwillow, 1981. Also others in the series.
Hoban, Russell. *A Bargain for Frances*. Harper & Row, 1970. Also others in the series.
Lobel, Arnold. *Frog and Toad Are Friends*. Harper & Row, 1970. Also others in the series.
Luttrell, Ida. *Tillie and Mert*. Harper & Row, 1985.
Rylant, Cynthia. *Henry and Mudge*. Bradbury, 1987. Also others in the series.

Chapter Books

Berrill, Margaret. *The Three Musketeers*. Raintree, 1985.
Cleary, Beverly. *Ellen Tebbits*. Morrow, 1951.
Scieszka, Jon. *Knights of the Kitchen Table*. Viking, 1991. Also other books about the Time Warp Trio.

Folklore

San Souci, Robert D. *The Faithful Friend*. Simon & Schuster, 1995.

Poetry

Grimes, Nikki. *Meet Danitra Brown*. Lothrop, 1994.

Just for Fun

McCoy, Sharon. *50 Nifty Super Friendship Crafts*. Contemporary, 1997.
Smolinski, Jill. *Girls Wanna Have Fun: Friendship Origami*. Laurel House, 1999.

Other Resources

"Circle of Friends" *Copycat*. Copycat Press. Jan./Feb. 1997.
Cook, Deanna F., ed. *Disney's Family Fun Crafts*. Hyperion, 1997. Contains an alternative method of making friendship bracelets by twisting yarn instead of stringing beads.
Fournier, Catherine. *The Coconut Thieves*. Scribner, 1964.
La Fontaine, Jean de. *The Complete Fables of Jean de la Fontaine*. Northwestern University Press, 1988. See "The Lion and the Rat."
Dallas, Patti. *Playtime Parade* (sound recording). Golden Glow, 1989.
Grunsky, Jack. *Dream Catcher* (sound recording). Youngheart, 1993.
Paxton, Tom. *Aesop's Fables*. Morrow, 1988. See "The Whispering Bear."
Raffi. *Singable Songs for the Very Young* (sound recording). MCA, 1976. Track: "The More We Get Together."

Sitarz, Paula Gaj. *More Picture Book Story Hours*. Libraries Unlimited, 1990. See "Getting Together: Stories About Friends."

Thomas, Marlo, et al. *Free to Be ... You and Me* (sound recording). Arista, 1972.

Thomas, Marlo, et al. *Free to Be ... You and Me*. McGraw-Hill, 1974. See "Glad to Have a Friend Like You."

The Big Meow

Wildcats

Bulletin Board

Construct a larger version of the Krazy Kat craft detailed below or post pictures of lions, tigers, panthers, leopards, and other wild felines. Caption the bulletin board "Wild, Wild Cats!"

Background Music

Record "The Lion Sleeps Tonight" (various artists), "The Tiger" (Greg Brown), "Lions and Tigers and Bears" (from *The Wizard of Oz*), "Wimoweh" (*Red Grammer's Favorite Sing Along Songs*), or play the soundtrack from Disney's *The Lion King*.

Opening Activity

Use William Blake's poem "The Tyger" as a call and response poem. Teach the children to recite the first verse of the poem. The librarian then reads the poem aloud and the whole group chants the first verse as a refrain between each verse of the poem.

Story

Tell "The Lion on the Path" from *The Story Vine*, by Anne Pellowski.
Materials: An African thumb piano (see Other Resources).

There are many other folk tales about wildcats. You may wish to use a well-known fable from Aesop such as "Androcles and the Lion" or "The Lion and the Mouse." Or use something that is less well known such as *Nine in-One, Grr! Grr! A Folktale from the Hmong People of Laos*, a tiger story by Blia Xiong.

Participation Activity

Hold a Wildcat Milk Cap Toss.
Materials: Plastic caps from plastic milk or juice jugs; poster board; paints or markers; craft knife.

Before the program, draw or paint the faces of a leopard, a lion, and a tiger onto two large pieces of poster board. At each cat's mouth, cut an open–mouth–shaped hole that is large enough for plastic milk caps to pass through when they are thrown from a short distance away. Divide the children into two teams and have them name their teams after types of wildcat—suggest Lynxes and Bobcats, for instance—and give each child three milk caps. Allow the children to take turns tossing milk caps into the mouths of the cats. Whichever team gets the most milk caps through the mouths of the wildcats wins.

Craft—Krazy Kat

Materials: Poster board; single-hole punch; crayons, markers or colored pencils; two brass fasteners.
Procedure: Ahead of time cut out poster board into wildcat body, head, legs, and tail (see patterns). Punch holes where indicated.

At the program explain to the children that they are going to create a brand new type of wildcat. They may, for example, want to draw leopard spots on the legs and tiger stripes on the body and give it a black panther's tail. Remind them about white tigers and snow leopards. After the children have finished coloring

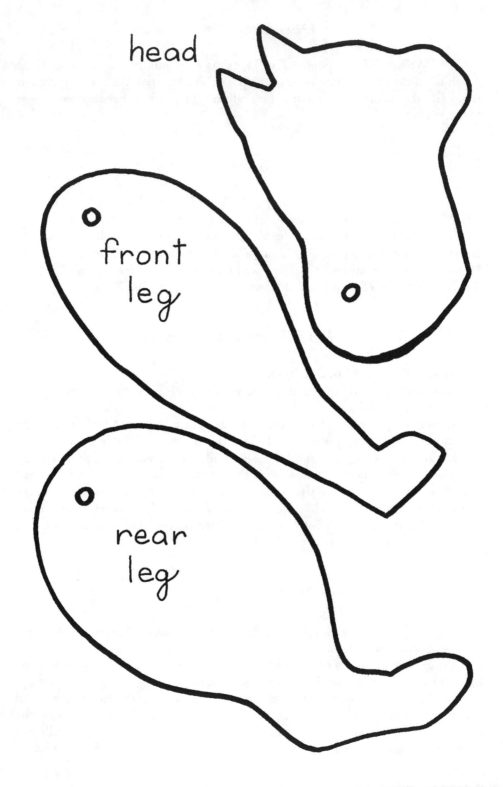

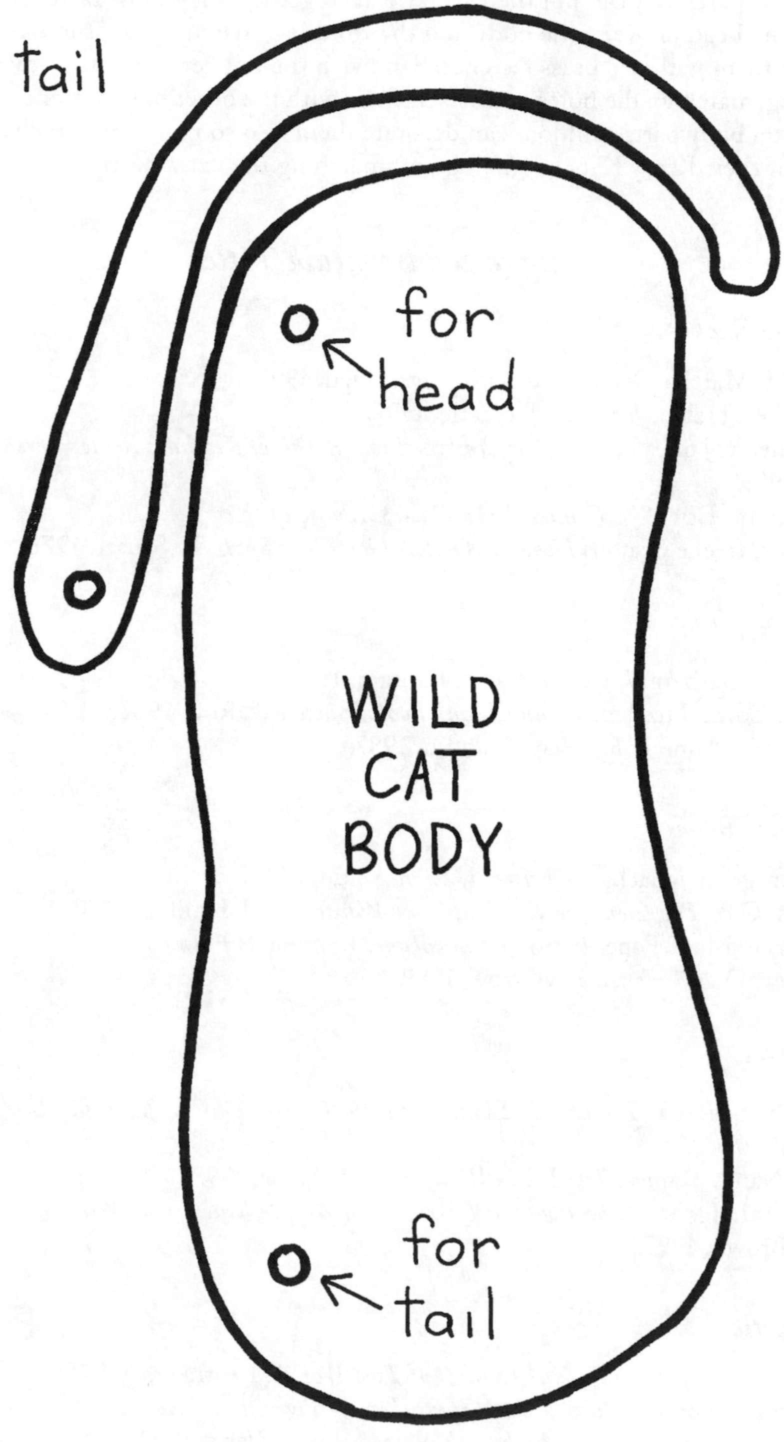

tail

for
head

WILD
CAT
BODY

for
tail

the body parts they can put their Krazy Kats together using brass fasteners. Sandwich the head between the body and the front leg, match up the three holes and attach them with one brass fastener. Sandwich the tail between the body and the rear leg, match up the holes and attach them with the other brass fastener. If there are extra body parts, children can decorate them also so that they can change the look of their Krazy Kats by mixing and matching the extra parts.

Suggested Booktalk Titles

Picture Books

Arnold, Marsha Diane. *Heart of a Tiger*. Dial, 1995.
Cowcher, Helen. *Jaguar*. Scholastic, 1997.
Daugherty, James Henry. *Andy and the Lion: A Tale of Kindness Remembered*. Puffin, 1989.
Rohmann, Eric. *The Cinder-Eyed Cats*. Crown, 1997.
Wicker, Ireene Seaton. *How the Ocelots Got Their Spots*. L. Stuart, 1976.

Easy Readers

Brenner, Barbara. *Lion and Lamb*. Bantam, 1989.
Hurd, Edith Thacher. *Johnny Lion's Book*. Harper & Row, 1965.
Rockwell, Anne F. *Big Boss*. Aladdin, 1987.

Chapter Books

Morpurgo, Michael. *The Butterfly Lion*. Viking, 1997.
Lewis, C.S. *The Lion, the Witch and the Wardrobe*. Macmillan, 1950.
Osborne, Mary Pope. *Lions at Lunchtime*. Random, 1998.
Stanley, Diane. *Fortune*. Morrow, 1989.

Folklore

Aardema, Verna. *The Lonely Lioness and the Ostrich Chicks: A Masai Tale*. Knopf, 1996.
Day, Nancy Raines. *The Lion's Whiskers*. Scholastic, 1995.
Souhami, Jessica. *The Leopard's Drum: An Asante Tale from West Africa*. Little, Brown, 1995.

Nonfiction

Adamson, Joy. *Born Free: A Lioness of Two Worlds*. Pantheon, 1987.
Cajacob, Thomas. *Close to the Wild: Siberian Tigers in a Zoo*. Carolrhoda, 1986.
Hilker, Cathryn Hosea. *A Cheetah Named Angel*. Watts, 1992.

Hodge, Deborah. *Wild Cats: Cougars, Bobcats and Lynx*. KidsCan, 1997.
Ryden, Hope. *Your Cat's Wild Cousins*. Lodestar, 1991.

Other Resources

Blake, William. *The Tyger*. Harcourt, 1993. Or find the poem in any edition of Blake's *Songs of Innocence and Experience*.
Brown, Marcia. *Once a Mouse: A Fable Cut in Wood*. Scribner, 1961.
Galdone, Paul. *Androcles and the Lion*. McGraw-Hill, 1970.
Harris, Franklin W. *Great Games to Play with Groups: A Leader's Guide*. Fearon, 1990. See "El Tigre, la Persona, y la Camara" (The Tiger, the Man, and the Camera).
Herman, Gail. *The Lion and the Mouse*. Random, 1998.
John, Elton, and Tim Rice. *The Lion King* (sound recording). Walt Disney, 1994.
Leach, Maria. *The Lion Sneezed: Folktales and Myths of the Cat*. Crowell, 1977.
Pellowski, Anne. *The Story Vine: A Source Book of Unusual and Easy-to-Tell Stories from Around the World*. Macmillan, 1984. See "The Lion on the Path."
Royds, Caroline, ed. *The Animal Tale Treasury*. Putnam, 1986. See "The Lion and the Mouse."
Sierra, Judy. *Multicultural Folktales: Stories to Tell Young Children*. Oryx, 1991. See "The Lion and the Mouse."
Stevens, Janet. *Androcles and the Lion: An Aesop Fable*. Holiday House, 1989.
Xiong, Blia. *Nine in-One, Grr! Grr! A Folktale from the Hmong People of Laos*. Children's Book Press, 1989.

African thumb pianos or gourd pianos (also known as kalimba, mbira, likembe, marimbula and other names) are commonly sold in gift shops that specialize in African imports, especially UNICEF or museum shops. Check in the Yellow Pages for local music stores. Two companies that sell lots of folk instruments, including thumb pianos, are Catania Folk Instruments at www.netstuff.com/catania and Lark in the Morning at www.larkinam.com.

Blast Off!

Outer Space

Bulletin Board

On a navy blue background, tack up pictures of the planets in our solar system circling the sun. At the far right and left, add pictures of galaxies and constellations. Hang 3-D models of rocket ships or flying saucers above the book display. Caption: Blast Off with Books!

Background Music

Play the soundtrack from *Star Wars* or another space themed movie. *The Planets* by Gustav Holst is a good classical choice. Or, play a compilation of music such as "Fly Me to the Moon" (Frank Sinatra), "Rocket Man" (Elton John), and other popular tunes.

Opening Activity

The children can help write the words to a new song, "I'm Blasting into Space Today," developed by Martha Simpson.

Materials: Large art pad, easel, markers.

Ask children to name some things they might see on a voyage into outer space. Write down one item for each letter of the alphabet. For example: alien, Big Dipper, crater, etc. When the list is complete, sing the following introduction and the alphabetical list to the tune of "Twinkle, Twinkle Little Star."

> *I'm blasting into space today*
> *To see new worlds so far away*
> *As I leave the Earth behind*
> *Here's a list of what I find:*
> (sing items on your list)

Story

Keepers of the Night by Michael J. Caduto and Joseph Bruchac is a compilation of Native American folktales. Stories about astronomy include "Oot-Kwah-Tah, the Seven Star Dancers," "The Creation of the Moon," and "How Grizzly Bear Climbed the Mountain." The book also contains related activities.

Participation Activity

Tell children to pretend they are going on a voyage to the moon and other planets. First, they will mime putting on their space suits. Next, have them squat on the floor, to simulate a rocket at the launch pad. You are the commander at Mission Control. Slowly, lead them through the countdown, from "T-minus 10" to "zero, ignition, blast off." At "blast off," the children will jump up and zoom around the room. Then tell the children they have landed on the moon and are going to walk on the surface. Explain that there is less gravity on the moon than on Earth, so they will bounce with each step. Let them practice moon-hopping and gathering moon rocks. Then, have children blast off again to visit Jupiter. Here, the gravity is much stronger than on Earth, so it is more difficult to walk. Now they should drag their feet and walk very slowly. What do they think the atmosphere of Jupiter is like? If you want, you can have them pretend to visit other planets, get tossed around while passing through the asteroid belt, experience a storm on Mars, and have other space adventures before they splash down in the Atlantic Ocean on their return to Earth.

Craft—NASA Rockets

Materials: Toilet paper tube; construction paper; small half circle of sturdy colored paper and a larger half-circle of construction paper (see patterns); small strips of paper with *NASA* printed in red or blue; small pieces of paper cut into triangles, crescents, and other shapes; stick-on dots and stars in assorted colors; glitter; glue stick; liquid glue poured in a tray; markers; scissors.

Procedure: Ahead of time, cover toilet paper tube with construction paper and cut two one-and-a-half-inch slits opposite each on one end, where the fins will be inserted. Fold and glue the larger construction paper half circle into a cone.

At the program, children can use the glue sticks to decorate the cone, tube, and fin with the other materials. Place the fin (small half circle) into slits so that the tube will stand upright. Dip the edge of the tube that does not have the fin into the tray of liquid glue, then place the cone on top so it will stick.

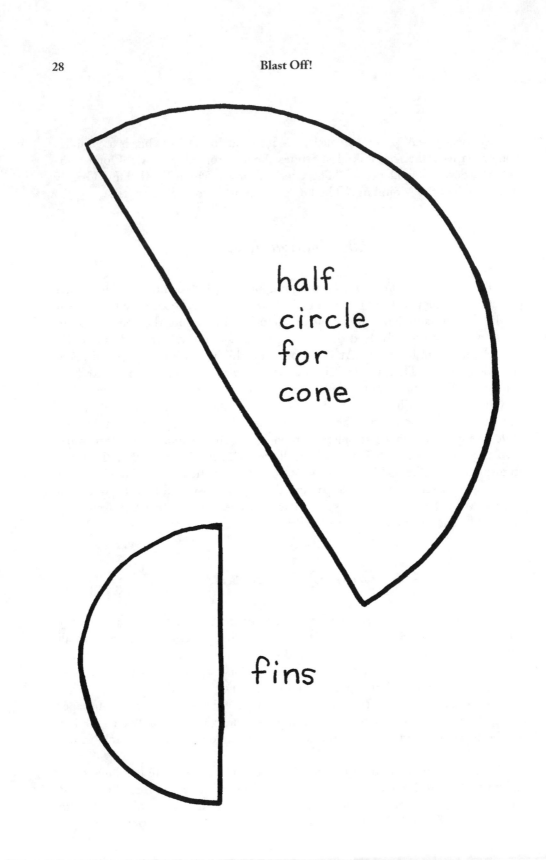

half
circle
for
cone

fins

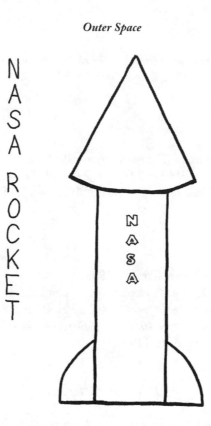

Suggested Booktalk Titles

Picture Books

Agee, Jon. *Dmitri, the Astronaut.* HarperCollins, 1996.
Sadler, Marilyn. *Alistair and the Alien Invasion.* Simon & Schuster, 1994.

Easy Reader

Yolen, Jane. *Commander Toad in Space.* Coward, 1980. Also others in series.

Chapter Books

Osborne, Mary Pope. *Midnight on the Moon.* Random, 1996.
Pilkey, Dav. *Captain Underpants and the Invasion of the Incredibly Naughty Cafeteria Ladies from Outer Space.* Scholastic, 1999.
Slote, Alfred. *My Trip to Alpha I.* Lippincott, 1978.

Nonfiction

Branley, Franklyn. *Floating in Space.* HarperCollins, 1998.
Cannat, Guillaume. *Be Your Own Astronomy Expert.* Sterling, 1996.

Cole, Joanna. *The Magic School Bus: Lost in the Solar System*. Scholastic, 1990.

Simon, Seymour. *Comets, Meteors, and Asteroids*. Morrow, 1994. Also, Simon's other books about planets, etc.

Biographies

Hanson, Rosanna. *Astronauts Today*. Random, 1998.

Kramer, Barbara. *Neil Armstrong: The First Man on the Moon*. Enslow, 1997.

Vogt, Gregory. *John Glenn's Return to Space*. Millbrook, 2000. Also other titles by this author.

Just for Fun

Biddle, Steve. *Planet Origami*. Barrons, 1998.

Blocksma, Mary, and Dewey Blocksma. *Space-Crafting*. Prentice Hall, 1986.

Keller, Charles. *Astronuts: Space Jokes and Riddles*. Prentice Hall, 1985.

Wiese, Jim. *Cosmic Science: Over 40 Gravity-Defying, Earth-Orbiting, Space-Cruising Activities for Kids*. Wiley, 1997.

Other Resources

Caduto, Michael J., and Joseph Bruchac. *Keepers of the Night: Native American Stories and Nocturnal Activities for Children*. Fulcrum, 1994. See "Oot-Kwah-Tah, the Seven Star Dancers," "The Creation of the Moon," and "How Grizzly Bear Climbed the Mountain."

Holst, Gustav. *The Planets* (sound recording).

"Lift-Off to Learning." *Copycat*. Copycat Press, Sept./Oct. 1995.

"The Night Sky." *Copycat*. Copycat Press, Nov./Dec. 1995.

Rovin, Jeff. *Aliens, Robots, and Spaceships*. Facts on File, 1995.

Sitarz, Paula Gaj. *More Picture Book Story Hours*. Libraries Unlimited, 1990. See "To the Moon."

The Starlite Orchestra. *Space Trax: The Best from Science Fiction Movies & TV*. Madacy Entertainment, 1997.

Symphonic Star Trek: Music of the Motion Pictures and Television Series (sound recording). Telarc, 1996.

Williams, John. *Star Wars Soundtrack* (sound recording). 20th Century, 1977.

Bon Voyage!

Travel

Bulletin Board

Use old maps for a background and a series of large compasses for a border. Make a mock suitcase from a large, flat box. Cover the suitcase with travel stickers representing various exotic places (stickers can be made from construction paper or pictures cut from travel magazines). Position the suitcase to one side of the bulletin board and secure it so that it is partially open. Have some real clothes tumbling out of the suitcase. Create a trail of construction paper clothes and other travel accouterments (binoculars, camera, maps, books, etc.) strewn across the length of the bulletin board. Let your imagination run wild and include some wacky items as well (maybe a pink flamingo!). Fill the empty space with the caption "Bon Voyage!"

Background Music

Play a compilation of traveling songs such as "Oh, Susanna" (James Taylor), "Roam" (B-52s), "On the Road Again" (Willie Nelson), "Ease on Down the Road" (from *The Wiz* soundtrack), "Sentimental Journey" (Dinah Shore or Doris Day), "Shuffle Off to Buffalo" (from *42nd Street*), "Side by Side" (Kay Starr or Mitch Miller), or "Travelin' Prayer" (Billy Joel), or play the soundtrack from the film *Around the World in Eighty Days*.

Opening Activity

Sing "The Happy Wanderer (Valderi, Valdera)." The words to this cheerful song vary in the different English translations, but the "Valdera hahaha haha" in the refrain always sounds like laughter. A great song!

Story

Tell *Traveling to Tondo: A Tale of the Nkundo of Zaire*, retold by Verna Aardema.

Materials: Flannel board; flannel board characters created as described in the craft below (the storyteller should use larger figures than the ones the children create for their craft).

Before telling this story, tell the children to watch how you use the flannel board characters to illustrate the action in the story. Later, the children will be creating their own flannel board characters and learning how to tell the story themselves.

Participation Activity

Play Alphabet Countries.

Hand out 26 books about countries to represent each letter of the alphabet. Make sure each book is colorfully illustrated. Give the children a few minutes to flip through the books. Starting with a child who has a book about a country whose name starts with the letter "A," have each child show an interesting picture from that country. Continue through the alphabet until you reach "Z."

Craft—Traveling Storyteller Flannel Board

Materials: Legal-size file folder; translucent paper; card stock; black flannel (flannel is less expensive if bought by the yard off a large bolt); white interfacing (nonwoven, nonfusible, medium to heavy weight—also available by the yard); pencil; colored markers; medium-tip black permanent marker; glue stick; sharp scissors; ribbon; clear tape.

Procedure: Ahead of time use a pencil and translucent paper to trace characters from Verna Aardema's book *Traveling to Tondo*. On the paper, outline the figures and their most prominent features with black marker. Use a photocopier to reduce the size of the figures so that they are small enough to fit within 8.5" × 14" all together (you may need to eliminate some detail to keep the outlines of the figures clear.) Trace a set of characters onto a piece of interfacing. With your sharp scissors, cut a shape such as an oval or a rectangle around each character so that the characters are separate from each other. Cut the flannel into pieces measuring 8.5" × 14". Cut card stock into 2" × 11" wide strips.

At the program have the children hold the file folder horizontally. Glue the flannel to the top half of the inside of the file folder. Tape the strip of card stock horizontally onto the bottom half, making a pocket to hold the figures. Use markers to color in the figures, accentuating all outline lines with the black permanent marker. If you have time afterward, you may wish to tell the story again so that the children can tell it along with you, using their own flannel boards as they follow along. Have them pair up and take turns telling the story to each other. Encourage the children to share the story with their friends and family whenever they get a chance. Remind them that they can design other characters and make up their own stories to use on their flannel boards. Storytelling is a great way to pass the time on a long trip in a car, train, or plane.

Suggested Booktalk Titles

Picture Books

Bunting, Eve. *The Traveling Men of Ballycoo*. Harcourt, 1983.
Day, Alexandra. *Frank and Ernest: On the Road*. Scholastic, 1994.
Kalman, Maria. *Ooh-La-La (Max in Love)*. Viking, 1991.
Mahy, Margaret. *The Three-Legged Cat*. Viking, 1993.
Priceman, Marjorie. *How to Make an Apple Pie and See the World*. Knopf, 1994.
Say, Allen. *Grandfather's Journey*. Houghton, 1993.
Thompson, Kay. *Eloise in Paris*. Simon & Schuster, 1957.
Tusa, Tricia. *Maebelle's Suitcase*. Macmillan, 1987.

Easy Readers

Brandenberg, Franz. *Everyone Ready?* Greenwillow, 1979.
Byars, Betsy Cromer. *The Golly Sisters Ride Again*. HarperCollins, 1994.
Cushman, Doug. *Aunt Eater's Mystery Vacation*. HarperCollins, 1992.
Schwartz, David M. *Supergrandpa*. Lothrop, 1991.

Folklore

Day, Edward C. *John Tabor's Ride*. Knopf, 1989.

Nonfiction

Adventures in Your National Parks. National Geographic Society, 1988.
Haskins, James. *Count Your Way Through...* (series with various countries, from Carolrhoda).
Keller, Laurie. *The Scrambled States of America*. Holt, 1998.
Krull, Kathleen. *Wish You Were Here: Emily's Guide to the 50 States*. Doubleday, 1997.

Poetry

Field, Rachel. *A Road Might Lead Anywhere*. Little, Brown, 1990.

Just for Fun

Lobel, Anita. *Away from Home*. Greenwillow, 1994.
Robbins, Ken. *City/Country: A Car Trip in Photographs*. Viking, 1985.
Mahoney, Judy. "Teach Me...." and "Teach Me More...." Foreign language kits

that include a book and a tape. Languages include Chinese, Hebrew, German, Russian, Italian, French, Spanish, and Japanese.

Other Resources

Aardema, Verna. *Traveling to Tondo: A Tale of the Nkundo of Zaire*. Knopf, 1991.

Around the World in Eighty Days (sound recording).

Boatness, Marie. *Travel Games for the Family*. Canyon Creek, 1993.

Brokaw, Meredith, and Anne Gilbar. *The Penny Whistle Traveling with Kids Book: Whether by Boat, Train, Car, or Plane—How to Take the Best Trip Ever with Kids of All Ages*. Simon & Schuster, 1994.

Butler, Arlene Kay. *Traveling with Children and Enjoying It: A Complete Guide to Family Travel by Car, Plane, and Train*. Globe Pequot, 1991. Describes kids traveling with flannel board stories.

"Let's Play Passport." *Copycat*. Copycat Press, Nov./Dec. 1995.

"Mad About Maps" and "Oh, the Places We Can Go with Books." *Copycat*. Copycat Press, Nov./Dec. 1996.

Sierra, Judy. *The Flannel Board Storytelling Book*. Wilson, 1987.

Sierra, Judy, and Robert Kaminski. *Multicultural Folktales: Stories to Tell to Young Children*. Oryx, 1991. Detailed directions for making flannel boards and how to encourage children to tell stories using flannel boards.

Staines, Bill. *The Happy Wanderer: Songs for Kids, Cars, and Campfires* (sound recording). Red House Records, 1993.

Weissman, Jackie. *Joining Hands with Other Lands: Multicultural Songs and Games* (sound recording). Kimbo, 1993.

Bookworms

Books and Libraries

Bulletin Board

Create a giant worm from large circles cut from various colors of construction paper and then stapled to the board in a long, wavy line. Have the worm eating its way through the pages of a giant book with a cardboard cover and pages made from newsprint. Use a clip art program to print out rows of colorful books for a border.

Background Music

Make a tape of library and book related songs such as "Love in the Library" (Jimmy Buffett), "Brush Up Your Shakespeare" (from *Kiss Me Kate*), "I Could Write a Book" (Frank Sinatra), "The Book I Read" (Talking Heads), "If You Could Read My Mind" (Gordon Lightfoot), "Marion the Librarian" (from *The Music Man*), "Paperback Writer" (The Beatles), "Book of Love" (Monotones), and "Tore Down à la Rimbaud" (Van Morrison). As an alternative, you may wish to play a recording of Gregorian chants to evoke the atmosphere of the monks who created illuminated manuscripts in the Middle Ages.

Opening Activity

Invite the children to participate in a song or chant about books, reading or libraries. You can also sing the following song to the tune of "This Old Man."

"WE LOVE BOOKS"
Lyrics by Martha Simpson

We love books,
We love books
Stories and all kinds of books.
We love fairy tales, fantasy, mysteries and more,
Humorous stories and folklore!

Teach the children the words to the song. Divide them into two or more groups and sing the song as a round.

Story

Tell "The Three Riddles" from *The Wily Witch: And All the Other Fairy Tales and Fables*, by Godfried Bomans. Or use a true story from one of the books by Elizabeth Rider Montgomery listed in Other Resources.

Participation Activity

Ask a local antiquarian book dealer to come in and show the children a selection of very old, rare, or valuable books, especially any with gilt-edged pages and fine or unusual bindings. As a librarian, you may be able to borrow a few items from a rare book room in the library where you work. If such items are unavailable, try finding a nice reproduction of an ancient text such as the *Book of Kells*. Talk about the parts of a book (spine, pages, cover, etc.) Ask the children to guess the prices for some of the rare books. Discuss how to properly care for books.

Craft—Bookworm Bookends

Materials: Two half-gallon juice or milk cartons; construction paper or self-adhesive shelf paper; white copy paper; patterns; glue; scissors; markers; craft knife.

Procedure: Ahead of time use a craft knife to cut the two cartons in half. Cover each half with construction paper or self-adhesive shelf paper. Discard the tops of the cartons. Make photocopies of the worm pattern and the words "BOOK" and "WORM."

At the program have the children color the worm and the words "BOOK" and "WORM" and cut them out. Glue the front half of the worm to one of the cartons and glue the word "BOOK" below it. Glue the back half of the worm to the other carton and glue the word "WORM" below it. Tell the children that when they get home they can weight the bookends by filling them with rocks.

Suggested Booktalk Titles

Picture Books

Deedy, Carmen Agra. *The Library Dragon*. Peachtree, 1994.
Duke, Kate. *Aunt Isabel Tells a Good One*. Dutton, 1992.
Duvoisin, Roger. *Petunia*. Random, 1973.
O'Neill, Catharine. *Mrs. Dunphy's Dog*. Viking, 1987.
Stewart, Sarah. *The Library*. Farrar, 1995.

FRONT

REAR

Easy Readers

Bonsall, Crosby Newall. *Tell Me Some More*. HarperCollins, 1989.
Hulbert, Jay. *Armando Asked, "Why?"* Raintree, 1990.

Chapter Books

Cleary, Beverly. *Emily's Runaway Imagination*. Morrow, 1961.
Clifford, Eth. *Help! I'm a Prisoner in the Library!* Houghton, 1979.
Dahl, Roald. *Matilda*. Viking, 1988.
Greenwald, Sheila. *The Mariah Delaney Lending Library Disaster*. Houghton, 1977.
Scieszka, Jon. *Summer Reading Is Killing Me!* Viking, 1998.

Nonfiction

Aliki. *How a Book Is Made*. Crowell, 1986.
Brookfield, Karen. *Book*. Knopf, 1993.
Christelow, Eileen. *What Do Authors Do?* Clarion, 1995.
Christelow, Eileen. *What Do Illustrators Do?* Clarion, 1999.
Munro, Roxie. *The Inside-Outside Book of Libraries*. Dutton, 1996.

Biographies

Aardema, Verna. *A Bookworm Who Hatched*. R.C. Owen, 1992. Also other author
    biographies in this series.
Lasky, Kathryn. *The Librarian Who Measured the Earth*. Joy Street, 1994.
Wheeler, Jill C. *Dr. Seuss*. Abdo, 1992.

Poetry

Hopkins, Lee Bennett, ed. *Good Books, Good Times*. Harper & Row, 1990.
Scieszka, Jon. *The Book That Jack Wrote*. Viking, 1994.

Just for Fun

Diehn, Gwen. *Making Books That Fly, Wrap, Pop Up, Twist, and Turn: Books for
    Kids to Make*. Lark, 1998.

Other Resources

Benedictine Monks of Santa Domingo de Silos. *Chant* (sound recording). Musi-
    cal Heritage Society, 1994.
Bomans, Godfried. *The Wily Witch: And all the Other Fairy Tales and Fables*. Stem-
    mer, 1977. A good source for "The Three Riddles."
"Books By Me." *Copycat*. Copycat Press, March/April 1997.
Freeman, Judy. *Hi Ho Librario: Songs, Chants and Stories to Keep Kids Humming*.
    Rock Hill, 1997. Chapter One has lots of songs about libraries, books, and
    reading.
Gaylord, Susan Kapuscinski. "Festive Gift Books for Kids to Make and Give."
    Instructor. November/December 1997, pp. 62+.
"The Journal Connections" and "Writer's Corner." *Copycat*. Copycat Press,
    Sept./Oct. 1995.
Montgomery, Elizabeth Rider. *The Story Behind Great Books*. Dodd, Mead, 1946,
    1947.
Montgomery, Elizabeth Rider. *The Story Behind Modern Books*. Dodd, Mead, 1949.

Celebrate Families

Family

Bulletin Board

Find pictures from magazines, greeting cards, and calendars that illustrate the concept of family. Frame each picture with construction paper and staple a length of yarn to the top two corners of the frame. On a brightly colored background create a large, branched tree from brown construction paper or cardboard tubes. Decorate the tree with flowers, green leaves, colored leaves, or snow to harmonize with the season. Hang the pictures in the tree by looping the yarn over push pins located along the branches.

Background Music

Record family songs on tape. Here are some favorites: "Cousins" (Tom Chapin), "When I Grow Up to Be a Man" (Beach Boys), "Baby Mine" (from *Dumbo*), "Mother and Child Reunion" (Paul Simon), "Triplets" (from *The Bandwagon*), "Danny's Song" (Loggins and Messina), "Teach Your Children" (Crosby, Stills, Nash, and Young), "Que Sera" (Doris Day), "Cat's in the Cradle" (Harry Chapin), "Leader of the Band" (Dan Fogelberg), and "Hacklebarney Tune" (Greg Brown).

Opening Activity

Sing "Something for Everyone" and let the children join in after teaching them the chorus. The words and music to this song can be found in the book or the sound recording of Marlo Thomas' *Free to Be ... a Family*.

Story

Tell "Naughty Marysia" from *The Story Vine*, by Anne Pellowski.
Materials: For this story you need a set of nesting dolls (see Other Resources).

Participation Activity

Talk about the concept of family and how the word "family" may mean many different things. Look at pictures from *Celebrating Families* by Rosmarie Hausherr or *Family Pictures* by Carmen Lomas Garza. You may wish to share an album of personal family pictures from a special occasion such as a wedding or a family reunion.

Craft—Family Tree

Materials: Pattern pieces; brown construction paper; green construction paper; white, beige or some other pale color of paper; a piece of 12" × 18" construction paper in any color; yarn; stapler or tape; glue stick; crayons, markers or colored pencils.

Procedure: Ahead of time enlarge the tree trunk and tree top patterns on a photocopier. Trace and cut the pattern pieces as follows: brown construction paper for tree trunk shapes, green construction paper for tree tops; pale-colored paper into larger and smaller ovals (see patterns). Cut the yarn into 20-inch pieces.

At the program each child will glue the tree trunk and tree top vertically to the large piece of construction paper. Children may then create representations of different family members by writing names or drawing portraits on the ovals. They may use larger ovals for adults and smaller ovals for children if they like. They may include pets, extended family, or whomever they feel fulfills their own idea of "family." Have children glue the finished ovals in the tree tops and finish by taping or stapling the two yarn ends to the top two corners of the background construction paper (see drawing). At home, the children can hang their family trees by simply slipping the yarn over a nail or a thumbtack.

tree top

ENLARGE
PATTERNS
ON
PHOTO-
COPIER

tree
trunk

FAMILY PORTRAITS

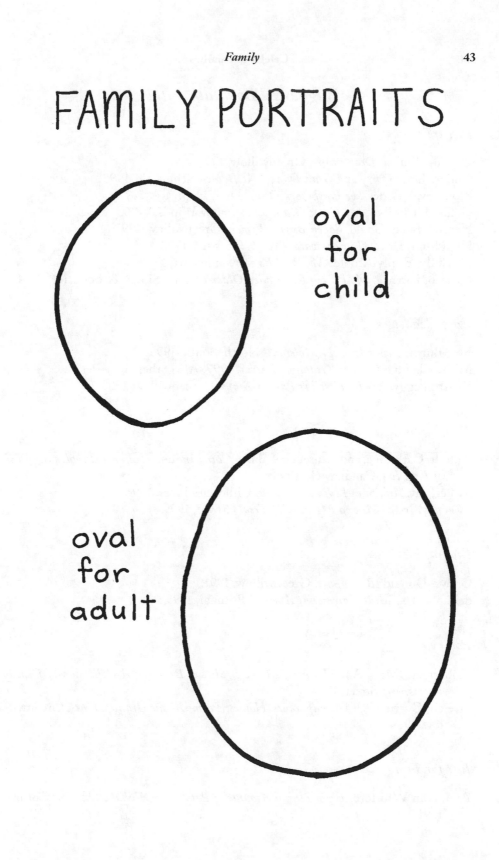

oval
for
child

oval
for
adult

Suggested Booktalk Titles

Picture Books

Caseley, Judith. *Dear Annie*. Greenwillow, 1991.
Cutler, Jane. *Darcy and Gran Don't Like Babies*. Scholastic, 1993.
Flourney, Valerie. *The Patchwork Quilt*. Dial, 1985.
Gelfand, Marilyn. *My Great Grandpa Joe*. Four Winds, 1986.
Hearne, Betsy Gould. *Seven Brave Women*. Greenwillow, 1997.
Houghton, Eric. *The Backwards Watch*. Orchard, 1992.
McCully, Emily Arnold. *My Real Family*. Harcourt, 1994.
Polacco, Patricia. *My Rotten Redheaded Older Brother*. Simon & Schuster, 1994.

Easy Readers

Bos, Burny. *Leave It to the Molesons!* North-South, 1995.
Mills, Claudia. *Gus and Grandpa*. Farrar, 1997. Also others in series.
Parish, Peggy. *Amelia Bedelia's Family Album*. Greenwillow, 1988.

Nonfiction

Anholt, Catherine, and Laurence Anholt. *Catherine and Laurence Anholt's Big Book of Families*. Candlewick, 1998.
Miller, Jay. *American Indian Families*. Children's Press, 1996.
Sweeney, Joan. *Me and My Family Tree*. Crown, 1999.

Biographies

Crews, Donald. *Bigmama's*. Greenwillow, 1991.
dePaola, Tomie. *26 Fairmount Avenue*. Putnam, 1999.

Poetry

Hoberman, Mary Ann. *Fathers, Mothers, Sisters, Brothers: A Collection of Family Poems*. Joy Street, 1991.
Streich, Corrine, ed. *Grandparents' Houses: Poems About Grandparents*. Greenwillow, 1984.

Just for Fun

Paul, Ann Whitford. *Eight Hands Around: A Patchwork Alphabet*. HarperCollins, 1991.

Other Resources

Hausherr, Rosmarie. *Celebrating Families*. Scholastic, 1997.

Lomas Garza, Carmen. *Family Pictures*. Children's Book Press, 1990.

"My Family Tree." *Copycat*. Copycat Press, March/April 1999.

"1994 … Year of the Family." *Copycat*. Copycat Press, Jan./Feb. 1994.

Pellowski, Anne. *The Story Vine: A Source Book of Unusual and Easy-to-Tell Stories from Around the World*. Macmillan, 1984. See "Naughty Marysia."

Sitarz, Paula Gaj. *More Picture Book Story Hours*. Libraries Unlimited, 1990. See "Meet My Family."

Thomas, Marlo, et al. *Free to Be … a Family* (sound recording). A&M, 1988.

Thomas, Marlo, et al. *Free to Be … a Family*. Bantam, 1987. The words and music for "Something for Everyone" are available both in the book and on the sound recording. The book is also a good source for stories and poems about families.

Nesting dolls (also known as matreska, matryoska, or matrioshka) commonly come from Russia, Poland, Czechoslovakia, and other Slavic countries, so you may find them in gift shops that carry imports from these countries. Here are some Internet sources for nesting dolls (prices range from reasonable to very expensive):

Matryoska Nesting Dolls from Russia has a website at www.importspecialist.com/dolls.htm.

Hearthsong sells kits for making nesting dolls through their website at www.hearthsong.com.

Choo Choo Boogie

Railroads and Trains

Bulletin Board

Make a train in bright rainbow colors. Cut each car from a large piece of construction paper starting with a black engine followed by cars of different shapes in blue, green, yellow, and orange, ending with a red caboose. Create a plume of smoke that comes out of the top of the engine and contains the caption: "Choo Choo Boogie!"

Background Music

Since train music is a genre in itself, take your pick from the many recordings of train music that are available. Two recordings that are geared specifically toward children are John Denver's *All Aboard* and Kevin Roth's *Train Songs and Other Tracks*.

Opening Activity

Sing "I've Been Working on the Railroad."

Story

Tell *Death of the Iron Horse*, by Paul Goble.
Materials: Use a train whistle or have the kids whistle for the train.

Participation Activity

Give the children rhythm instruments to play and sing "John Henry," "Freight Train," or some other classic train song. Make good use of a train whistle if you have one. Depending on your song choice, you can have the children line up in single file, like the cars in a train, and grab on to a piece of rope with one hand. Let them shake their instruments as you lead them around the room in a choo choo boogie.

Craft—Collage Train of Good Things

Materials: White copy paper; patterns; old magazines; 12" × 18" piece of construction paper; crayons; glue stick; scissors.

Procedure: Ahead of time photocopy and cut out the train pieces and cut out lots of pictures from the old magazines.

At the program allow the children some time to color their trains and glue them onto the piece of construction paper. They may then "fill up" the freight cars by gluing on magazine pictures so that the freight cars are filled up with lots of goodies.

Suggested Booktalk Titles

Picture Books

Bunting, Eve. *Train to Somewhere*. Clarion, 1996.
Fleischman, Paul. *Time Train*. HarperCollins, 1991.
Peet, Bill. *The Caboose That Got Loose*. Houghton, 1971.
Peet, Bill. *Smokey*. Houghton, 1984.
Pinkney, Gloria Jean. *The Sunday Outing*. Dial, 1994.

Easy Readers

Hoff, Syd. *Barney's Horse*. Harper & Row, 1987.
Hutchins, Pat. *The Best Train Set Ever*. Greenwillow, 1978.
Mills, Claudia. *Gus and Grandpa Ride the Train*. Farrar, 1998.
Murphy, Mary. *My Puffer Train*. Houghton, 1999.
Rosenbloom, Joseph. *Deputy Dan Gets His Man*. Random, 1985.
Rylant, Cynthia. *Mr. Putter and Tabby Take the Train*. Harcourt, 1998.

Chapter Books

Warner, Gertrude Chandler. *The Caboose Mystery*. Whitman, 1966. Also others in the Boxcar Children series.

Folklore

Lester, Julius. *John Henry*. Dial, 1994.

TRAIN ENGINE

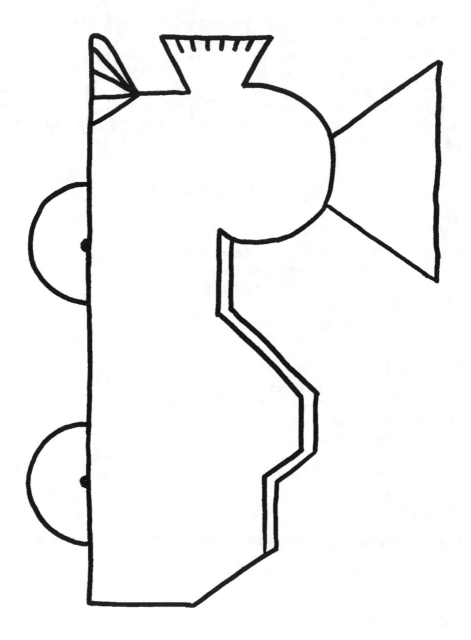

FREIGHT CAR

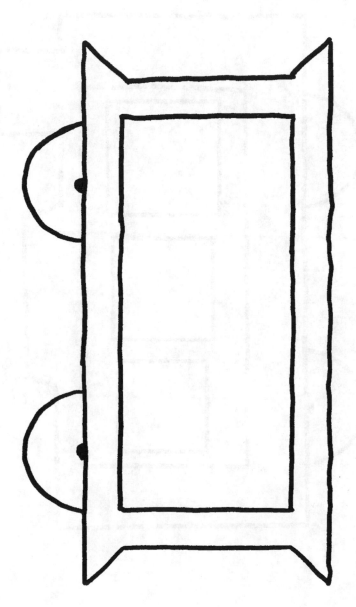

CABOOSE

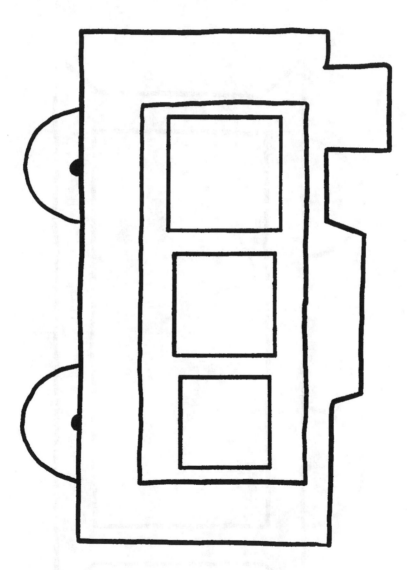

Nonfiction

Balkwill, Richard. *The Best Book of Trains*. Kingfisher, 1999.

Coiley, John. *Train*. DK, 2000.

Mosely, Keith. *Steam Locomotives: A Three-Dimensional Book*. Orchard, 1989.

O'Brien, Patrick. *Steam, Smoke, and Steel: Back in Time with Trains*. Charterbridge, 2000.

Otfinoski, Steven. *Riding the Rails: Trains Then and Now*. Benchmark, 1997.

Biographies

Ott, Virginia. *Man with a Million Ideas: Fred Jones, Genius/Inventor*. Lerner, 1977.

San Souci, Robert D. *Kate Shelley: Bound for Legend*. Dial, 1995.

Just for Fun

Micklethwait, Lucy. *I Spy a Freight Train: Transportation in Art*. Greenwillow, 1996.

Other Resources

Denver, John. *All Aboard* (sound recording). Sony, 1997.

Cohn, Amy, ed. *From Sea to Shining Sea*. Scholastic, 1993. See "I've Been Working on the Railroad" section and words and music for "John Henry."

Goble, Paul. *Death of the Iron Horse*. Bradbury, 1987.

Krull, Kathleen. *Gonna Sing My Head Off! American Folk Songs for Children*. Knopf, 1992. Words and music for the song "Freight Train."

McCutcheon, John. *Howjadoo* (sound recording). Rounder, 1987. Track: "John Henry."

Roth, Kevin. *Train Songs and Other Tracks* (sound recording). Marlboro, 1994.

Seeger, Mike. *American Folksongs for Children* (sound recording). Rounder Records, 1996. Tracks: "The Train Is a-Coming," "The Little Black Train," "When the Train Comes Along," and "John Henry."

Watson, Doc. *Doc Watson Sings Songs for Little Pickers* (sound recording). Alacazam, 1990. Track: "John Henry."

Zydeco, Buckwheat. *Choo Choo Boogaloo* (sound recording). Music for Little People, 1994.

Circus Time

Bulletin Board

A large circus poster makes a good centerpiece. Tack up a clown figure on either side and a circus train along the bottom of the bulletin board. Fill in the display with pictures of circus scenes and balloons.

Background Music

Play selections from the Broadway musical *Barnum*. Calliope music of familiar circus or merry-go-round tunes is also fun.

Opening Activity

Divide the children into three groups for this circus calliope sing-along. Instruct the first group to chant, in deep bass voices, "Boom (pause), boom (pause), boom (pause), boom (pause)." In each couplet, the first "boom" should be in a deep voice, and the second "boom" even deeper. After a rhythm is established, the second group will come in a few beats later with "Oom-pa-pa, oom-pa-pa." When both groups are going strong, the third group trill in high voices, "Oom-diddle-dee-dee, oom-diddle-dee-dee." Then, the librarians sing or hum the melody of a popular circus tune, such as "Did You Ever See a Lassie?" or "When You Are in Love, It's a Wonderful Time of the Year." The four-part harmony sounds great.

Story

The Man on the Flying Trapeze: The Circus Life of Emmett Kelly, Sr. by Robert M. Quackenbush is a biography set to music. You can tell it as a story or a song. Have the children sing along parts of it with you, to the tune of "The Daring Young Man on the Flying Trapeze."

Participation Activity

Have the children act out a mini-circus.

Materials: Rope for the tightrope act; lion heads made out of brown paper bags; a twig for the lion tamer's whip; a Hula Hoop.

With a librarian acting as ringmaster, assign children to be acrobats, tightrope walkers, a lion tamer, and lions. The acrobats start off with a series of rolls, tumbles, and cartwheels. Next, lay the rope on the floor and let the tightrope walkers pretend to walk, run, hop, or ride a bicycle across. Last, announce the brave lion tamer and his or her fierce lions. The lion tamer will order the beasts to sit, roar, roll over, and jump through the hoop. You can add more acts so all the children can be in the circus.

Craft—Clown Marionettes

Materials: Clown pieces (see patterns); white copy paper; card stock; five brass fasteners; yarn; colored pencils and crayons; hole punch; glue stick; dots, stars, and other decorations.

Procedure: Ahead of time photocopy and cut out the clown pattern pieces and mount them on card stock. Punch holes at the places indicated for the brass fasteners and yarn. Cut three 12-inch lengths of yarn.

At the program let children color and decorate the clown pieces. Then connect the clown arms and legs to the body using the brass fasteners. Finally, help the children tie pieces of yarn onto the puppets' arms and legs. Make a loop at the other end of the yarn through which the children can put their fingers. Show them how to move the yarn to make the marionette dance.

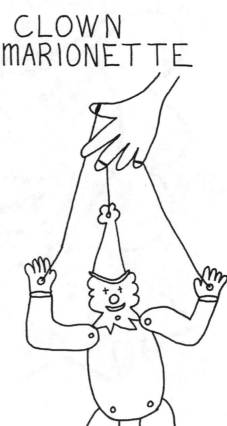

CLOWN MARIONETTE

Suggested Booktalk Titles

Picture Books

Freeman, Don. *Bearymore*. Viking, 1976.

CLOWN BODY

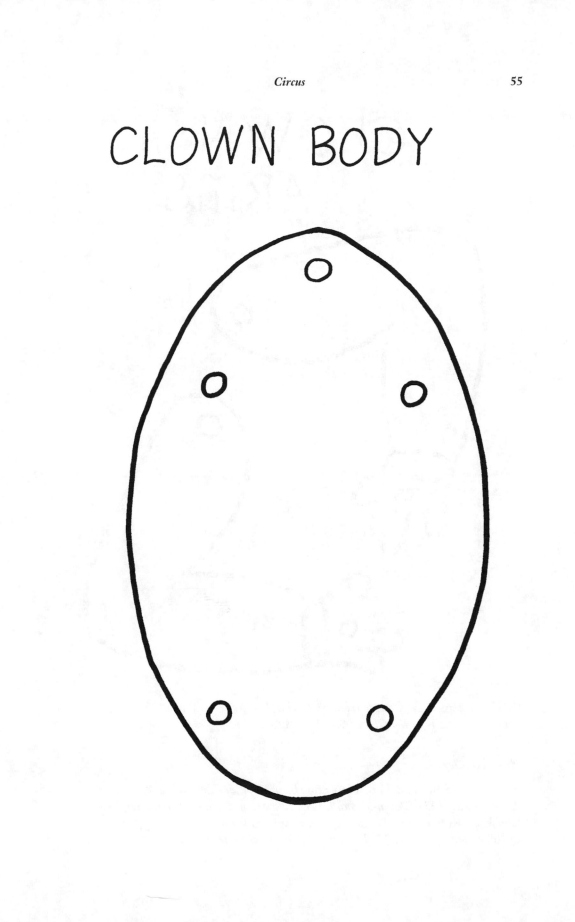

CLOWN ARMS

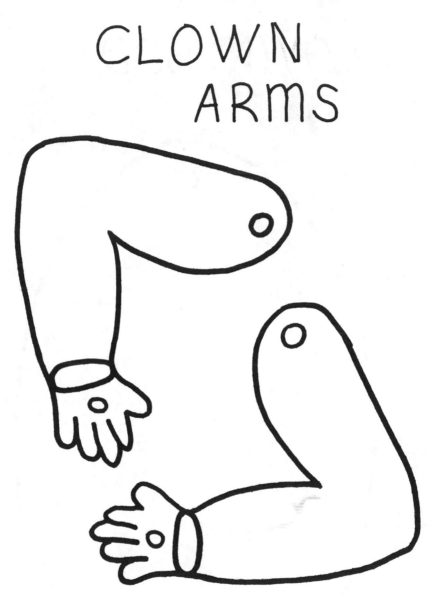

McCully, Emily Arnold. *Mirette on the High Wire*. Putnam, 1992.
Seuss, Dr. *If I Ran the Circus*. Random, 1984.

Easy Readers

Berenstain, Stan, and Jan Berenstain. *Bears on Wheels*. Grolier, 1969.
Cole, Joanna. *The Clown-Arounds Go on Vacation*. Parents Magazine, 1993.
Lopshire, Robert. *Put Me in the Zoo*. Random, 1988.
Quackenbush, Robert M. *Detective Mole and the Circus Mystery*. Lothrop, 1985.

CLOWN LEGS

Chapter Book

Mahy, Margaret. *The Greatest Show Off Earth*. Viking, 1994.

Nonfiction

Blumberg, Rhoda. *Jumbo*. Macmillan, 1992.
Presnall, Judith Janda. *Circuses: Under the Big Top*. Watts, 1996.
Sutton, Felix. *The Big Show: A History of the Circus*. Doubleday, 1971.

Biography

Wright, David. *P.T. Barnum*. Raintree, 1997.

Poetry

Prelutsky, Jack. *Circus*. Collier, 1978.

Just for Fun

Ames, Lee J. *Make 25 Crayon Drawings of the Circus*. Doubleday, 1980.
Granseth, Sandra, and Mary Williams. *At the Circus*. Meredith Corp., 1991.
Klayer, Connie. *Circus Time! How to Put on Your Own Show*. Lothrop, 1979.
Perkins, Catherine. *The Most Excellent Book of How to Be a Clown*. Copper Beach, 1996.
Walton, Rick. *Clowning Around: Jokes About the Circus*. Lerner, 1989.
West, Robin. *Paper Circus: How to Create Your Own Circus*. Carolrhoda, 1984.

Other Resources

Circus Time: The Greatest Show on Earth (sound recording). MCA, 1980.
Cleveland, John. *The Calliope Cassette* (sound recording). J. Cleveland, 1988.
Coleman, Cy. *Barnum: Original Broadway Cast* (sound recording). CBS, 1980.
Go In and Out the Window: An Illustrated Songbook for Young People. Holt, 1987. See "Did You Ever See a Lassie."
Miss Carol and the Wonderland Orchestra and Chorus. *Travelling Sing-a-Lings* (book and cassette). Wonderland Records, 1987. Tracks: "Did You Ever See a Lassie?" and "The Daring Young Man on the Flying Trapeze."
Quackenbush, Robert M. *The Man on the Flying Trapeze: The Circus Life of Emmett Kelly, Sr.* Lippincott, 1975.
Sitarz, Paula Gaj. *More Picture Book Story Hours*. Libraries Unlimited, 1990. See "Under the Big Top: Circus Stories."

Creepy Crawlies
———— Bugs, Worms, and Slimy Critters

Bulletin Board

Put up a green construction paper background, with fringes of green paper here and there to simulate grass. Add some trees made of corrugated cardboard, vines made of twisted green crepe paper, and paper leaves. Add a blue paper pond with lilypads. Make them all oversized, since this represents a forest from a bug's eye view. Then add cartoon-like bugs, snakes, frogs, lizards, and other creepy crawlies of all sorts. They can be doing silly things, such as the ants marching in formation toward an ant hill ("The Ants Go Marching…"), frogs dancing on lily pads, snakes doing a trapeze act through the trees, etc.

Background Music

Play the soundtrack of *A Bug's Life* or *Antz*.

Opening Activity

Sing one or more silly songs about creepy, crawly critters, such as "Baby Bumble Bee," "Lots of Worms," or "Coming of the Frogs."

Story

Tell one of the many stories about Anansi the Spider.

Participation Activity

Adapt the song "The Ants Go Marching" to include all types of creepy crawlies.

Materials: Easel, art pad, marker.

Ask the children to name some crawling critters and a word describing how they move. Assign each critter to a number (one through ten), come up with a rhyme, and write them on the art pad. For example, "The toads go hopping one by one... The little one stops to bounce on a drum," "The snakes go slithering two by two... The little one stops to inspect a shoe," or "The spiders go spinning three by three... The little one stops to climb a tree," etc. Then sing the song and let the children act out the verses.

Craft—Cork and Egg Carton Bugs

Materials: Corks in assorted sizes and shapes; egg carton bottoms; plastic eyes; little pom-poms; pipe cleaners in various colors; liquid glue; toothpicks; stick-on dots; other decorations.

Procedure: Ahead of time cut the egg cartons into various sizes (one or more sections per piece). Make several sample bugs, using corks as well as carton sections.

At the program show your samples to the children. They can make bugs similar to the samples or make up their own designs. If you have a lot of materials, each child can make a few bugs.

Suggested Booktalk Titles

Picture Books

Banks, Kate. *Spider, Spider*. Farrar, 1996.
Cannon, Janell. *Verdi*. Harcourt, 1997.
Coxe, Molly. *The Great Snake Escape*. HarperCollins, 1994.
McDonald, Megan. *Insects Are My Life*. Orchard, 1996.
Noble, Trinka Hakes. *The Day Jimmy's Boa Ate the Wash*. Dial, 1980.
Van Laan, Nancy. *Big Fat Worm*. Knopf, 1995.
Yolen, Jane. *Beneath the Ghost Moon*. Little, Brown, 1993.

Easy Readers

Lobel, Arnold. *Frog and Toad Are Friends*. Harper & Row, 1974.

Chapter Books

Coville, Bruce. *Jennifer Murdley's Toad*. Harcourt, 1992.
Naylor, Phyllis Reynolds. *Beetles, Lightly Toasted*. Atheneum, 1987.
Rockwell, Thomas. *How to Eat Fried Worms*. Watts, 1973.

Nonfiction

Coldrey, Jennifer. *Discovering Worms*. Bookwright, 1986.
Facklam, Margery. *Bugs for Lunch*. Charlesbridge, 1999.
Facklam, Margery. *Creepy, Crawly Caterpillars*. Little, Brown, 1996.
Johnston, Ginny. *Slippery Babies: Young Frogs, Toads, and Salamanders*. Morrow, 1991.
Markle, Sandra. *Outside and Inside Snakes*. Macmillan, 1995.
Wechsler, Doug. *Bizarre Bugs*. Cobblehill, 1995.

Poetry

Fleischman, Paul. *Joyful Noise: Poems for Two Voices*. Harper & Row, 1988.

Just for Fun

Ames, Lee J. *Draw 50 Creepy Crawlies*. Doubleday, 1991.
Woodworth, Viki. *Bug Riddles*. Child's World, 1993.

Other Resources

Arkhurst, Joyce Cooper. *The Adventures of Spider: West African Folk Tales*. Little, Brown, 1964.
Arnold, Linda. *Sing Along Stew* (sound recording). Ariel Records, 1996. Tracks: "Baby Bumble Bee" and "The Ants Go Marching."
Gregson-Williams, Harry. *Antz: Original Film Music* (sound recording). Angel Records, 1998.
GuideZone website, www.guidezone.skl.com/i_bv_songs.htm. See Other Silly Songs (including "Worms," "It's an Insect World," and "Coming of the Frogs").
Kimmel, Eric A. *Anansi and the Moss-Covered Rock*. Holiday, 1988.
Nelson, Esther L. *The Funny Songbook*. Sterling, 1984. See "Baby Bumble Bee," "The Grasshopper Song," and other songs.
Newman, Randy. *A Bug's Life: An Original Walt Disney Records Soundtrack* (sound recording). Disney, 1998.
Oram, Hiawyn. *A Creepy Crawly Song Book*. Farrar, 1993.
Sharon, Lois, and Bram. *Stay Tuned* (sound recording). Elephant Records, 1987. Track: "Lots of Worms."
Sherman, Joseph, and T.K.F. Weisskopf. *Greasy Grimy Gopher Guts*. August House, 1995. See chapter "Gopher Guts, and Other Gross-Outs" for yucky songs.

Day by Day

Calendars

Bulletin Board

We suggest using this unit in January to celebrate the new year. Caption the bulletin board "Happy New Year" and decorate it with party hats, streamers, noise makers, etc. You may also wish to include pages from a calendar of the current year.

Background Music

Record songs that have days, months, or years in the title. For years, try David Bowie's "1984." For months, use songs such as "April Come She Will" (Simon and Garfunkel), or "Try to Remember" (from *The Fantastiks*). For days, use "Pleasant Valley Sunday" (The Monkees), "Monday, Monday" (The Mamas and the Papas), "Tuesday Afternoon" (Moody Blues), "Come Saturday Morning" (Sandpipers), "Another Saturday Night" (Sam Cooke), "Blue Monday" (Fats Domino), "Ruby Tuesday" (Rolling Stones), "Rainy Days and Mondays" (The Carpenters), "Saturday Night" (Bay City Rollers), etc.

Opening Activity

Discuss birthdays. Ask the children if they know their birthstones or astrological signs. Have a source handy that has these things listed so that you can look them up. Use *Chase's Calendar of Events* to look up the children's birthdays and find out different festivals and events taking place on those days. You may also wish to discuss calendars from various cultures. For instance, show a picture of the Aztec calendar. Describe the Chinese tradition of naming years after animals and then look up the corresponding animal's year for each child. Also look up the current year to see which animal is listed for that year.

Story

Tell the story of Marushka and the Twelve Month Brothers. Many different versions are available (see Other Resources).

Materials: A bunch of—artificial or real—violets (another spring flower, such as crocuses or snow drops, may be substituted); a basket of strawberries; two apples; a wooden staff.

Participation Activity

Sing or recite "Chicken Soup with Rice" by Maurice Sendak. Make a print-out of the song lyrics with type large enough to be read from a distance. Have a sound system (CD or cassette player) and a recording of the song if you'd like to play it in the background. The librarian can hold up the words to the song so that the children may recite it as a poem or sing along. The musical version is available in the soundtrack for the stage play or video "Really Rosie." Prepare ahead of time pictures for each month based on Maurice Sendak's poem/song "Chicken Soup with Rice." Create one picture for each child that you expect in the program with the name of a month across the top and a pertinent picture underneath that illustrates the poem (Examples: January—picture of ice skates, February—picture of snowman, etc.). If you don't have a good clip art program in your computer, try finding pictures in old calendars or magazines. During the program, seat the children in a circle. Give each child a picture and explain that they are to hold up their month when they hear it mentioned in the song.

Craft—Calendars

Materials: Old magazines or greeting cards; calendar pages for all 12 months of the year; 12" × 18" construction paper; stickers or precut tiny clip art illustrating various holidays; hole punch; scissors; two brass fasteners; glue stick.

Procedure: Ahead of time create 12 calendar pages for each child by photocopying from a calendar or printing from a computer program. Punch two holes at the top of each calendar page. Looking at the construction paper vertically, punch two holes about halfway down that correspond to the holes in the calendar pages (see drawing). Cut out pictures from magazines and greeting cards, etc. If necessary, print and cut out holiday clip art pictures small enough to fit in the calendars' daily spaces.

At the program let the children attach their calendar pages together in the proper order to the bottom half of the construction paper using two brass fasteners. The children can decorate the top half of the calendar by making collages from their favorite pictures from magazines or greeting cards. They can use stickers or tiny precut clip art to mark family birthdays, holidays, etc., on the different days of the year on the calendar months.

CALENDAR PAGES

punch holes at circles

Suggested Booktalk Titles

Picture Books

Bacon, Ethel. _To See the Moon_. Bridgewater, 1996.
Cocca-Leffler, Maryann. _Wednesday Is Spaghetti Day_. Scholastic, 1990.
Gerstein, Mordicai. _The Story of May_. HarperCollins, 1993.

Giff, Patricia Reilly. *I Love Saturday*. Viking, 1989.
Seuss, Dr. *My Many-Colored Days*. Knopf, 1996.
Stevenson, James. *Un-Happy New Year, Emma!* Greenwillow, 1989.
Viorst, Judith. *Alexander and the Terrible, Horrible, No Good, Very Bad Day*. Atheneum, 1972.
Wiesner, David. *June 29, 1999*. Clarion, 1992.

Easy Readers

Galbraith, Kathryn Osebold. *Holding onto Sunday*. McElderry, 1995.
LeSieg, Theo. *Please Try to Remember the First of Octember!* Beginner Books, 1977.
Pomerantz, Charlotte. *The Half-Birthday Party*. Clarion, 1984.

Chapter Books

Regan, Dian Curtis. *Monster of the Month Club*. Scholastic, 1994.
Rodgers, Mary. *Freaky Friday*. Harper & Row, 1972.

Folklore

Gilchrist, Cherry. *A Calendar of Festivals*. Barefoot Books, 1998.
Perl, Lila. *Blue Monday and Friday the Thirteenth*. Clarion, 1986.

Nonfiction

Gibbons, Gail. *The Reasons for Seasons*. Holiday House, 1995.
Weiss, Malcolm E. *Solomon Grundy, Born on Oneday: A Finite Arithmetic Puzzle*. Crowell, 1977.

Biography

Stevenson, James. *July*. Greenwillow, 1990.

Poetry

Otten, Charlotte F. *January Rides the Wind: A Book of Months*. Lothrop, 1997.
Singer, Marilyn. *Turtle in July*. Macmillan, 1989.

Just for Fun

Bjork, Christina. *Linnea's Almanac*. Farrar, 1989.

Other Resources

Chase's Calendar of Events. Contemporary (annual).

King, Carole. *The Broadway Cast Album of Maurice Sendak's Really Rosie* (sound recording). Caedmon, 1981. Track: "Chicken Soup with Rice."

Perl, Lila. *Candles, Cakes, and Donkey Tails: Birthday Symbols and Celebrations.* Clarion, 1984.

Sendak, Maurice. *Chicken Soup with Rice: A Book of Months.* Harper & Row, 1962.

Sendak, Maurice. *Maurice Sendak's Really Rosie Starring the Nutshell Kids.* Harper & Row, 1975. Includes sheet music for "Chicken Soup with Rice."

Travers, P.L. *Mary Poppins Opens the Door.* Harcourt, 1943. "Happy Ever After," Chapter 7, recounts an adventure that the children have while they are in the "crack" between the Old Year and the New Year.

Vittorini, Domenico. *The Thread of Life: Twelve Old Italian Tales.* Crown, 1995.

Whitfield, Susan, and Philippa-Alys Browne. *The Animals of the Chinese Zodiac.* Crocodile, 1998.

Here are a few versions of the story of Marushka and the Twelve Month Brothers:

Haviland, Virginia. *Favorite Fairy Tales Told in Czechoslovakia.* Little, Brown, 1966. "The Twelve Months."

Marshak, Samual. *The Month Brothers: A Slavic Tale.* Morrow, 1983.

Vojtech, Anna, and Philomen Sturges. *Marushka and the Month Brothers.* North-South Books, 1996.

Delightful Dragons

Bulletin Board

Using construction paper, make a green dragon with gold scales. Layer large, flame-shaped pieces of red, orange, and yellow construction paper so that the flames shoot out of the dragon's mouth. Use the flames as a background for a caption in black letters. Make extra blue or purple dragon scales to use as a border.

Background Music

Make a recording of music about dragons such as "St. George and the Dragonet" (Stan Freberg), "Purple People Eater" (Sheb Wooley), Jack Prelutsky's musically enhanced recording of poems from his book *The Dragons Are Singing Tonight*, or songs from Kevin Roth's *Dinosaurs and Dragons*.

Opening Activity

Talk about dragons in different cultures. Explain how Chinese dragons differ from European dragons because Chinese dragons are considered to be regal and wise instead of greedy and monstrous. Sing "Puff the Magic Dragon."

Story

Tell *The Dragon Kite*, by Nancy Luenn.
Materials: Dragon puppet.

Participation Activity

Have a dragon parade.
Materials: Large brown paper shopping bag; construction paper; crepe paper streamers; toy drums and cymbals.

Construct ahead of time a dragon head made from a shopping bag decorated with dragon features such as scales on the back of the neck, a mouth with fangs and flames, etc. Affix two 20-foot-long pieces of crepe paper streamers to each side of the head. During the program, choose a child to wear the head and have other children line up behind the dragon head and hold one of the streamers overhead in each hand. Choose a few children to stay out of the parade to play the drums and cymbals as the dragon parade progresses. Switch the children around so that everyone has a chance to be in the parade or to play the instruments.

Craft—Dragon Puppets

Materials: A cardboard paper towel tube; green and yellow (or red) construction paper; glue stick; plastic googly eyes; patterns; scissors.

Procedure: Ahead of time cover the cardboard tube with green construction paper. Trace the patterns and cut out from green construction paper two sets each of dragon scales, belly, head, and tail (see patterns). Fold along the lines indicated to make tabs on all the green pieces. Trace and cut one dragon flame from yellow construction paper (see pattern).

At the program have the children glue the pairs of dragon parts facing together (sandwich the flame into the mouth before gluing the two dragon heads

DRAGON HEAD

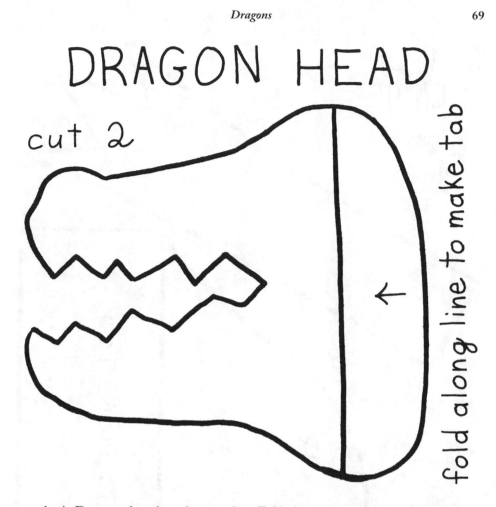

cut 2

fold along line to make tab

together). Do not glue the tabs together. Fold the tabs away from each other so that they spread outward and form a flat surface. Cover the flat surface with glue and wrap the tabs around the tube to affix the dragon parts as follows: the head and flames on one side near the top of the tube; the belly under the head; the scales on the opposite side of the tube starting near the top; the tail beneath the scales on the same side. Make sure the children leave about three inches free near the bottom of the tube for a hand grip.

Suggested Booktalk Titles

Picture Books

Deedy, Carmen Agra. *The Library Dragon*. Peachtree, 1994.
Nunes, Susan Miho. *The Last Dragon*. Clarion, 1995.
Peet, Bill. *How Droofus the Dragon Lost His Head*. Houghton, 1971.
Pilkey, Dav. *Dragon Gets By*. Orchard, 1991.

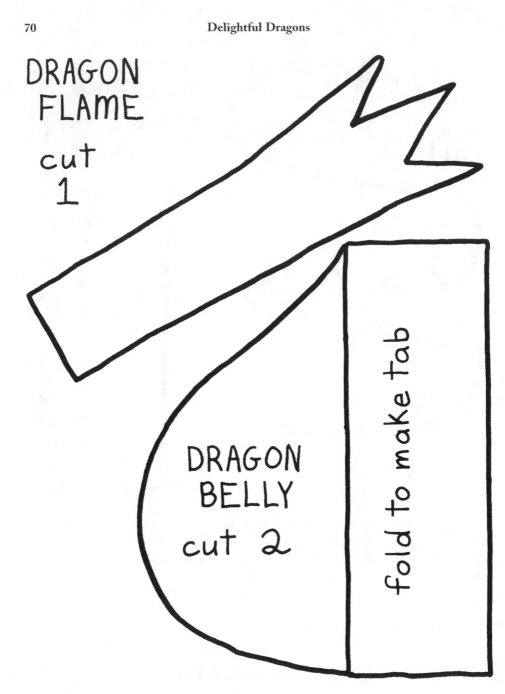

DRAGON
FLAME

cut
1

DRAGON
BELLY

cut 2

fold to make tab

Sis, Peter. *Komodo!* Greenwillow, 1993.
Wilson, Sarah. *Beware the Dragons.* Harper & Row, 1985.

Easy Readers

Brandenberg, Franz. *Leo and Emily and the Dragon.* Greenwillow, 1984.

DRAGON SCALES

cut 2

fold to make tab

Chapter Books

Coville, Bruce. *Jeremy Thatcher, Dragon Hatcher*. Pocket, 1992.
Dadey, Debbie. *Dragons Don't Cook Pizza*. Scholastic, 1997.
Koller, Jackie French. *A Dragon in the Family*. Little, Brown, 1993.

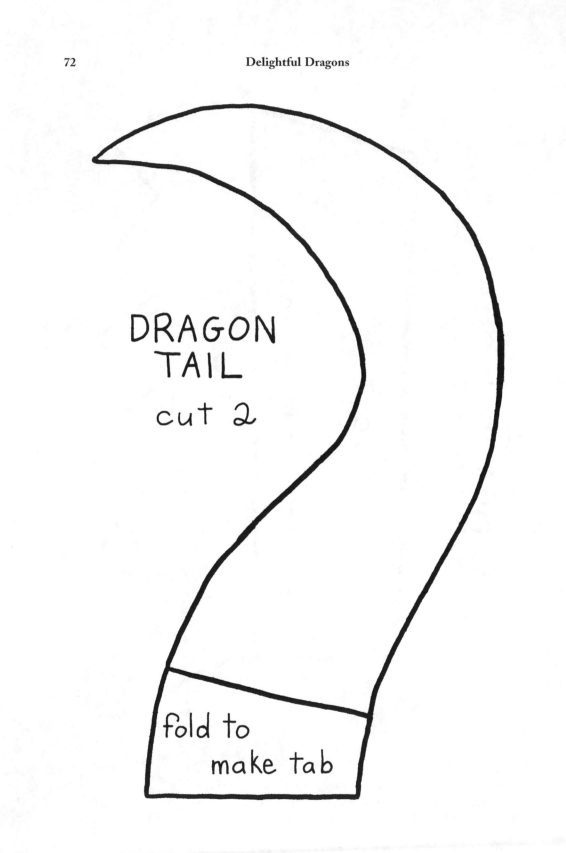

DRAGON
TAIL

cut 2

fold to
make tab

McMullan, Kate. *Revenge of the Dragon Lady*. Grosset & Dunlap, 1997. Also others in the Dragon Slayers Academy series.
Osborne, Mary Pope. *Day of the Dragon King*. Random, 1998.

Folklore

Baskin, Hosie. *A Book of Dragons*. Knopf, 1985.
Hodges, Margaret. *Saint George and the Dragon: A Golden Legend*. Little, Brown, 1984.
Ragache, Gilles. *Myths and Legends of Dragons*. Marshall Cavendish, 1991.

Nonfiction

Demi. *Demi's Dragons and Fantastic Creatures*. Holt, 1993.
Gibbons, Gail. *Behold—The Dragons!* Morrow, 1999.

Poetry

Nash, Ogden. *Custard the Dragon*. Little, Brown, 1959.
Prelutsky, Jack. *The Dragons Are Singing Tonight*. Greenwillow, 1993.

Just for Fun

Cohen, Shari. *Draw Fantasy: Dragons, Centaurs and Other Mythological Characters*. Contemporary, 1997.
Walton, Rick. *Kiss a Frog: Jokes About Fairy Tales, Knights, and Dragons*. Lerner, 1989.

Other Resources

Brokaw, Meredith, and Annie Gilbar. *The Penny Whistle Any Day Is a Holiday Party Book*. Simon & Schuster, 1996. See "Day of the Dragon."
Carton, Carol Elaine. *Super Storytelling: Creative Ideas Using Finger Plays, Flannel Board Stories, Pocket Stories, and Puppets with Young Children*. Denison, 1986. See "10 Dizzy Dragons."
"Dazzling Dragons." *Copycat*. Copycat Press, Jan./Feb. 1999.
"Dragons, Kites, and Lanterns." *Copycat*. Copycat Press, May/June 1997.
Luenn, Nancy. *The Dragon Kite*. Harcourt, 1982.
Manning-Sanders, Ruth. *A Book of Dragons*. Dutton, 1964.
Nesbit, E. *The Book of Dragons*. Random, 1961.
Peter, Paul, and Mary. *Peter, Paul & Mommy, Too* (sound recording). Warner, 1993. Track: "Puff the Magic Dragon."
Prelutsky, Jack. *The Dragons Are Singing Tonight: Poems and Music* (sound recording). Listening Library, 1994.
Roth, Kevin. *Dinosaurs and Dragons* (sound recording). Sony music, 1997.
Silverstein, Shel. *A Light in the Attic*. Harper, 1981. See "The Dragon of Grindly Grun."

Dynamic Dinosaurs

—— *Dinosaurs and Prehistoric Creatures*

Bulletin Board

Create a mural of a land where dinosaurs rule. Construct a smoking volcano on the left side of the bulletin board, a lake in the center, and vegetation here and there. Post pictures of various dinosaurs all around.

Background Music

Play music from the soundtrack of *The Land Before Time* and its sequels, or music from *Jurassic Park*. Several recordings of songs about dinosaurs for children, such as *Dinosaur Choir* (Bonnie Phipps), are also available.

Opening Activity

Teach the children the chorus to the poem "Gotta Find a Footprint" by Jeff Moss. Chant or sing it to the tune of the *Jeopardy!* theme. You can do the alternating verses and have the children chime in for the chorus.

Story

Read *Stone Girl, Bone Girl*, a fictionalized account of the life of Mary Anning. Or, read a chapter from *The Enormous Egg* by Oliver Butterworth.

Participation Activity

Do the following fill-in-the-blanks story, developed by Martha Simpson. Ask the children to supply adjectives, nouns, etc. (explain these terms if necessary), and read the story aloud.

Dinosaur Facts

Dinosaurs lived _____ years ago. The word "dinosaur" means
          [number]

_____ _____. There were many different dinosaurs. Some were
[adjective]   [noun]

_____-eaters, which means they ate only _____. Others were
   [noun]   [plural noun]

_____ -eaters, that ate _____. Some examples of these were the
   [noun]   [plural noun]

_____*osaurus* and the _____ *raptor*, which were very _____.
   [noun]   [noun]   [adjective]

The most _____ dinosaur of all was the _____ *osaurus rex* because it
            [adjective]   [noun]

_____ other dinosaurs. Some dinosaurs were much more _____,
  [past tense verb]   [adjective]

like the _____ *adon* and the _____ *oducus*. The largest dinosaur of
            [adjective]   [verb]

all was the _____ *osaurus*, which grew to about _____ feet long
              [nonsense word]   [number]

and weighed _____ pounds. My favorite dinosaur is the
              [number]

_____ *ceratops* because it had _____ _____on its head.
  [nonsense word]   [adjective]   [plural noun]

Dinosaurs are no longer alive today, but you can see their _____
                                                                  [plural noun]

in a _____.
      [building]

Craft—Apatosaurus

Materials: White nine-inch paper plate; two legs, neck/head and tail (see patterns); card stock; four brass fasteners; crayons and markers; stapler; paper hole punch.

APATOSAURUS

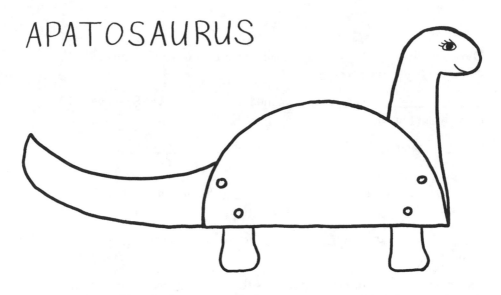

Procedure: Ahead of time trace and cut out pattern pieces from card stock. Fold paper plate in half (insides touching) and staple edges together, leaving openings for the pattern pieces (see drawing). Punch holes for brass fasteners on the paper plate and pattern pieces as shown.

At the program children can color the paper plate and pattern pieces. Then help them attach the legs, neck/head, and tail with the fasteners.

Suggested Booktalks

Picture Books

Ahlberg, Allan. *Dinosaur Dreams*. Greenwillow, 1991.
Carrick, Carol. *Patrick's Dinosaurs*. Clarion, 1983.
Joyce, William. *Dinosaur Bob and His Adventures with the Family Lazardo*. Harper & Row, 1988.
Pfister, Marcus. *Dazzle the Dinosaur*. Scholastic, 1994.
Shields, Carol Diggory. *Saturday Night at the Dinosaur Stomp*. Candlewick, 1997.
Yolen, Jane. *How Do Dinosaurs Say Good Night?* Blue Sky Press, 2000.

Easy Readers

Hoff, Syd. *Danny and the Dinosaur*. Harper & Row, 1958. Also sequels.

Chapter Books

Adler, David A. *Cam Jansen and the Mystery of the Dinosaur Bones*. Viking, 1981.
Carusone, Al. *The Boy with Dinosaur Hands*. Clarion, 1998. See title story.

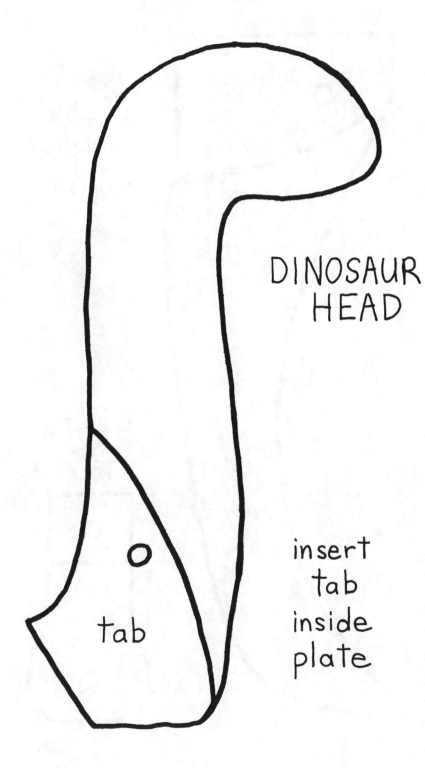

DINOSAUR
HEAD

insert
tab
inside
plate

tab

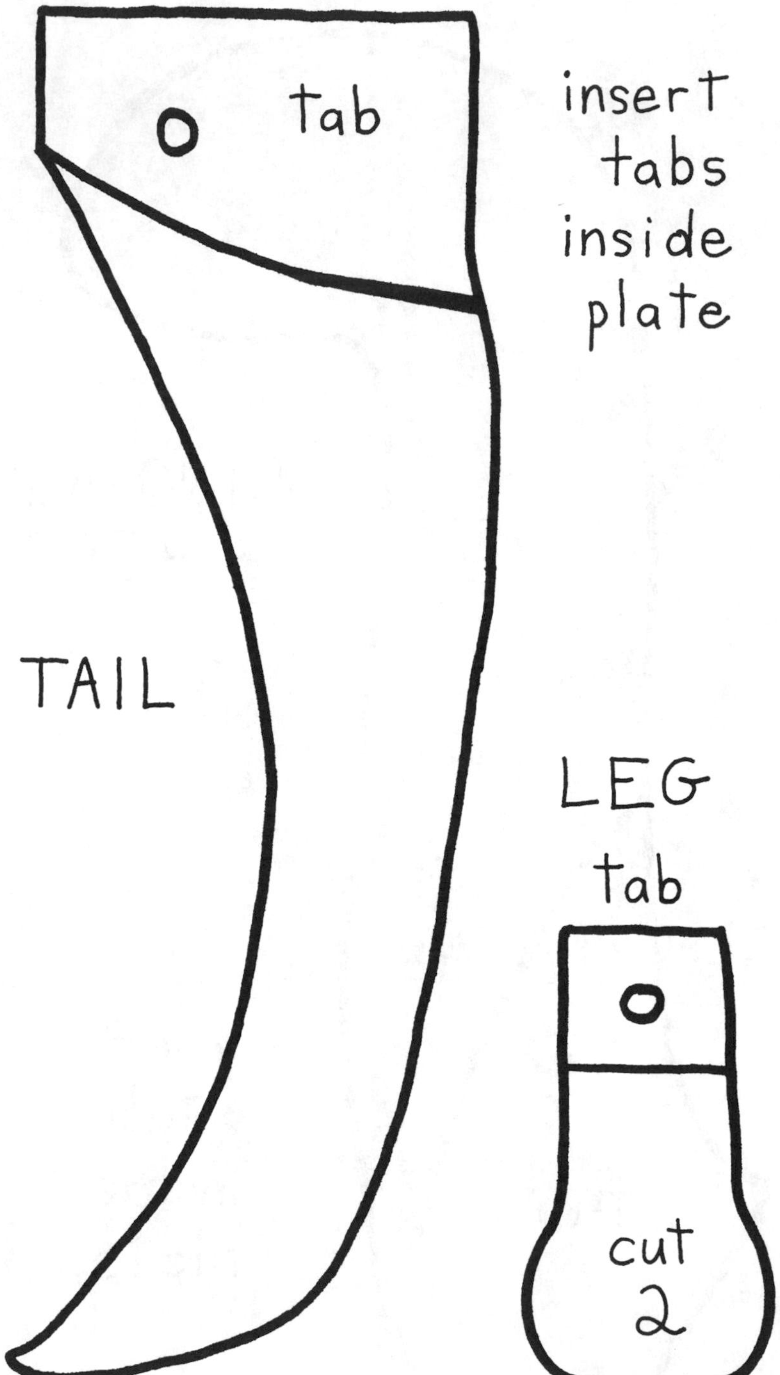

tab

insert
tabs
inside
plate

TAIL

LEG
tab

cut
2

Gurney, James. *Dinotopia: A Land Apart from Time*. Turner, 1992.
Packard, Edward. *Choose Your Own Adventure: Dinosaur Island*. Bantam, 1993.

Nonfiction

Aliki. *Dinosaur Bones*. Crowell, 1988.
Harrison, Carol. *Dinosaurs Everywhere!* Scholastic, 1998.
Most, Bernard. *Dinosaur Questions*. Harcourt, 1995. Also other dinosaur books.

Poetry

Yolen, Jane. *Dinosaur Dances*. Putnam, 1990.

Just for Fun

Emberley, Michael. *Dinosaurs! A Drawing Book*. Little, Brown, 1980.
Rosenbloom, Joseph. *The Funniest Dinosaur Book Ever!* Sterling, 1987.
Ross, Kathy. *Crafts for Kids Who Are Wild About Dinosaurs*. Millbrook, 1997.
Saurus, Alice. *1001 Dinosaur Jokes for Kids*. Ballentine, 1993.

Other Resources

Anholt, Laurence. *Stone Girl, Bone Girl*. Orchard, 1999.
Butterworth, Oliver. *The Enormous Egg*. Little, Brown, 1984.
"Dinomania." *Copycat*. Copycat Press, Nov./Dec. 1993.
Horner, James. *The Land Before Time* (sound recording). MCA, 1988.
Moss, Jeffrey. *Bone Poems*. Workman, 1997. See "Gotta Find a Footprint" and other poems.
Phipps, Bonnie. *Dinosaur Choir* (sound recording). WF Kids, 1992.
Williams, John. *Jurassic Park* (sound recording). MCA, 1993.

Fantastic Creatures

—— *Unicorns and Other Fantasy Beasts*

Bulletin Board

Create a fantasy land populated by imaginary creatures. Place the phoenix atop a mountain, and a dragon guarding the entrance to a cave. The Loch Ness Monster can be visible in a lake. A unicorn can stand by the edge of a forest, and Pegasus flies above. Add pictures of other fantastic creatures.

Background Music

Play *Symphony No. 6 ("Pastoral") Op. 68* by Beethoven. Children may recognize this as the music for the flying horses scene in *Fantasia*.

Opening Activity

Sing "The Unicorn" (The Irish Rovers), "Puff (the Magic Dragon)" (Peter, Paul, and Mary), or another song about a creature of fantasy.

Story

Relate the story of *Pegasus*, from the book by Marianna Mayer.

Participation Activity

Play a game in which children must Name the Fantastic Creature.
Materials: Pictures of several creatures from fantasy literature and mythology, including the lesser-known ones such as wyvern, phoenix, Ganesha, and griffin, labeled with the beasts' names; clues you have written.

Display all the pictures. Then read clues and let the children guess which beast you are describing. For example:

Head like a dragon, end like a snake. One roar from me, and you'll be awake!
(wyvern)

I have the head of an elephant and four arms. In India, they believe in my charms.
(Ganesha)

Craft—Invent-a-Creature

Materials: 12" × 18" construction paper; assorted heads, wings, legs, feet, and other body parts from various beasts (see patterns); white copy paper; colored pencils or crayons; glue stick; scissors.

Procedure: Ahead of time photocopy the patterns on white paper (enlarge them if you wish) and cut them out. You may want to draw additional body parts for the children to choose from.

At the program let the children choose whatever body parts they want to use

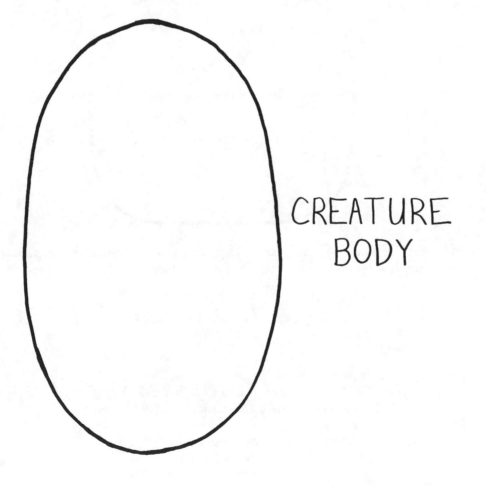

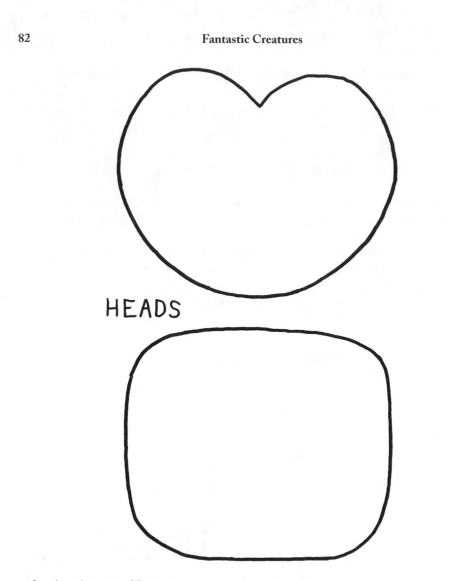

HEADS

and color them in. Then they can arrange the parts on construction paper and glue them down to create their own fantastic creature.

Suggested Booktalk Titles

Picture Books

Base, Graeme. *Animalia*. Abrams, 1993.
Cherry, Lynne. *The Dragon and the Unicorn*. Gulliver, 1995.
Demi. *Demi's Dragons and Fantastic Creatures*. Holt, 1993.
Demi. *The Firebird*. Holt, 1994.
Mayer, Marianna. *The Unicorn and the Lake*. Dial, 1990.
Pilkey, Dav. *God Bless the Gargoyles*. Harcourt, 1996.

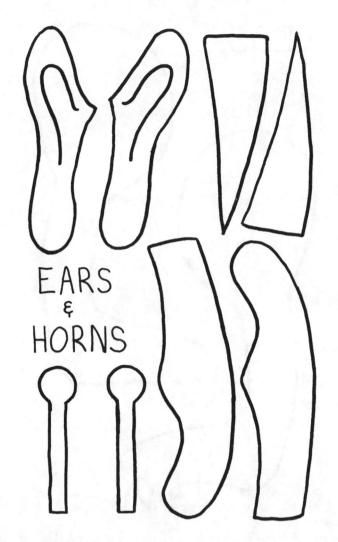

EARS
&
HORNS

Chapter Books

Cooper, Susan. *The Boggart and the Monster*. Simon & Schuster, 1997.

Dadey, Debbie. *Gremlins Don't Chew Bubblegum*. Scholastic, 1995. Also others in Bailey School Kids series.

Rowling, J.K. *Fantastic Beasts and Where to Find Them by Newt Scamander*. Scholastic, 2001.

Wrede, Patricia. *Book of Enchantments*. Harcourt, 1996.

Yolen, Jane. *Here There Be Unicorns*. Harcourt, 1994.

Folklore

Marx, Doug. *Mythical Beasts*. Capstone, 1991.

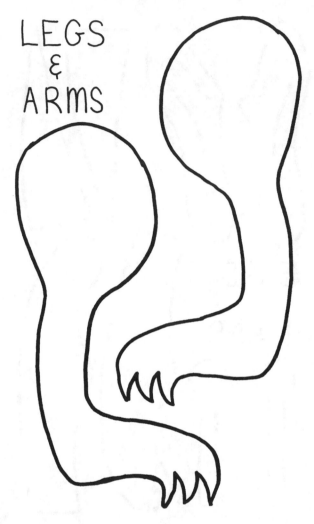

Mayo, Margaret. *Mythical Birds & Beasts from Many Lands*. Dutton, 1997.

Ross, Stewart. *Dragons and Demons (Myths and Legends from Asia Brought to Life with a Wild Text and Awesome Facts)*. Copper Beach, 1998.

San Souci, Robert D. *Sukey and the Mermaid*. Four Winds, 1992.

Weil, Lisl. *Of Witches and Monsters and Wondrous Creatures*. Atheneum, 1985.

Nonfiction

Carle, Eric. *Eric Carle's Dragons Dragons and Other Creatures That Never Were*. Philomel, 1991.

Krishnaswami, Uma. *The Broken Tusk: Stories of the Hindu God Ganesha*. Linnet, 1996.

Rockwell, Anne F. *The One-Eyed Giant and Other Monsters from the Greek Myths*. Greenwillow, 1996.

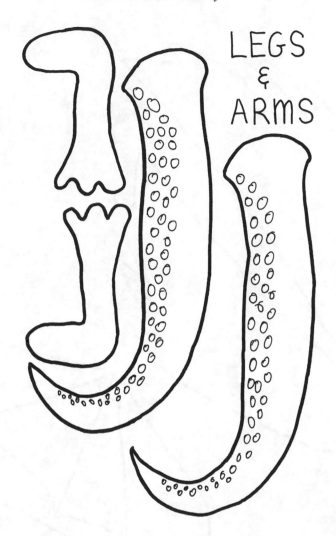

LEGS & ARMS

Just for Fun

Cohen, Shari. *Draw Fantasy: Dragons, Centaurs & Other Mythological Characters.* Lowell House, 1997.

Montroll, John. *Mythological Creatures and the Chinese Zodiac in Origami.* Dover, 1996.

Other Resources

Beethoven. *Symphony No. 6 ("Pastoral") Op. 68* (sound recording).

Giblin, James Cross. *The Truth About Unicorns.* HarperCollins, 1991.

Irish Rovers, The. *A Child's Celebration of the World* (sound recording). Music for Little People, 1998. Track: "The Unicorn."

WINGS

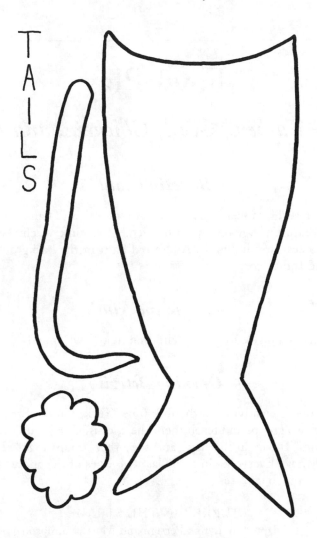

McHargue, Georgess. *The Beasts of Never*. Delacorte, 1988.

Mayer, Marianna. *Pegasus*. Morrow, 1998.

Peter, Paul, and Mary. *Peter, Paul & Mommy* (sound recording). Warner Bros., 1969. Track: "Puff (the Magic Dragon)."

Silverstein, Shel. *Where the Sidewalk Ends*. Harper & Row, 1974. See "The Unicorn."

See also: Resources for "Delightful Dragons."

Fowl Play

—— *Turkeys, Geese, Chickens, and Ducks*

Bulletin Board

This barnyard bird scene makes a great November (Thanksgiving Day) bulletin board. Feature a large turkey, with several other turkeys, chickens, geese, and ducks of all sizes surrounding it. Add a red barn in the background with some haystacks and Indian corn.

Background Music

Play bluegrass music to get the children in a "fowl" mood.

Opening Activity

We wrote our own lyrics to the folk tune "Turkey in the Straw." Divide the children into two groups and teach them the chorus. One group sings "Turkey in the straw" and "Turkey in the hay," and the other group sings "Haw haw haw" and "Hey hey hey." Everyone sings the last two lines of the chorus together. The librarians sing the four verses.

"TURKEY IN THE STRAW"
Adapted by Lynne Perrigo and Martha Simpson

Oh I had a little chicken and she wouldn't lay an egg
No matter how I cried, no matter how I begged
So I boiled me some water
And I grabbed her by the leg
And that gosh darn chicken laid a hard-boiled egg!

(CHORUS)
Turkey in the Straw (haw haw haw)
Turkey in the hay (hey hey hey)
Funniest thing I ever saw
Here's a little ditty called "Turkey in the Straw."

Did you ever go a-swimming on a sunny sunny day
When all the little goosies are a-swimmin' in the bay
With their hands in their pockets
And their pockets in their pants
And all the little goosies do the hootchie kootchie dance!

(CHORUS)

Oh I took me to the market and I bought myself a duck
And I taught him how to gobble and I taught him how to cluck
Oh but when we practiced how to quack
His little throat got stuck
He wasn't good at quacking, but he learned to drive a truck!

(CHORUS)

Oh the most amazing turkey that I ever ever saw
Was the tom that belonged to my dear grandpaw
He would gobble out a tune
And pluck a banjo with his claw
And that's why I'm a-singing 'bout the Turkey in the Straw!

(CHORUS)

Story

Tell *The Golden Goose* by Linda M. Jennings.
Materials: A large, stuffed toy goose; a crown for the princess.
Have children act out the part where someone gets stuck to the goose, and then other people get stuck to the person in front of them. Invent enough roles so that all the children become stuck and form a long line around the storyteller, who is carrying the goose. A child or a teen volunteer can be the princess.

Participation Activity

Dance "The Chicken Dance" with the children.

Craft—Paper Bag Turkeys

Materials: Lunchbag-size brown paper bag; construction paper used as follows: red head, orange feet, red wattle and yellow beak (see patterns), and yellow strips for legs; eyes (see drawing); white copy paper; small white paper plate; crayons; liquid glue; twist tie; newspaper scraps.
Procedure: Ahead of time trace and cut out the construction paper parts. Fold

the strips of yellow paper for the turkey legs accordion-style. Fold the beak in half. Photocopy the eyes and cut them out.

At the program, children can crumple up some newspaper to stuff their paper bags. Close the bag with the twist tie. Color the paper plate to use for the tail. Glue the bottom half of the beak onto the turkey's face so that the top half moves freely. Glue the wattle alongside the beak. Then glue the head, tail, and legs onto the bag as shown in the drawing.

Suggested Booktalk Titles

Picture Books

Auch, Mary Jane. *Peeping Beauty*. Holiday, 1993.
Bang, Molly. *Goose*. Scholastic, 1996.

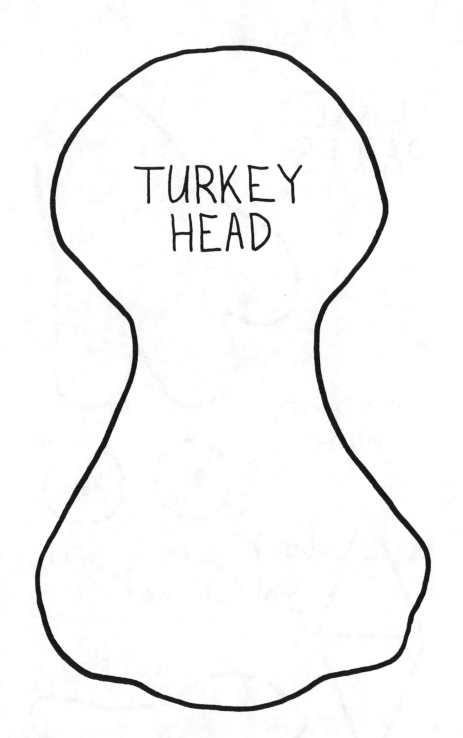

TURKEY
HEAD

Bunting, Eve. *A Turkey for Thanksgiving*. Clarion, 1991.
Kroll, Steven. *One Tough Turkey: A Thanksgiving Story*. Holiday, 1982.
Schatell, Brian. *Farmer Goff and His Turkey Sam*. Lippincott, 1982.
Silverman, Erica. *Don't Fidget a Feather!* Macmillan, 1994.

TURKEY PARTS

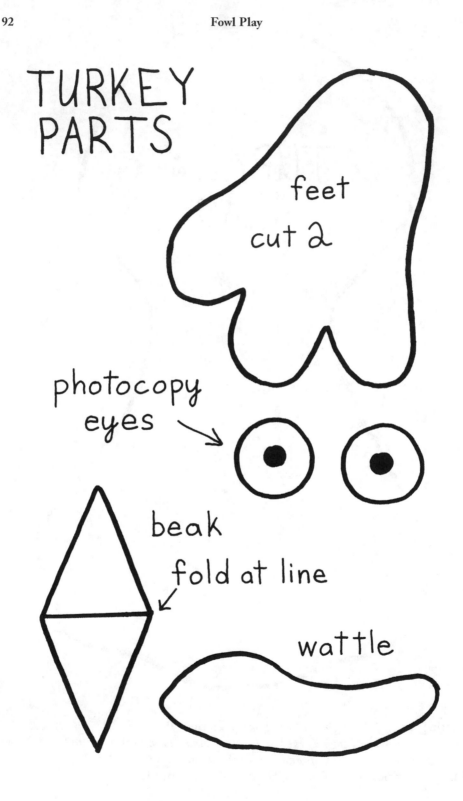

feet
cut 2

photocopy
eyes

beak
fold at line

wattle

Easy Readers

Benchley, Nathaniel. *The Strange Disappearance of Arthur Cluck*. Harper & Row, 1967.

Quackenbush, Robert M. *Stairway to Doom: A Miss Mallard Mystery*. Prentice Hall, 1983. Also others in series.

Chapter Book

Karr, Kathleen. *The Great Turkey Walk*. Farrar, 1998.

Folklore

Cauley, Lorinda Bryan, reteller. *The Goose and the Golden Coins*. Harcourt, 1981.

Nonfiction

Arnosky, Jim. *All About Turkeys*. Scholastic, 1998.

Fowler, Allan. *The Chicken or the Egg?* Children's Press, 1993.

Potter, Tessa. *Ducks and Geese*. Steck-Vaughn, 1990.

Just for Fun

Morrison, Sol. *The World's Greatest Book of Chicken Jokes and Other Fowl Humor*. Poetry Center, 1995.

Walton, Rick, and Ann Walton. *Dumb Clucks! Jokes About Chickens*. Lerner, 1987.

Other Resources

Greg & Steve Big Fun (sound recording). Youngheart, 1998. Track: "The Chicken Dance."

"The Henny Penny Players." *Copycat*. Copycat Press, March/April 1995.

Jennings, Linda M. *The Golden Goose*. Silver Burdett, 1985.

Rosenthal, Phil. *Turkey in the Straw* (sound recording). American Melody, 1985.

"Spring, Chickens, and Eggs … Oh My!" *Copycat*. Copycat Press, March/April 1998.

"Tabletop Turkey." *Copycat*. Copycat Press, Nov./Dec. 1994.

"Take Home Turkeys." *Copycat*. Copycat Press, Nov./Dec. 1996.

"Two Little Turkeys." *Copycat*. Copycat Press, Nov./Dec. 1997.

Fractured Fairy Tales

Fairy Tales Revisited

Bulletin Board

Parody several popular fairy tales with this amusing display. On the right of the bulletin board, construct a large paper model of Cinderella's castle, but with a slight difference. Instead of making the turrets stand straight up, place some of them at an angle as if they are cracked and tipping over. (The March/April 1996 issue of *Copycat* has a great castle pattern that can be enlarged.) Make the giant's leg equal to the size of the castle. The leg (pants) should start below the knee and end with a boot. Tack up the giant's leg so that it looks like he is crashing through the ceiling, and stepping on the castle, causing it to crack. To the left of the fractured castle, pin up several pairs of easily identifiable fairy tale characters, but switch their heads. For example, Little Red Riding Hood wears the wolf's head, and the wolf's body has a girl's head with a red hood. Use large green paper leaves (from Jack's beanstalk) to decorate the borders.

Background Music

Play tunes from Disney fairy tale movies, such as *Cinderella* and *Sleeping Beauty*. Or play *Mainly Mother Goose* by Sharon, Lois, & Bram.

Opening Activity

Sing "With Apologies to Mother Goose" with the children.

Story/Participation Activity

Do the following fill-in-the-blanks story, developed by Martha Simpson, with the children. Don't tell them in advance what the story is. Ask them to contribute adjectives, nouns, colors, etc. (explain these terms if needed). When all the blanks are filled in, have some children briefly recount the story of *Snow White and the Seven Dwarfs*. Then read the version you and the children created.

SNOW _____ AND THE SEVEN _____
      [color #1]   [plural noun #1]

Once upon a time, there was a beautiful young princess named Snow

_____. Her stepmother, the queen, was jealous of Snow _____
[color #1]   [color #1]

because she wanted to be the most _____ lady in the kingdom. Every
                                    [adjective]

day, the queen would look into her _____ mirror and say, "Mirror,
                                    [adjective]

mirror, on the _____, who is the _____ one of all? The
            [noun]   [adjective -est #1]

mirror always said, "You queen, are the _____ one of all." But one
                              [adjective-est #1]

day, when Snow _____ was _____ years old, the mirror had a
            [color #1]   [number]

different answer. It said, "Snow _____ is the _____lady
                     [color #1]   [adjective-est #1]

in the kingdom." This made the queen so angry, she turned _____
                                        [color]

with rage. She told one of her servants to take Snow _____ into the
                                  [color #1]

woods and _____ her. But instead, the servant let Snow _____
        [verb]   [color #1]

escape. Afraid and _____, Snow _____ ran through the
            [adjective]   [color #1]

_____ woods until she came to the _____ cottage of the
[adjective]   [adjective]

seven _____. Snow _____ lived happily with the seven
     [plural noun #1]   [color #1]

_____ until the queen discovered that Snow _____ was
[plural noun #1]   [color #1]

still alive. The _____ queen drank a _____ potion that turned
       [adjective]   [adjective]

her into an old _____ woman. Disguised, the queen went to the
                  [occupation #1]

cottage where Snow _____ lived, and offered her a _____
                    [color #1]   [food #1]

to eat. The seven _____ were not there to protect Snow
                  [plural noun #1]

_____. She trusted the old _____ and took a bite of the
[color #1]   [occupation #1]

_____. But the _____ was poisoned, and Snow _____
[food #1]   [food #1]   [color # 1]

fell into a _____ sleep. Snow _____ slept for _____
            [adjective]   [color #1]   [number]

years, until a handsome _____ came by. When he saw her, he was so
                        [occupation #2]

overcome by her beauty that he kissed her on her _____. Instantly,
                                                  [body part]

Snow _____ awoke. The seven _____ were so happy, they
      [color #1]   [plural noun #1]

_____ for joy. Then the handsome _____ and Snow _____
[past tense verb]   [occupation #2]   [color #1]

were married. And they lived _____ ever after.
                              [adverb]

Craft—Fractured Fairy Tale Characters Flip Book

Materials: Flip book pages of these popular fairy tale characters—Little Red Riding Hood, the Big Bad Wolf, Cinderella, Prince Charming, one of the Three Little Pigs, and a witch (see drawings); white copy paper; colored pencils or crayons; scissors; stapler.

Procedure: Ahead of time photocopy the flip book pages, making sure the dotted lines on each page match up.

At the program give each child copies of all the pictures to color. When the children are done coloring, staple the pages together at the left side, like a book. An adult should use a good pair of scissors to cut through the dotted lines, leaving a margin on the left so that the book does not fall apart. Then the children can flip the sections of their books to mix up the heads, torsos, and legs of the fairy tale characters.

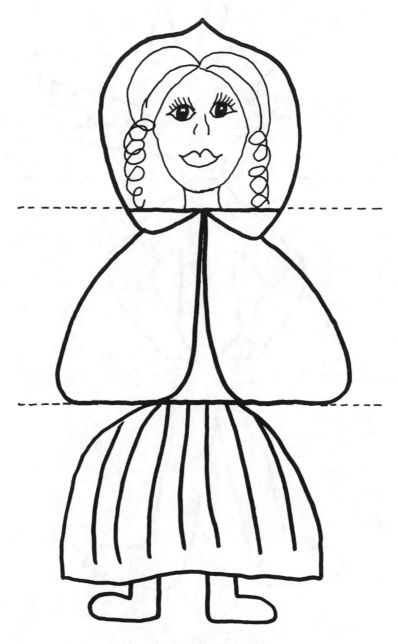

Suggested Booktalk Titles

Picture Books

Ada, Alma Flor. *Dear Peter Rabbit*. Macmillan, 1994.
Bloom, Becky. *Wolf!* Orchard, 1999.
Lowell, Susan. *The Bootmaker and the Elves*. Orchard, 1997.

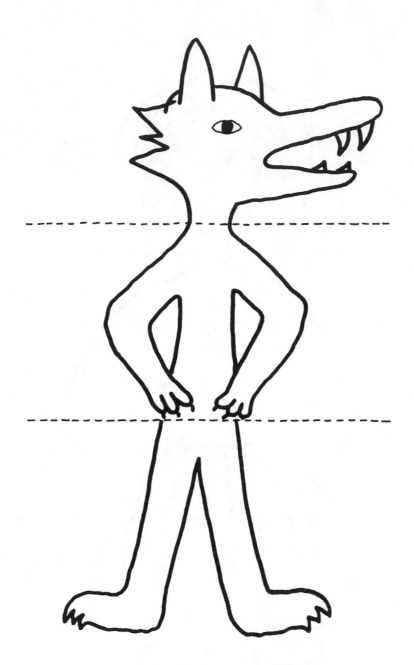

MacDonald, Alan. *Beware of the Bears!* Little Tiger, 1998.

Perlman, Janet. *The Emperor Penguin's New Clothes*. Viking, 1995.

Rosen, Michael. *Little Rabbit Foo Foo*. Simon & Schuster, 1990.

Scieszka, Jon. *The Frog Prince, Continued*. Viking, 1991.

Scieszka, Jon. *The Stinky Cheese Man and Other Fairly Stupid Tales*. Viking, 1992.

Scieszka, Jon. *The True Story of the Three Little Pigs*. Scholastic, 1989.

Stanley, Diane. *Rumpelstiltskin's Daughter*. Morrow, 1997.

Trivizas, Eugene. *The Three Little Wolves and the Big, Bad Pig*. Macmillan, 1993.

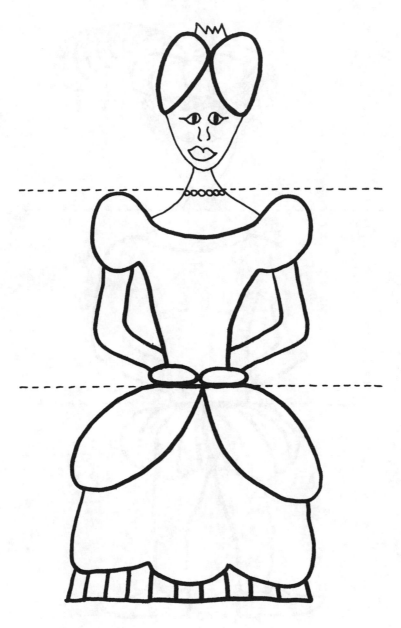

Easy Readers

Harris, Jim. *Jack and the Giant: A Story Full of Beans*. Rising Moon, 1997.
Jackson, Ellen B. *Cinder Edna*. Lothrop, 1994.
Rankin, Laura. *Merl and Jasper's Supper Caper*. Simon & Schuster, 1997.
Yolen, Jane. *Sleeping Ugly*. Coward, 1981.

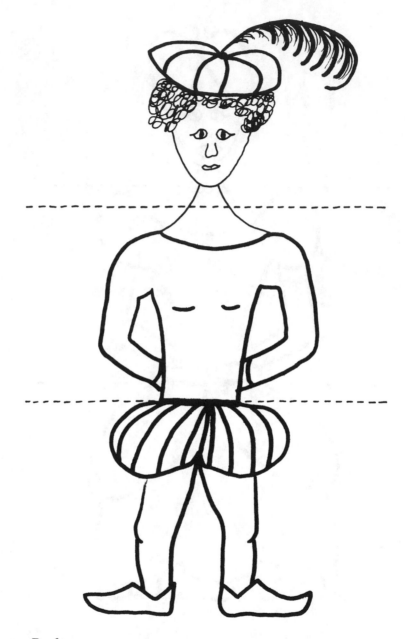

Chapter Books

Brooke, William J. *A Telling of the Tales: Five Stories*. Harper & Row, 1990.
Napoli, Donna Jo. *The Prince of the Pond*. Dutton, 1992.

Poetry

Lansky, Bruce. *The New Adventures of Mother Goose: Gentle Rhymes for Happy Times*.
    Simon & Schuster, 1993.

Just for Fun

MacGregor, Carol. *The Fairy Tale Cookbook*. Macmillan, 1982.
Ross, Kathy. *Crafts from Your Favorite Fairy Tales*, Millbrook, 1997.
Vogt, Anke. *Fairy Tale Fancy Dress*. Players, 1989.
Walton, Rick. *Kiss a Frog: Jokes About Fairy Tales, Knights, and Dragons*. Lerner, 1989.

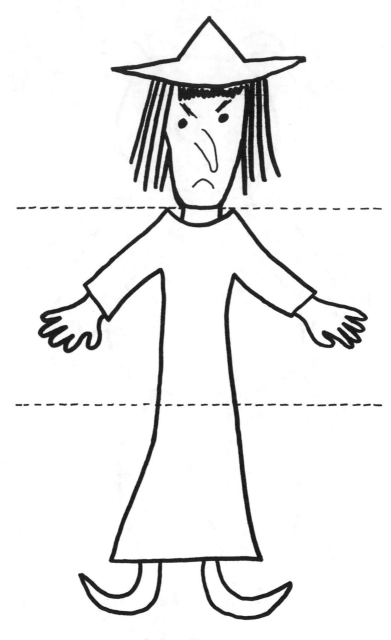

Other Resources

Children's Favorite Songs performed by Larry Groce and the Disneyland Children's
  Sing-along Chorus (sound recording). Buena Vista, 1979–1990. Track: "With
  Apologies to Mother Goose."
Freeman, Judy. *Hi Ho Librario! Songs, Chants and Stories to Keep Kids Humming.*
  Rock Hill Press, 1997. See: "Prinderella and the Cince."

"Hans Christian Andersen: The Fairy Tale Prince." *Copycat.* Copycat Press, March/April 1996.

"Little Red Riding Hood—The Musical." *Copycat.* Copycat Press, March/April 1998.

"Mother Goose Games." *Copycat.* Copycat Press, May/June 1996.

Sharon, Lois, & Bram. *Mainly Mother Goose* (sound recording). A&M Records, 1984.

Sitarz, Paula Gaj. *Story Time Sampler.* Libraries Unlimited, 1997. See "Fractured Fairy Tales."

Gardens Grow

Gardens and Gardening

Bulletin Board

If you have a collection of house plants, try to incorporate one or more of them into this bulletin board. A long philodendron is a natural choice for a border (but you may use cut-out green construction paper leaves as an alternative). Make an enormous spider plant by cutting white paper into narrow leaves. Make green stripes on the leaves with a marker, gather them into a bunch and secure the bunch with wire. If you wish to add spider plant babies, make each "baby" using the same technique as for the large plant. Use a very long piece of wire (one to three feet) to wrap the base of each baby spider plant, leaving most of the wire free. Tuck the free ends of the wires into the base of the mother plant. From orange construction paper cut out a large flower pot. Place the spider plant in the center of the bulletin board and then secure the flower pot over the base so that the spider plant is growing out of the pot. For the rest of the board, make green grass with construction paper and add colorful origami flowers.

Background Music

Use songs about plants and gardening in a recording of background music: "The Garden Song" (Peter, Paul, and Mary), "Where Have All the Flowers Gone?" (various artists), "Tip-toe Through the Tulips with Me" (Tiny Tim), "Crimson and Clover" (Tommy James), "Being Green" (Kermit the Frog), "Octopus's Garden" (The Beatles), or play the sound recording *Family Garden* by John McCutcheon.

Opening Activity

Sing "The Green Grass Grew All Around."
Materials: large art pad; markers.
As you progress through the song, draw the part described in each verse.

Story

Tell "Princess Dicentra in the Bleeding Heart" from *Sunflower Houses* by Sharon Lovejoy.

Materials: Flower from bleeding heart plant (*Dicentra spectabilis*).

This story is best told in the late spring when the old-fashioned variety of the bleeding heart is in bloom. Bring a bouquet of bleeding heart flowers to the program so you can use one of the flowers at the end of the story for the Princess Dicentra being set free from the inside of the flower. Many similar stories using flowers as props are in *Hidden Stories in Plants*, by Anne Pellowski (see Other Resources). Or tell *The Magic Grove: A Persian Folktale* by Libuse Palecek.

Participation Activity

Have the children pretend to be seeds that grow into plants. They start as seeds curled up into little balls on the floor. Play the theme music from *2001: A Space Odyssey* and talk them through the process of sprouting, growing stems, reaching up to the sun on the tips of their toes, and finally, blossoming.

Craft—Pot of Flowers

Materials: Small terra cotta pot (or pressboard paper pot, margarine tub, detergent bottle lid, or any other suitable container); foam egg carton; chenille stems or pipe cleaners; green construction paper; modeling dough (see Appendix I for recipe); glue stick; crayons or markers; push pin.

Procedure: Ahead of time cut the foam egg carton into cups with scalloped edges. Punch a pinhole in the bottom of each cup. Cut the chenille stems or pipe cleaners into six-inch lengths. Cut pairs of leaves from green construction paper (see pattern).

At the program let the children decorate the pots with crayons or markers (if using pressboard, markers will be better). To make a flower, insert a chenille stem through the pinhole in the base of a foam egg cup so that about one half inch of the stem emerges from the center of the cup (it should look like a pistil or stamen). Fold a pair of leaves in half around flower stem so that it becomes one leaf and glue facing sides of leaf together. Children may make several flowers if they want. Put a lump of dough in the bottom of the pot and stick the flower stems into it to make a flower arrangement.

POT OF FLOWERS— LEAF

fold leaf around stem

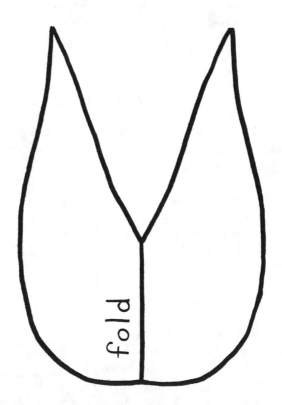

fold

Suggested Booktalk Titles

Picture Books

Anderson, Janet. *Sunflower Sal*. Whitman, 1997.
Cooney, Barbara. *Miss Rumphius*. Viking, 1982.

Ernst, Lisa Campbell. *Miss Penny and Mr. Grubbs*. Collier, 1991.
Glass, Andrew. *Folks Call Me Appleseed John*. Doubleday, 1995.
Perkins, Lynn Rae. *Home Lovely*. Greenwillow, 1995.

Easy Readers

Buller, Jon. *Felix and the 400 Frogs*. Random, 1996.
Himmelman, John. *The Clover County Carrot Contest*. Silver Press, 1991.
Rockwell, Anne F. *How My Garden Grew*. Macmillan, 1982.

Chapter Books

Burnett, Frances Hodgson. *The Secret Garden*. Harper & Row, 1987.
Dadey, Debbie. *Frankenstein Doesn't Plant Petunias*. Scholastic, 1993.
Fleischman, Sid. *McBroom's Ear*. Norton, 1969.
Quattlebaum, Mary. *Jackson Jones and the Puddle of Thorns*. Delacorte, 1994.

Folklore

dePaola, Tomie. *The Legend of the Poinsettia*. Putnam, 1994.
Morris, Winifred. *The Magic Leaf*. Atheneum, 1987.
Kellogg, Steven. *Jack and the Beanstalk*. Morrow, 1991.
Stevens, Janet. *Tops and Bottoms*. Harcourt, 1995.

Nonfiction

Bjork, Christina. *Linnea's Windowsill Garden*. Farrar, 1988.
Lerner, Carol. *My Backyard Garden*. Morrow, 1998.
Wilkes, Angela. *Growing Things*. Osborne, 1984.

Biography

Bjork, Christina. *Linnea in Monet's Garden*. Farrar, 1987.
Croll, Carolyn. *Redouté: The Man Who Painted Flowers*. Putnam, 1995.

Poetry

Lindbergh, Reeve. *Johnny Appleseed: A Poem*. Joy Street, 1990.

Just for Fun

Lobel, Arnold. *The Rose in My Garden*. Greenwillow, 1984.
Mallett, David. *Inch by Inch: The Garden Song*. HarperCollins, 1995.

Other Resources

Bomans, Godfried. *The Wily Witch: And All the Other Fairy Tales and Fables*. Stemmer House, 1977. See "The Sunday Child."

Bruchac, Joseph. *Native Plant Stories*. Fulcrum, 1995.

Caduto, Michael J., and Joseph Bruchac. *Keepers of Life: Discovering Plants Through Native American Stories and Earth Activities for Children*. Fulcrum, 1994.

Gary, Charles L. *Flower Fables*. EPM, 1978.

"Grass in the Class." *Copycat*. Copycat Press, March/April 1998.

"Growing Like a Sunflower." *Copycat*. Copycat Press, Sept./Oct. 1994.

Lewis, Shari. *One-Minute Favorite Fairy Tales*. Doubleday, 1985. See "Baba Yaga and the Hedgehog."

Lovejoy, Sharon. *Sunflower Houses: Garden Discoveries for Children of all Ages*. Interweave, 1991. See "Princess Dicentra in the Bleeding Heart."

Palecek, Libuse. *The Magic Grove: A Persian Folktale*. Neugebauer, 1985.

Pellowski, Anne. *Hidden Stories in Plants: Unusual and Easy-to-Tell Stories from Around the World Together with Creative Things to Do While Telling Them*. Macmillan, 1990.

Rhoades, Diane. *Garden Crafts for Kids: 50 Great Reasons to Get Your Hands Dirty*. Sterling, 1995.

Rosenthal, Phil. *The Green Grass Grew All Around* (sound recording). American Melody, 1995.

Sitarz, Paula Gaj. *More Picture Book Story Hours*. Libraries Unlimited, 1990. See "How Does Your Garden Grow?"

"Soil Science." *Copycat*. Copycat Press, March/April 1996.

2001: A Space Odyssey (sound recording). CBS Records, 1990. Track: "Also Sprach Zarathustra."

Go Team!

Sports

Bulletin Board

Display posters, game schedules, caps, and other memorabilia of the major and minor league and school sports teams in your area. Or, you may choose to concentrate on one sport, such as baseball.

Background Music

Play a recording of team sports songs, such as *Hail to the Victors!* (football) or *Baseball's Greatest Hits.*

Opening Activity

If you have some teen volunteers who are cheerleaders at their schools, have them teach the children some of the cheers they use. You can also sing popular sports songs, such as "Take Me Out to the Ball Game."

Story

Choose a story or a chapter from a novel about a sport that is played at the time of year you are conducting the program. For football, basketball, or baseball, you could look at some books by Matt Christopher. Bruce Brooks has a series of books about young hockey players, or tell the story *Atalanta's Race.*

Participation Activity

Play a couple of sports-themed games with the children. Start with The Sports Equipment Matching Game. Hold up various balls, racquets, helmets, and clubs, and let the children identify which sport uses the items.

Next, play Sports Talk. Call out some sports terms and let the children tell you what sport the word or phrase comes from, and what it means. Some terms may have different meanings for different sports. For example, "strike" is used in both baseball and bowling.

Craft—Sports Pennants

Materials: Large sheet of construction paper; dowel; print-outs of various major and minor league and school team logos; magazine pictures of sports players, team mascots, and equipment; markers; colored pencils or crayons; glue stick; scissors; masking tape.

Procedure: Ahead of time cut the construction paper in half diagonally, to make two triangular pennants per sheet. Print and cut out names of various teams.

At the program let the children color and glue pictures on their pennants. Help them attach the dowels with masking tape.

Suggested Booktalk Titles

Picture Books

Brown, Marc. *D.W. Flips!* Little, Brown, 1988.
Isenberg, Barbara, and Marjorie Jaffe. *Albert the Running Bear's Exercise Book.* Clarion, 1984.

Chapter Books

Brooks, Bruce. Various hockey titles in *The Wolf Bay Wings* series.
Christopher, Matt. Various sports titles.

Nonfiction

Jackman, Joan. *The Young Gymnast*. DK, 1995. Also others in series.
Kiralfy, Bob. *The Most Excellent Book of How to Be a Cheerleader*. Copper Beach, 1997.
Owens, Tom. *Collecting Baseball Cards*. Millbrook, 1998.
Schiffer, Don. *Football Rules in Pictures*. Perigee, 1994. Also others in series.

Biographies

Dunham, Montrew. *Abner Doubleday: Young Baseball Pioneer*. Aladdin, 1995.
Grolier All-Pro Biographies, various titles in series.

Poetry

Ernest L. Thayer's Casey at the Bat. Handprint Books, 2000.
Hopkins, Lee Bennett. *Opening Days: Sports Poems.* Harcourt, 1996.
Korman, Gorden. *The Last-Place Sports Poems of Jeremy Bloom: A Collection of Poems About Winning, Losing, and Being a Good Sport.* Scholastic, 1996.

Just for Fun

Christopher, Matt. *Baseball Jokes and Riddles.* Little, Brown, 1996.
Cohen, Paul. *Sporty Riddles.* Whitman, 1989.
Hall, Katy. *Really, Really Bad Sports Jokes.* Candlewick, 1998.
Sullivan, George. *Don't Step on the Foul Line: Sports Superstition.* Millbrook, 2000.
Tallarico, Tony. *Drawing and Cartooning All-Star Sports.* Perigee, 1998.

Other Resources

Baseball's Greatest Hits (sound recording). Rhino Records, 1989.
Brokaw, Meredith, and Annie Gilbar. *The Penny Whistle Any Day Is a Holiday Party Book.* Simon & Schuster, 1996. See "Play Ball."
Climo, Shirley. *Atalanta's Race: A Greek Myth.* Clarion, 1995.
Cohn, Amy L., compiler. *From Sea to Shining Sea.* Scholastic, 1993. See "Go Team!" section.
Diagram Group. *Rules of the Game: The Complete Illustrated Encyclopedia of All the Sports of the World.* St. Martin's, 1995.
Hail to the Victors! (sound recording). Columbia, 1978.
Paxton, Tom. *Balloon-alloon-alloon* (sound recording). Pax Records, 1987. Track: "The Monkey's Baseball Game."
Paxton, Tom. *The Jungle Baseball Game.* Morrow, 1999.
Sitarz, Paula Gaj. *Story Time Sampler.* Libraries Unlimited, 1997. See "Games and Sports."

Gulp!

—— *People, Animals, and Things Eating Stuff They Shouldn't*

Bulletin Board

Start with a sea green background. Tack up a series of fish, with their mouths wide open, in a straight line across the bulletin board. The one on the far left will be small, and each fish to the right will grow progressively larger, until the one at the far right is a giant monster fish. The effect should look like each fish is ready to gobble up the one in front of it. You can add sea shells, rocks, coral, seaweed and other underwater items to decorate the display.

Background Music

Since this is a rather absurd theme for a program, play a compilation of novelty songs about unusual eating habits. Look for songs such as "Eat It" (Weird Al Yankovic), "Purple People Eater" (Sheb Wooley), and "Junk Food Junkie" (Larry Groce).

Opening Activity

Recite "Boa Constrictor" from *Where the Sidewalk Ends* by Shel Silverstein. **Materials:** A large blanket.

Have everyone sit together in a big circle, feet in the middle. Place the blanket in the center of the circle—it will be the boa. Each person should hold onto an edge of the blanket. Recite the poem, moving the blanket up to cover the part of the body mentioned in each line. When you get to the last line, everyone will throw the blanket over their heads. Your kids will probably want to do this a second time!

Story

Tell "The Parrot and the Cat" from *Nursery Tales from Around the World* or one of the other stories mentioned under Other Resources. You can also read some humorous poems from the chapter "Never Eat More Than You Can Lift" from the anthology *Never Take a Pig to Lunch: Poems About the Fun of Eating*, or the Shel Silverstein poems noted below.

Participation Activity

"THERE ONCE WAS A BABY WHO SWALLOWED SOME DOUGH"
Developed by Martha Simpson

Ask the children if they know the rhyme, "There Was an Old Lady Who Swallowed a Fly." Quickly recap the verses if necessary. Show the children some alternate versions that have been published, such as *I Know an Old Lady Who Swallowed a Pie* and *There Was an Old Lady who Swallowed a Trout*. Next, tell them they are going to write their own song in this style. Using the same tune as the popular song, sing:

> *There once was a baby who swallowed some dough*
> *I don't know why he swallowed it so—*
> *Perhaps he'll grow.*

Divide the children into two groups. One will think of things the baby can swallow, and the other will think of a rhyme to go with it. Alternate turns so each group has an equal chance at both tasks. Remind the children to start with small items and end with something really big for the baby to swallow. On a large pad of paper, list the items and rhymes for all to see. When you have about eight items, have everyone sing the new song together. Link the verses this way (for example):

> *There once was a baby who swallowed a car*
> *He couldn't go far when he swallowed a car,*
> *Then he swallowed a ...*
> *And he swallowed a ...*
> *And he swallowed a ...*
> *And he swallowed some dough*
> *With one big gulp he swallowed it so—*
> *Perhaps he'll grow.*

Craft—"There Was an Old Lady Who Swallowed a Fly" Puppet

Materials: Plain brown paper lunch bag; pattern pieces for fly and other animals (see patterns), as well as the lady's eyes; white copy paper; crayons, colored pencils or markers; glue stick; plastic sandwich bag (gusseted type, not zippered); scissors; material and lace scraps; masking tape.

Procedure: Ahead of time hold the paper bag on your hand like a puppet and decide where the mouth will be. Draw an oval wide enough for the animal pieces to fit through and cut out the hole. Open the bag and tape a plastic bag to the inside of the mouth, so that the animals will fall into it. Cut scraps of material that the children can use as hair and dresses for their puppets. Photocopy the animals on white paper and cut them out.

At the program let the children draw and color in the faces and mouths of their puppets. They can draw or glue on fabric for the lady's dress and hair, and glue on the eyes. Children can also color the animals that the lady will swallow. If there is time, sing "There Was an Old Lady Who Swallowed a Fly" so the children can use their puppets.

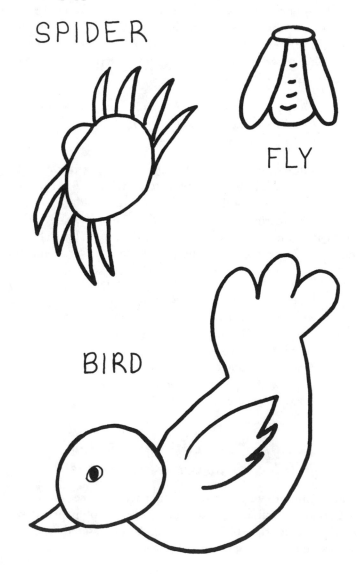

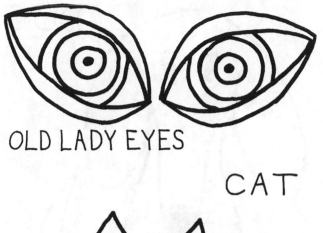

Suggested Booktalk Titles

Picture Books

Allan, Nicholas. *The Thing That Ate Aunt Julia*. Dial, 1991.
Bender, Robert. *A Most Unusual Lunch*. Dial, 1994.
Egielski, Richard. *Buz*. HarperCollins, 1995.

DOG

Grossman, Bill. *My Little Sister Ate One Hare*. Crown, 1996.
Jackson, Alison. *I Know an Old Lady Who Swallowed a Pie*. Dutton, 1997.
Noble, Trinka Hakes. *The Day Jimmy's Boa Ate the Wash*. Dial, 1980.
Sharmat, Mitchell Weinman. *Gregory the Terrible Eater*. Four Winds Press, 1980.
Sloat, Teri. *There Was an Old Lady Who Swallowed a Trout*. Holt, 1998.
Taback, Simms. *There Was an Old Lady Who Swallowed a Fly*. Viking, 1997.

Chapter Books

Naylor, Phyllis Reynolds. *Beetles, Lightly Toasted*. Atheneum, 1987.
Rockwell, Thomas. *How to Eat Fried Worms*. Watts, 1973.

Folklore

Bishop, Claire Huchet. *The Five Chinese Brothers*. Coward, 1965.
Yep, Laurence. *The Boy Who Swallowed Snakes*. Scholastic, 1994.

COW

HORSE

Nonfiction

Facklam, Margery. *Bugs for Lunch*. Charlesbridge, 1999.
Hutton, Warwick. *Jonah and the Great Fish*. Atheneum, 1984.
Showers, Paul. *What Happens to a Hamburger*. Harper & Row, 1985.
Stille, Darlene R. *The Digestive System*. Children's Press, 1997.

Other Resources

Cohn, Amy L., ed. *From Sea to Shining Sea*. Scholastic, 1993. See "The Boy Who Ate Too Much," retold by Edward L. Keithahn.

Dr. Demento 20th Anniversary Collection (sound recording). Rhino Records, 1991. This has a great assortment of novelty songs, including "Eat It" by Weird Al Yankovic, "Purple People Eater" by Sheb Wooley, and "Junk Food Junkie" by Larry Groce.

Pepper, Dennis, ed. *The Oxford Book of Scary Tales*. Oxford University, 1992. See "The Great Swallowing Monster."

Peter, Paul, and Mary. *Peter, Paul & Mommy* (sound recording). Warner, 1971. Track: "There Was an Old Lady Who Swallowed a Fly."

Sierra, Judy, reteller. *Nursery Tales from Around the World*. Clarion, 1995. See "The Parrot and the Cat," "I Know an Old Lady Who Swallowed a Fly," "The Boy Who Tried to Fool His Father, " and "Sody Sallyraytus."

Silverstein, Shel. *Where the Sidewalk Ends*. Harper & Row, 1974. See "Boa Constrictor," "Melinda Mae," and "Hungry Mungry."

Westcott, Nadine Bernard, ed. *Never Take a Pig to Lunch: Poems About the Fun of Eating*. Orchard, 1994. See the section called "Never Eat More Than You Can Lift."

Harvest Fair

Bulletin Board

Ask some children to help you with this one. Have them draw pictures of things that they saw or did at a local harvest fair. Mount the drawings on the bulletin board along with posters, flyers, tickets, photos, and other fair memorabilia.

Background Music

Play carousel or calliope music, similar to what you would hear on the midway of the county fair. Ragtime music is another good choice to promote an upbeat atmosphere.

Opening Activity

Ask the children if they have gone to any local harvest fairs. Discuss things you might see there: displays of fruits and vegetables grown by area residents during the summer, food contests, animal shows, amusement rides, arcade games, entertainment, etc. There are several traditional songs about fairs, such as "Oh, Dear, What Can the Matter Be?" and "Animal Fair." Sing some of these with the children.

Story

Relate this story of a magical fair ride: "The Merry-Go-Round" from *The Girl with the Green Ear* by Margaret Mahy.

Participation Activity

Hold a mini-fair. Set up areas for various activities resembling things people might see and do at a harvest fair, such as:

119

- Petting zoo—Let children pet stuffed animals.
- Baked goods contest—Have three or four different cookies, brownies or other baked items cut into small pieces. Let children taste each item and vote for their favorite. Award a blue ribbon to the winning dessert.
- Best home-grown vegetable—Display several pieces of one type of vegetable (six tomatoes, for example). Tell children to judge which one deserves the blue ribbon. They should consider size, ripeness, color, freshness, and other factors when awarding the prize.
- Arcade games—Set up one or more simple games, such as a ring toss or a fishing pond. Give each child a chance to win a small prize.

Craft—Carousel Horses

Materials: Card stock in pastel and bright colors; pattern pieces; one pound margarine tub with lid (the decorated kind is best); colorful plastic drinking straw; modeling dough; colored pencils, crayons or markers; glue stick; scissors; hole punch; glitter, stick-on dots, or pieces of lace trim; the smallest rubber band you can find; yarn or ribbon; sharp pencil.

Procedure: Ahead of time trace and cut out two horses from the pastel card stock. Punch a hole on each horse as shown. Cut out the circle from the bright card stock. Use a sharp pencil to punch a hole in the center that is just slightly larger in diameter than the straw. Also punch two holes opposite each other near the edge of the circle. Purchase or make modeling dough (see Appendix I for recipe). In the center of the plastic margarine tub lid, use the sharp pencil to poke a hole just large enough for the straw to go through (but not so large that the straw will be able to move around). Tightly wrap a rubber band around the straw, about one half inch from one end. Cut two seven-inch pieces of yarn or thin ribbon and tie one end of each one onto an outer edge hole on the circle.

At the program let the children color their horses. Children can also decorate the circles with glitter, dots, and ribbon, and glue lace trim to the outside of their margarine tubs. To put the carousel together, place a wad of modeling dough inside the margarine tub. Hold the straw so that the rubber band is near the top. Press the bottom end of the straw through the hole of the margarine tub lid and then into the dough. Secure the lid onto the top of the tub so the straw stands up straight. Place the circle on top of the straw and press it down to rest on the rubber band to make a roof for the carousel. Help children tie the horses onto the yarn or ribbon that is attached to the roof so that the horses dangle down.

Suggested Booktalk Titles

Picture Books
Calhoun, Mary. *Blue Ribbon Henry*. Morrow, 1999.
Crews, Donald. *Night at the Fair*. Greenwillow, 1998.

CAROUSEL

Lunn, Janet Louise Swoboda. *Come to the Fair*. Tundra, 1997.
Martin, Bill, Jr. *Up and Down on the Merry-Go-Round*. Holt, 1988.
Schatell, Brian. *Farmer Goff and His Turkey Sam*. Lippincott, 1982.
Tudor, Tasha. *The County Fair*. Walck, 1964.
Wilder, Laura Ingalls. *County Fair: Adapted from the Little House Books*. Harper-
    Collins, 1997.

Easy Readers

Cooper, Elisha. *Country Fair*. Greenwillow, 1997.
Himmelman, John. *The Clover County Carrot Contest*. Silver, 1991.

CAROUSEL HORSE

Chapter Books

Kehret, Peg. *Danger at the Fair*. Cobblehill, 1995.
Spinelli, Jerry. *Blue Ribbon Blues: A Tooter Tale*. Random, 1998.
White, E.B. *Charlotte's Web*. Harper & Row, 1952.

Nonfiction

Alter, Judy. *Meet Me at the Fair: Country, State, and World's Fairs & Expositions*.
     Watts, 1997.
Bial, Raymond. *County Fair*. Houghton, 1992.

CAROUSEL TOP

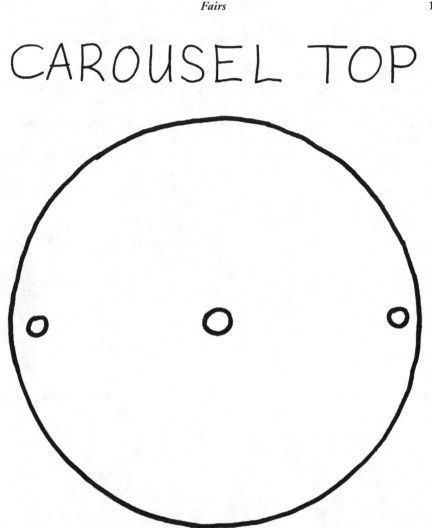

Gibbons, Gail. *Country Fair*. Little, Brown, 1994.
Lewin, Ted. *Fair!* Lothrop, 1997.
Pierce, Jack. *The State Fair Book*. Carolrhoda, 1980.

Just for Fun
Peterson, Chris. *Harvest Year*. Boyds Mills, 1996.

Other Resources

Cleveland, John. *The Calliope Cassette* (sound recording). MCA, 1980.
Fox, Dan, music arranger. *The Grandma Moses American Songbook*. Abrams, 1985.
    See "Animal Fair."

Groce, Larry. *Children's Favorites* (sound recording). Buena Vista, 1990. Track: "Animal Fair."

"Harvest Festival." *Copycat*. Copycat Press, Sept./Oct. 1994.

Joplin, Scott. *The Entertainer & Other Scott Joplin Favorites* (sound recording). Intersound, 1996. Great ragtime music.

Mahy, Margaret. *The Girl with the Green Ear*. Knopf, 1992. See "The Merry-Go-Round."

Sharon, Lois, & Bram. *Mainly Mother Goose* (sound recording). Elephant Records, 1984. Track: "Oh, Dear, What Can the Matter Be?"

Strawberry Fair: 51 Traditional Songs. A & C Black, 1985. See "Strawberry Fair," "Scarborough Fair," and "Widdicombe Fair."

Stevens, Janet. *I Went to the Animal Fair*. Holiday, 1981.

Wellstood, Dick. *Ragtime Piano Favorites* (sound recording). Special Music, 1988.

Hats Off to You!

Hats, Caps, and Crowns

Bulletin Board

Tack up five long strips of brown construction paper in a row, placing them at diagonals to the right. Make sure they are spaced evenly apart. Over this, tack up five more strips of paper at the opposite diagonal, so that the effect is of a hat rack in a criss-cross design. At the points where the strips of paper intersect, pin different hats. If your bulletin board is large enough, pin more hats along the borders.

Background Music

You may have to do some digging to find hat songs, but they're out there. Look for "Golden Helmet of Mambrino" from *The Man of La Mancha*, "Top Hat, White Tie and Tails" from *Cheek to Cheek*, "Easter Parade" from the movie of the same name, and others.

Opening Activity

Sing "My Hat, It Has Three Corners." The gestures for each word or phrase are:

MY (point to yourself)

IT (point straight out)

THREE (hold up three fingers)

AND (put palms of hands together)

BE (put thumb and fingers together and motion like a bee flying)

HAT (put hands on head)

HAS or *HAD* (make a fist)

CORNERS (left hand touches right elbow)

NOT and *WOULD NOT* (shake your head)

Sing the song with gestures once through with the children. Then say that they will sing the song and do the movements again, but instead of speaking the first

125

word (*MY*), they will do only the gesture. Repeat this process, staying silent on one additional word each time, until the whole song is done only in movement.

Story

Tell *Caps for Sale* by Esphyr Slobodkina.
Materials: Circles of poster board in assorted colors to use as hats.
At the part of the story where the monkeys take the hats, let each child take a circle. They can throw them down at the corresponding point of the story. Or, tell "For Each a Hat" from *Folding Stories: Storytelling & Origami Together as One* while making the origami shapes as directed.

Participation Activity

Dance "The Mexican Hat Dance" with the children.
Materials: A large sombrero; sound recording of "The Mexican Hat Dance."

Craft—Fancy Hats

Materials: 12" × 18" pieces of construction paper in assorted colors; lots of decorating material such as glitter, cut paper shapes, feathers, buttons, bows, pom-poms and whatever else you have on hand; liquid glue; stapler; scissors; clear tape.
Procedure: Ahead of time cut out wide strips of construction paper (length-wise) with the tiaras (see patterns) in the center.
At the program children can choose one tiara style and use whatever materials they want to decorate their hat. Then fit the hat around each child's head and carefully staple or tape the paper ends to size. Have the children parade through the library to show everyone their fancy hats.

Suggested Booktalk Titles

Picture Books

Blos, Joan W. *Martin's Hats*. Morrow, 1984.
Brett, Jan. *The Hat*. Putnam, 1997.
Greenstein, Elaine. *Mattie's Hats Won't Wear That!* Random, 1997.
Johnston, Tony. *The Witch's Hat*. Putnam, 1984.
Lowell, Susan. *Little Red Cowboy Hat*. Holt, 1996.
Seuss, Dr. *The 500 Hats of Bartholomew Cubbins*. Random, 1990.
Wildsmith, Brian. *Whose Hat Is That?* Mulberry, 1993.

HATS

TIARA STYLE #1

HATS

TIARA STYLE
#2

Easy Readers

Cushman, Doug. *Uncle Foster's Hat Tree*. Dutton, 1988.
Geringer, Laura. *A Three Hat Day*. Harper & Row, 1985.
Venn, Cecilia. *That Is Not My Hat!* Millbrook, 1998.

Chapter Books

Dadey, Debbie. *Elves Don't Wear Hard Hats*. Apple, 1995.
Haywood, Carolyn. *Eddie's Menagerie*. Morrow, 1978.

Folklore

Uchida, Yoshiko. *The Magic Listening Cap*. Harcourt, 1955.

Nonfiction

Charlesworth, Liza. *Hats Around the World*. Scholastic, 1997.
Miller, Margaret. *Whose Hat?* Morrow, 1997.

Biography

Brenner, Martha. *Abe Lincoln's Hat*. Random, 1994.
Christian, Mary Blount. *Hats Off to John Stetson*. Macmillan, 1992.

Just for Fun

Newbold, Patt, and Anne Diebel. *Paper Hat Tricks, Vol. 4: A Big Book of Hat Patterns, Folklore, Fairytales, Foreign Lands & Long Ago Hats*. Start Reading, 1992.

Other Resources

Courlander, Harold, and Albert Kofi Prempeh. *The Hat-Shaking Dance and Other Tales of the Gold Coast*. Harcourt, 1957. See "Anansi's Hat-Shaking Dance."
Kallevig, Christine Petrell. *Folding Stories: Storytelling & Origami Together as One*. Storytime Ink, 1991. See "For Each a Hat."
Reichmeier, Betty. *Sing with Me* (sound recording). Random, 1987. Track: "My Hat, It Has Three Corners."
Sitarz, Paula Gaj. *More Picture Book Story Hours*. Libraries Unlimited, 1990. See "What's On Top? Stories About Hats."
Slobodkina, Esphyr. *Caps for Sale: A Tale of a Peddler, Some Monkeys, and Their Monkey Business*. Harper & Row, 1985.
Stewart, Georgiana Liccione. *Folk Dance Fun* (sound recording). Kimbo Educational, 1984. Track: "The Mexican Hat Dance."

Here Comes a Wedding

Weddings

Bulletin Board

Drape white crepe paper along the sides and top of the bulletin board, coming together above the center with paper wedding bells. Build a giant white wedding cake in the middle of the area, decorated elaborately with doilies and lace, with a bride and groom figure on top. On either side of the cake, post cutouts of doves, his and her wedding rings, and other wedding symbols.

Background Music

You can play a selection of tunes that suggest weddings, such as "Sunrise, Sunset" (*Fiddler on the Roof*), "I'm Getting Married in the Morning" (*My Fair Lady*), or "Chapel of Love" (The Dixie Cups). Or play classical wedding-themed music such as Mozart's "Overture to The Marriage of Figaro" and Nicolai's "Overture to the Merry Wives of Windsor."

Opening Activity

Many cultures have traditional dances that people do at weddings. Teach children the Israeli horah, Greek handkerchief dance, Italian tarantella, Polish polka, Irish jig, or another popular wedding dance. Dance steps for several of these can be found in *Quickstart to Social Dancing*. Or, sing "Frog Went A-Courtin'" with the children.

Story

Tell *A Japanese Fairy Tale* by Jane Hori Iké and Baruch Zimmerman or another story of how two people met and married. Or tell the story of "The Bartered Bride" while playing the music in the background.

Participation Activity

Perform *The Mouse Bride* by Joy Cowley as a reader's theater piece.
Materials: Six copies of the script.

Retype the story into play format. Assign the roles of the Mouse, the Sun, the Cloud, the Wind, and the House to children in the group, and read the part of the Narrator yourself.

Craft—Wedding Cake Tops

Materials: Cardboard cylinder box, such as the ones Quaker Oats, hot chocolate, or salt come in; bride and groom cutout (see pattern); colored pencils, crayons, or markers; glue stick; scissors; white construction paper; cut paper flowers, doilies, lace, bows, ribbons, sequins, pom-poms and other decorative material.

Ahead of time cut the cardboard cylinder three inches from the bottom. Keep the bottom half and discard the rest. Flip the bottom over so that it becomes the top of the cake. Cover all outside surfaces of the bottom cylinder part with white construction paper.

At the program let the children color in the bride and groom figures and decorate their cakes. Help them fold the bride and groom cutouts and glue them to stand up in the center of the cake.

Suggested Booktalk Titles

Picture Books

Brown, Marc. *D.W. Thinks Big*. Joy Street, 1993.
Cox, Judy. *Now We Can Have a Wedding!* Holiday, 1998.
dePaola, Tomie. *Helga's Dowry: A Troll Love Story*. Harcourt, 1977.
English, Karen. *Nadia's Hands*. Boyds Mills, 1999.
Friedman, Ina R. *How My Parents Learned to Eat*. Houghton, 1984.
Gibbons, Gail. *Mountain Wedding*. Morrow, 1996.
Heine, Helmut. *The Pigs' Wedding*. Atheneum, 1979.
Hines, Anna Grossnickle. *When We Married Gary*. Greenwillow, 1996.
Kirk, David. *Miss Spider's Wedding*. Scholastic, 1995.
Schick, Eleanor. *Navajo Wedding: A Diné Marriage Ceremony*. Marshall Cavendish, 1999.
Soto, Gary. *Snapshots from the Wedding*. Putnam, 1997.
Wright, Courtni C. *Jumping the Broom*. Holiday, 1994.

Chapter Books

Kline, Suzy. *Horrible Harry and the Kickball Wedding*. Viking, 1992.
Leverich, Kathleen, et al. *Flower Girls* series. HarperCollins, 1997.
Spinelli, Eileen. *Lizzie Logan Gets Married*. Simon & Schuster, 1997.

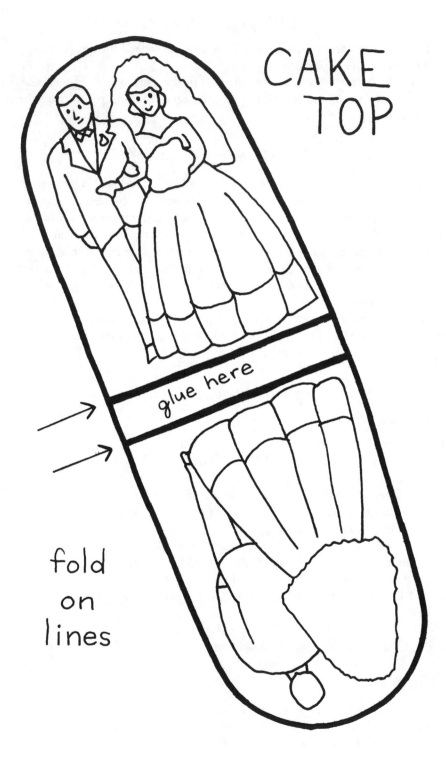

CAKE
TOP

glue here

fold
on
lines

Folklore

Jaffe, Nina. *The Way Meat Loves Salt*. Holt, 1998.

Nonfiction

Compton, Anita. *Marriage Customs*. Thomson Learning, 1993.
Gelber, Carol. *Love & Marriage Around the World*. Millbrook, 1998.
Jackson, Ellen B. *Here Come the Brides*. Walker, 1998.
Lasker, Joe. *Merry Ever After: The Story of Two Medieval Weddings*. Viking, 1976.
Plaisted, Caroline. *I'm in the Wedding, Too: A Complete Guide for Flower Girls & Junior Bridesmaids*. Dutton, 1997.

Other Resources

Allen, Jeff. *Quickstart to Social Dancing*. Qqs, 1998.
Cowley, Joy. *The Mouse Bride*. Scholastic, 1995.
Elliott, Doug. *Crawdads, Doodlebugs & Creasy Greens* (sound recording). Native Ground Music, 1995. Track: "Frog Went A-Courtin'."
Iké, Jane Hori, and Baruch Zimmerman. *A Japanese Fairy Tale*. Warne, 1982.
Langstaff, John M. *Frog Went A-Courtin'*. Harcourt, 1991.
London Symphony Orchestra. *Classical Weddings* (sound recording). Platinum Disc, 1998. Tracks: "The Bartered Bride" and other selections.
Sierra, Judy. *The Flannel Board Storytelling Book*. Wilson, 1987. See "Little Cockroach Martina."
Skalsky, Syd. *The Music Box Book*. Dutton, 1946. See "The Bartered Bride."

Hidden Treasure

Treasure

Bulletin Board

> There are more treasures in books than all the pirates' loot on Treasure Island … and best of all, you can enjoy these riches every day of your life.
>
> —*Walt Disney (1901–1966)*

Taking this quote as your credo, create a giant treasure chest from construction paper and have gilt-edged books and jewels heaped up inside and spilling out from the chest. You may wish to print the Disney quote in an attractive font on colored paper and tack it up in one corner of the bulletin board. In the other three corners hang a pirate flag (skull and crossbones), a colorful parrot, and a compass.

Background Music

Play songs about different kinds of treasure such as "Look for the Silver Lining" (Chet Baker), "Heart of Gold" (Neil Young), "Golden Years" (David Bowie), "Diamonds Are Forever" (Shirley Bassey), "Silver Threads and Golden Needles" (Linda Ronstadt), "Blue Money" (Van Morrison), "If I Were a Rich Man" (from *Fiddler on the Roof*), or "Brother Can You Spare a Dime" (various artists).

Opening Activity

The children can help write the words to a new song, "I've Been Digging for Some Treasure," developed by Martha Simpson.

Materials: Large art pad; easel; marker.

This activity lets the children help compose the words to the song. The tune is the chorus of "Battle Hymn of the Republic" (Glory, Glory Hallelujah).

> *I've been digging for some treasure*
> *I've been digging for some treasure*
> *I've been digging for some treasure*
> *And this is what I found…*

Ask the children to name some items from A to Z and list them on a large sheet of paper. Sing the song again incorporating the list of items.

Story

Tell *The Treasure*, by Uri Shulevitz.

Participation Activity

HIDDEN TREASURE GAME
Developed by Lynne Perrigo
and Martha Simpson

Create ahead of time a Hidden Treasure guessing game with clues. Gather ten containers of various shapes and sizes. Fill a coffee can with "treasure" (candy or some other small items that everyone will be able to share). Nine of your clues will reveal which containers do not contain the hidden treasure. By the last clue, the children should be able to guess which box contains the treasure through the process of elimination.

Below are ten clues you can adapt or use as they are.

Clues for "Hidden Treasure" Game

1. If you scrape your knee, look in me. (Band-Aid box)
2. Take me out to the ball game! (Cracker Jack box)
3. You might see me in February. (heart-shaped box)
4. Picture, picture on the wall—I'm small and round and not too tall. (film canister)
5. Open Sesame! I have jaws like a clam. (a carton for eggs, take-out food, etc.)
6. Long and thin and brown am I—I have two doors that you can try. (a cabinet or box with two doors or lids)
7. I have four flaps, but otherwise I'm very dull. (standard cardboard box with interlocking flaps for lid)
8. They say good things come in small packages, but not this time! (make sure this is your smallest box)
9. They say I look like my cousin, the ironing board. (a very flat box such as a tie box)
10. I would make a good drum (or "*Can* this be the container with the hidden treasure?") (coffee can)

Craft—Treasure Boxes

Materials: Cardboard egg carton; construction paper or wallpaper; old greeting cards and magazines; ribbons in various colors; bits of lace; pieces of gold and silver foil; any other decorative materials; liquid glue; scissors.

Procedure: Ahead of time cut the construction paper or wallpaper to fit over the lid of an egg carton. Cut pictures of flowers from the greeting cards and magazines. Cut the ribbon into short lengths and tie some of the pieces into small bows. Crumple pieces of gold and silver foil into tiny balls.

At the program let the children decorate the egg cartons so that they each have a treasure box for hiding their own special treasures.

Suggested Booktalk Titles

Picture Books

Allen, Pamela. *Hidden Treasure*. Putnam, 1986.

Balian, Lorna. *Leprechauns Never Lie*. Abingdon, 1980.

Cole, Joanna. *Don't Tell the Whole World!* Crowell, 1990.

Stroud, Jonathan. *The Lost Treasure of Captain Blood: How the Infamous Spammes Escaped the Jaws of Death and Won a Vast and Glorious Fortune*. Candlewick, 1996.

Turkle, Brinton. *Do Not Open*. Dutton, 1981.

Easy Readers

Burningham, John. *Come Away from the Water, Shirley*. Crowell, 1977.

Cosby, Bill. *The Treasure Hunt*. Scholastic, 1997.

Chapter Books

Avi. *Windcatcher*. Macmillan, 1991.

Byars, Betsy. *The Seven Treasure Hunts*. Harper & Row, 1991.

Sobol, Donald J. *Encyclopedia Brown and the Case of the Treasure Hunt*. Morrow, 1988.

Strickland, Brad. *Salty Dog*. Big Red Chair, 1997.

Wallace, Bill. *Danger in Quicksand Swamp*. Pocket, 1989.

Folklore

Ben-Ezer, Ehud. *Hosni the Dreamer: An Arabian Tale*. Farrar, 1997.

Carrick, Carol. *Aladdin and the Wonderful Lamp*. Scholastic, 1990.

Coombs, Patricia. *The Magic Pot*. Lothrop, 1977.

Wells, Ruth. *The Farmer and the Poor God: A Folktale from Japan*. Simon & Schuster, 1996.

Nonfiction

Donnelly, Judy. *True-Life Treasure Hunts*. Random, 1993.
Gibbons, Gail. *Sunken Treasure*. Crowell, 1988.

Just for Fun

Deem, James M. *How to Hunt Buried Treasure*. Houghton, 1992.
Hort, Larry. *Treasure Hunts! Treasure Hunts! Treasure and Scavenger Hunts to Play with Friends and Family*. HarperCollins, 2000.

Other Resources

There are several versions of the story of the treasure told in Uri Shulevitz's book:

Crossley-Holland, Kevin. *Pedlar of Swaffham*. Seabury, 1971.
Sawyer, Ruth. *The Way of the Storyteller*. Viking, 1942. See "The Peddler of Ballaghadereen."
Shulevitz, Uri. *The Treasure*. Farrar, 1978.

Hocus Pocus

Magic Tricks

Bulletin Board

Against a red background, create a white rabbit emerging from a giant black top hat. On each side of the hat place two giant white-gloved hands. Have one hand waving a magic wand over the hat. The wand should be topped with a star—make it shine with foil or glitter. Caption this board "Hocus Pocus!"

Background Music

You can choose from many magical tunes: "That Old Black Magic" (various artists), "Abracadabra" (Steve Miller Band), "Do You Believe in Magic?" (Lovin' Spoonful), "Magical Mystery Tour" (The Beatles), "Black Magic Woman" (Santana), "I Put a Spell on You" (Screamin' Jay Hawkins), "Every Little Thing She Does Is Magic" (The Police), "It's Magic" (Dinah Washington or Sarah Vaughan), "Love Potion #9" (The Searchers).

Opening Activity

Read the poem "Sybil the Magician's Last Show" from *Falling Up*, by Shel Silverstein. Demonstrate a couple of simple magic tricks such as the Rubber Pencil or the Disappearing Stamp.

Story

Tell "The Hungry Stranger: A Buddhist Story from India" from *The Family Storytelling Handbook*, by Anne Pellowski.

Materials: One sheet of plain white paper; juice of one lemon; toothpick; pen or colored pencil; desk lamp; matches.

A "magic trick" brings this story to its conclusion. Before the story, the storyteller should draw a circle on a piece of paper. Inside the circle use a toothpick dipped

138

in lemon juice to draw a picture of a rabbit and let the lemon juice dry. When the god Shakra in the story creates the image of the Rabbit on the face of the moon, the storyteller heats the piece of paper over the hot light bulb from the desk lamp (make sure you've given it time to heat up) and the image of the rabbit magically appears.

Participation Activity

Materials: Monopoly money; paper clips.

Give each child a Monopoly bill and two paper clips and teach them how to do this simple "magic" trick. Fold the bill into a "Z" shape. You now have three layers of paper. Clip one paper clip over the top two layers of paper and the other paper clip next to it over the bottom two layers of paper. Grasp either end of the paper in each hand and quickly pull it apart so that it snaps open. The paper clips should fly off the paper into the air. When you pick them up, they should be linked together.

Craft—"The-Hand-Is-Quicker-Than-the-Eye" Game

Materials: Three plastic cups; self-adhesive stickers; colored tape; markers; two pieces of foil.

Procedure: Ahead of time cut the pieces of foil to size. The size will depend on the cups—when a piece of foil is crumpled into a ball a cup should fit over it with just a little room to spare.

At the program have the children decorate the cups with stickers and markers. Crumple the two pieces of foil into two round balls that will fit underneath the cups. The children now have a magic swap game that they can use to fool their friends and family. To play the swap game, place the two balls of foil under two of the cups. Swap the cups around very quickly. Feel where the foil balls are by grasping the cups firmly during the swapping. Stop swapping and ask a spectator to point to a cup containing a ball. If the cup contains a ball, squeeze the sides of the cup so that the ball is lifted when the cup is lifted and the cup appears to be empty.

Suggested Booktalk Titles

Picture Books

Alexander, Sue. *World Famous Muriel and the Magic Mystery*. Crowell, 1990.
Bemelmans, Ludwig. *Madeline's Christmas*. Viking, 1985.
dePaola, Tomie. *Strega Nona's Magic Lesson*. Harcourt, 1982.
Grejniec, Michael. *Who Is My Neighbor?* Random House, 1994.

Houghton, Eric. *Walter's Magic Wand*. Watts, 1989.
Kroll, Steven. *Fat Magic*. Holiday House, 1978.
Laurin, Anne. *Perfect Crane*. Harper & Row, 1981.
Van Allsburg, Chris. *The Garden of Abdul Gasazi*. Houghton, 1979.

Easy Readers

Howe, James. *Rabbit-Cadabra!* Morrow, 1993.
Kessler, Ethel. *Grandpa Witch and the Magic Doobelator*. Macmillan, 1981.
Marzollo, Jean. *Robin of Bray*. Dial, 1982.
Thaler, Mike. *Madge's Magic Show*. Watts, 1978.
Walt Disney's The Sorcerer's Apprentice. Random House, 1973.

Chapter Books

Adler, David A. *Onion Sundaes*. Random, 1994.
Fleischman, Sid. *The Midnight Horse*. Greenwillow, 1990.
Levy, Elizabeth. *The Case of the Mindreading Mommies*. Simon & Schuster, 1989.
    Also other books in the Magic Mystery series.
Lewis, C.S. *The Magician's Nephew*. Macmillan, 1955.

Folklore

Cole, Joanna. *Doctor Change*. Morrow, 1986.
Langstaff, John M. *The Two Magicians*. Atheneum, 1973.
Moore, Inga. *The Sorcerer's Apprentice*. Macmillan, 1989.
San Souci, Robert D. *Young Merlin*. Doubleday, 1990.
Sierra, Judy. *Wiley and the Hairy Man*. Lodestar, 1996.
Turska, Krystyna. *The Magician of Cracow*. Greenwillow, 1975.

Nonfiction

Eldin, Peter. *The Most Excellent Book of How to Do Card Tricks*. Millbrook, 1996.
Lewis, Shari, and Dick Zimmerman. *Shari Lewis Presents 101 Magic Tricks for Kids to Do*. Random, 1990.
McMaster, Shawn. *60 Super Simple Magic Tricks*. Lowell House, 1996.

Biographies

Blackstone, Harry. *My Life as a Magician*. Pocket, 1992.
Woog, Adam. *Harry Houdini*. Lucent, 1995.

Just for Fun

Nozaki, Akihiro, and Mitsumasa Anno, illus. *Anno's Hat Tricks*. Philomel, 1985.
Magic Eye: 3D Illusions. N.E. Thing Enterprises, 1995. Also other books in the series.

Other Resources

Cobb, Vicki. *Magic ... Naturally! Science Entertainments & Amusements*. Lippincott, 1976. Has the disappearing stamp trick called "A Stamped-Out Stamp: Light Refraction."

Dukas, Paul. *The Sorcerer's Apprentice* (sound recording).

Eldin, Peter. *The Most Excellent Book of How to Be a Magician: With Easy Step-by-Step Instructions for a Brilliant Performance*. Millbrook, 1996. Has a version of the flying paper clip trick called "Link-up in Space" ; also contains a version of the "Magic Balls" trick that can double as a craft.

Jennings, Terry. *101 Amazing Optical Illusions: Fantastic Visual Tricks*. Sterling, 1996. Contains "Make a Stamp Disappear" and "The Rubber Pencil."

Lewis, Shari, and Dick Zimmerman. *Shari Lewis Presents 101 Magic Tricks for Kids to Do*. Random, 1990. Contains the flying paper clip trick called "The Linking Chain," "The Rubber Pencil" and a version of the disappearing stamp called "Under Water."

McMaster, Shawn. *60 Super Simple Magic Tricks*. Lowell House, 1996. Has "The Midair Paper Clip Collision" and "The Rubber Pencil."

Pellowski, Anne. *The Family Storytelling Handbook: How to Use Stories, Anecdotes, Rhymes, Handkerchiefs, Paper, and Other Objects to Enrich Your Family Traditions*. Macmillan, 1987. Contains the story "The Hungry Stranger: A Buddhist Story from India" as retold by Ruth Stotter.

Silverstein, Shel. *Falling Up*. HarperCollins, 1996. See "Sybil the Magician's Last Show."

Sitarz, Paula Gaj. *Picture Book Story Hours: From Birthdays to Bears*. Libraries Unlimited, 1987. See "Magic to Do."

Sitarz, Paula Gaj. *Story Time Sampler*. Libraries Unlimited, 1997. See "Magic and Magicians."

How's the Weather?

Bulletin Board

Divide the bulletin board into several areas to showcase different types of weather. For example, for WIND, show kites flying and pinwheels spinning; for RAIN show umbrellas and raindrops; and for SNOW put up snowmen and kids sledding.

Background Music

Play a compilation of songs that mention various types of weather, such as "Singin' in the Rain" from the movie of that name, "Stormy Weather" (Lena Horne), "Sunshine on My Shoulders" (John Denver), "Blowin' in the Wind" (Peter, Paul, and Mary), and "Let It Snow" (various artists).

Opening Activity

Sing to the tune of "If You're Happy and You Know It."

"IF IT'S RAINING AND YOU KNOW IT"
Lyrics adapted by Martha Simpson

If it's raining and you know it, clap your hands (repeat)
If it's raining and you know it you'll be soaking wet to show it
If it's raining and you know it, clap your hands.

If the streets are getting muddy, stamp your feet...
If the streets are getting muddy you can squish it just like putty...

If the wind is really blowing, shake your head...
If the wind is really blowing and your hair is wild and flowing...

If the temperature is falling, rub your hands...
If the temperature is falling and the cold is so appalling...

If the rain should turn to snow then dress up warm...
If the rain should turn to snow then out to shovel you will go...

If the sun begins to come out, yell "Hooray!"(Hooray!)....
If the sun begins to come out then it is a reason to shout....

Story

Tell *The Rain Player* by David Wisniewski, or a folktale about some aspect of the weather (see Other Resources).

Participation Activity

Divide the children into two or three groups to run a Weather Relay Race. For each team, set a pile of clothes that could be worn for cold weather conditions, such as snow boots, warm coat, scarf, hat, and mittens. The teams will line up to race. Each child, at his turn, must put on all the clothing, race to an appointed part of the room, turn around and race back, then take off all the winter clothing so the next person can use them. The team that finishes first is the winner. It is especially fun if the clothes are a couple of sizes too big for the kids.

Craft—Wind Chimes

Materials: Colorful plastic disposable plate, six inches in diameter; plastic lacing (gimp); a large amount of dry ziti and other pasta with large holes; a small amount of pasta with smaller holes; food dye; rubbing alcohol; scissors; awl or other implement to poke holes in plate; ruler.

Procedure: Ahead of time cut the plastic lacing into four 12-inch strands and one 18-inch strand. Dye the dry pasta in assorted colors using food dye and alcohol (see directions in Appendix I.) Punch holes in the plate that are just large enough for the lacing to go through—one in the center and four evenly spaced around the circumference (see drawing). Turn the plate upside down, so that the top (side A) is facing down, and the bottom (side B) is facing up. String the 12-inch laces through the outer holes and make a knot at side B. To be sure the laces don't come loose during the craft, you can also tie a knot close to the plate on side A. The laces should hang below the plate surface of side A. Then string the 18-inch lacing through the center hole but make a one inch loop before knotting on side B. Knot the strand again on side A as before. You should be able to hold up the plate by the center loop so that the strands of lacing hang down but do not fall though.

At the program let children string the colored pasta onto the five strands of lacing. Tell them to end each strand with a piece of small-holed pasta. Help them

WIND CHIMES

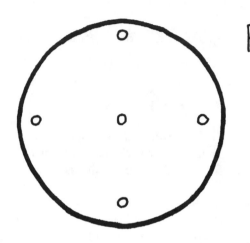

punched
holes in
plate

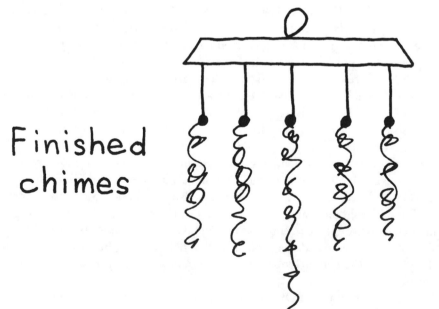

Finished
chimes

knot the ends of the lacing when they are through. Show them how they can hang their wind chimes from the loop at the top of the plate.

Suggested Booktalk Titles

Picture Books

Barber, Antonia. *The Mousehole Cat*. Macmillan, 1990.
Barrett, Judi. *Cloudy with a Chance of Meatballs*. Atheneum, 1978.
Desimini, Lisa. *My House*. Holt, 1994.
Lesser, Carolyn. *What a Wonderful Day to Be a Cow*. Random, 1995.

Easy Readers

Coombs, Patricia. *Dorrie and the Weather-Box*. Lothrop, 1966.
Hall, Malcolm. *Forecast*. Coward, 1977.
Rylant, Cynthia. *Henry and Mudge and the Wild Wind*. Macmillan, 1993.

Chapter Books

Stevens, Carla. *Anna, Grandpa, and the Big Storm*. Clarion, 1982.

Nonfiction

Ardley, Neil. *The Science Book of Weather*. Harcourt, 1992.
Arnold, Caroline. *El Niño: Stormy Weather for People and Wildlife*. Clarion, 1998.
Elsom, Derek M. *Weather Explained: A Beginner's Guide to the Elements*. Holt, 1997.
Gibbons, Gail. *Weather Words and What They Mean*. Holiday, 1990.
Greenberg, Keith. *Hurricanes and Tornadoes*. 21st Century, 1994.
Herman, Gail. *Storm Chasers: Tracking Twisters*. Grossett, 1997.
Wood, Jenny. *Storms: Nature's Fury*. Gareth Stevens, 1991.

Biographies

Martin, Jacqueline Briggs. *Snowflake Bentley*. Houghton, 1998.
Roop, Peter, and Connie Roop. *Keep the Lights Burning, Abbie*. Carolrhoda, 1985.

Poetry

Prelutsky, Jack. *Rainy Rainy Saturday*. Greenwillow, 1980.

Just for Fun

Walton, Rick, and Ann Walton. *Weather or Not: Riddles for Rain or Shine*. Lerner, 1990.

Other Resources

Caduto, Michael J., and Joseph Bruchac. *Keepers of the Earth: Native American Stories and Environmental Activities for Children*. Fulcrum, 1989. See "Gluscabi and the Wind Eagle."

La Fontaine, Jean de. *The North Wind and the Sun: A Fable*. Oxford University, 1984.

Ludwig, Warren. *Good Morning, Granny Rose: An Arkansas Folktale*. Putnam, 1990.

"Sky Watch." *Copycat*. Copycat Press, March/April 1995.

Sitarz, Paula Gaj. *More Picture Book Story Hours*. Libraries Unlimited, 1990. See "Rainy Days."

Wisniewski, David. *The Rain Player*. Clarion, 1991.

Jungle Safari

Rain Forests

Bulletin Board

Create a tropical rain forest of paper trees and other vegetation, with a canopy of leaves above. Throughout, post pictures of an assortment of jungle animals, hidden among the branches and leaves, and on the forest floor.

Background Music

Play a recording of rain forest nature sounds, such as *Voices of the Rain Forest*.

Opening Activity

"JUNGLE WALK"
Developed by Martha Simpson

Stand in a circle with the children. Teach them the chorus of the rhyme:

Walking through the jungle, what did I see?

Then add:

A great green crocodile snapping at me!

With your arms, make motions of crocodile jaws opening and closing, and tell the children to copy your movements. Continue to repeat the chorus and add the following verses and motions:

A long spotted boa sliding by me.

Put your hands together and snake them in front of you, while the children repeat the motion.

A jewel-colored hummingbird hovering near me.

Place a flat hand horizontally in the air and shimmy it.

A chattering monkey swinging by me.

147

Pretend to reach for vines like a monkey swinging through the trees.

A hive full of busy bees buzzing at me.

Put your thumb and fingers together and zip your hand through the air while you make a buzzing sound.

A sleek yellow tiger slinking toward me.

Rotate your shoulders up and down.

A tree full of parrots squawking at me.

Make talking motions with your hands.

A long row of army ants marching by me.

March in place.

A little brown fruit bat gliding toward me.

Put hands out flat on either side of you, and sway them in a gentle rocking motion.

A big-eyed lemur staring at me.

Curl your hands into fists and put them in front of your eyes.

A long-tongued tree frog flicking at me.

Hold hand horizontally in a fist, then open and close it in a flicking motion.

A dozen bright butterflies waving at me.

Put your hands together like a butterfly and flap them up and down.

Story

Tell *The Great Kapok Tree* by Lynne Cherry and have children act out the roles of the man and the animals. Or tell *The Story of Little Babaji* and let children be the tigers.

Participation Activity

"RAIN FOREST PRODUCT GUESSING GAME"
Developed by Martha Simpson

Display several products or pictures of items that originated in a rain forest. Give clues and ask children to identify the object. Sample clues:

- I am the fruit of a palm tree from the Pacific Islands. I may be hard and hairy on the outside, but I'm sweet on the inside. (coconut)
- I started out as sap from a tree in South America. I have a very bouncy personality. (rubber ball)
- I am made up of lots of ground up beans from Central America. I am a popular hot drink. (coffee)

- You will find me in the sweet-smelling pods of a vine that grows on trees in Mexico and several islands in the South Pacific. I'll bet you've tasted me in ice cream and lots of desserts! (vanilla)

- I am originally from Asia, but now I'm grown in tropical areas all over the world. I hang out with a bunch of friends. Monkeys and people find me very "a-peel-ing." (banana)

- If you like foods that are hot and spicy, you like me. I come from the bark of a tree that grows in Indonesia. People especially like my flavor in apple pie, gum, and candy. (cinnamon)

- I come from the sap of a chicle tree in Guatemala. I can be made into a chewy treat, but don't let a teacher catch you with me in class! (gum)

- My main ingredient comes from the seed of an evergreen tree that is native to West Africa. You know me as the popular soft drink that's the Real Thing. (Coca-Cola)

Craft—Rain Sticks

Materials: Cardboard tube—the longer the better—but a paper towel tube will do; cardboard; construction paper; liquid glue; round wooden toothpicks (they are sturdier than the flat kind); markers; a small artist's paint brush and a cheap two inch wide paint brush; a push pin; a nail clipper; scissors; uncooked rice; a coffee scoop; cut paper and other materials for decorating; colorful wide tape; yarn or ribbon.

Procedure: This craft takes a lot of advance preparation. Ahead of time cut two cardboard circles to cover the ends of the cardboard tubes. Cut two circles of construction paper about twice the diameter of the cardboard circles. Glue the cardboard circles to the centers of the paper circles and let dry. Cut four or five large notches in the paper circles from the outside edges to the cardboard inner circles. With the marker, place a dot about every inch along the spiral seam of the cardboard tube. Use the push pin to poke small holes at the marks and push the toothpicks through both sides of the tube so that the toothpicks will stick out on either side. After toothpicks have been stuck through all the marks, use the small artist's brush to place a dot of liquid glue around each place where the tooth-picks poke through the cardboard. Then set the tubes aside overnight so that the glue will dry the toothpicks into place. The next day, use a nail clipper to clip off the protruding toothpick ends, leaving the cardboard tubes relatively smooth on the surface. Wrap a piece of construction paper around each prepared tube and glue into place. (Use the paint brush to spread the glue—it's fast and easy.)

At the program let the children look inside the tubes to see how the tooth-picks cross back and forth. Then help them put on the end pieces. Take one cir-cle-within-a-circle and lay it on a table with the cardboard inner circle face up. Apply wet glue to the outer ring of construction paper. Carefully, place the circle

Cutaway
View
of
Rain
Stick

over one end of the cardboard tube, so that the inner cardboard circle fits neatly over the hole. Press down the construction paper notches, overlapping as needed, and smoothing out the glue. Secure the end cover to the tube with colorful tape. Turn the tube over so the uncovered end is up. Measure out a scoop of dry rice and pour it into the tube. Cover the open end with the circles as before, securing it with the tape. Now the children can glue decorations to the outside of the cardboard tubes. They can also tie ribbon or yarn on if desired. Tip the rain stick over and listen to the rain fall.

Suggested Booktalk Titles

Picture Books

Banks, Kate. *The Bird, the Monkey, and the Snakes in the Jungle*. Frances Foster, 1999.
Hamilton, Virginia. *Jaguarundi*. Scholastic, 1995.
Knutson, Kimberley. *Jungle Jamboree*. Marshall Cavendish, 1988.
Steig, William. *The Zabajaba Jungle*. Farrar, 1991.
Wundrow, Deanna. *Jungle Drum*. Millbrook, 1999.

Easy Readers

Engel, Diana. *The Shelf-Paper Jungle*. Macmillan, 1994.

Chapter Books

Talbott, Hudson, and Mark Greenberg. *Amazon Diary: The Jungle Adventures of Alex Winter*. Putnam, 1996.

Nonfiction

Baker, Lucy. *Life in the Rain Forest*. World Book, 1997.
Forsyth, Adrian. *How Monkeys Make Chocolate: Foods and Medicines from the Rain Forest*. Owl, 1995.
Gibbons, Gail. *Nature's Green Umbrella*. Mulberry, 1997.
Greenaway, Theresa. *Jungle* (Eyewitness Books.) Knopf, 1994.
Grupper, Jonathan. *Destination: Rain Forest*. National Geographic, 1997.
Lasky, Kathryn. *The Most Beautiful Roof in the World: Exploring the Rainforest Canopy*. Harcourt, 1997.
Lewington, Anne. *Antonio's Rain Forest*. Carolrhoda, 1993.

Just for Fun

DuBosque, D. *Draw! Rainforest Animals*. Peel, 1994.
Ross, Kathy. *Crafts for Kids Who Are Wild About Rainforests*. Millbrook, 1997.

Other Resources

Bannerman, Helen. *The Story of Little Babaji*. HarperCollins, 1996.
Cherry, Lynne. *The Great Kapok Tree*. Harcourt, 1990.
De Leeuw, Hendrik. *Java Jungle Tales*. Arco, 1956.
Sitarz, Paula Gaj. *More Picture Book Story Hours*. Libraries Unlimited, 1990. See "In the Jungle."
Tropical Rainforest (sound recording). Clair Entertainment, 1995.
Voices of the Rain Forest (sound recording). Relaxation, 1992.

Let's Dance!

Dance

Bulletin Board

On black construction paper, trace and cut out a pair of man's shoes and a pair of woman's shoes several times. Place the footprints in a pattern similar to the illustrations in books that teach ballroom dancing. Also tack up pictures of famous dancers such as Fred Astaire, Maria Tallchief, Alvin Ailey, Martha Graham, etc.

Background Music

Play a recording of popular dance tunes such as *Drew's "Famous" Kids' Birthday Party Music* or recordings of dance songs from Fred Astaire movies, MGM musicals, or any other type of dance music.

Opening Activity

Have everyone pull on imaginary dancing shoes and tie the laces. Then sprinkle everyone's feet with magic dancing dust. Do a simple dance such as the Hokey Pokey.

Story

Tell *The Red Heels*, by Robert D. San Souci, *The Dancing Man*, by Ruth Bornstein, or "The Dancing Horse" from *Terry Jones' Fantastic Stories*.

Participation Activity

Do the Macarena, the Electric Slide or any other popular party dance.

Craft—Dancing Horse

Materials: White poster board; white plastic straws; white yarn; one feather; four black pony beads; two googly eyes; a craft stick; scissors; stapler; markers; Scotch tape.

Procedure: Ahead of time cut five pieces of white yarn into four-inch lengths. Cut out the body of the horse from white poster board (see pattern). Punch two small holes in the horse cutout where indicated on the pattern. Cut the white plastic straws into ½" lengths. Cut two pieces of yarn into 12-inch lengths.

At the program explain to the children that they are going to make dancing Lipizzaner stallions. They may start by decorating the horses with markers. Have the children glue the googly eyes to each side of the horse's head. For the horse's legs children should tie a pony bead to one end of a piece yarn, thread six pieces of plastic straw down to the bead, insert free end of the yarn through one of the horse's leg holes and wind the yarn one extra turn through the hole in the horse so that the yarn won't slide around (this makes one leg). Continue by threading six plastic straw pieces onto the yarn on the other side, and finish by tying a pony bead to the end. This will make a pair of legs—the pony beads are the hooves. Repeat this process for the other pair of legs. Staple a feather to the horse's brow for a headdress. Tape a craft stick to the belly of the horse. Hold on to the stick and shake the horse to make the legs dance.

Suggested Booktalk Titles

Picture Books

Ackerman, Karen. *Song and Dance Man*. Knopf, 1988.
Blake, Quentin. *The Story of the Dancing Frog*. Knopf, 1984.
Isadora, Rachel. *Max*. Macmillan, 1976.
Martin, Bill, Jr., and John Archambault. *Barn Dance!* Holt, 1986.
Medearis, Angela. *Dancing with the Indians*. Holiday House, 1991.
Paxton, Tom. *Engelbert the Elephant*. Morrow, 1990.
Schroeder, Alan. *Ragtime Tumpie*. Joy Street, 1989.
Winslow, Barbara. *Dance on a Sealskin*. Alaska Northwest, 1995.

DANCING
HORSE

Easy Readers

Bottner, Barbara. *Bootsie Barker Ballerina*. HarperCollins, 1997.
Byars, Betsy Cromer. *The Golly Sisters Go West*. Harper, 1985.
O'Connor, Jane. *Nina, Nina, Star Ballerina*. Grosset & Dunlap, 1997.
Sandin, Joan. *Pioneer Bear: A True Story*. Random, 1995.

Chapter Books

Charbonnet, Gabrielle. *Tutu Much Ballet*. Holt, 1994.
Henry, Marguerite. *White Stallion of Lipizza*. Rand McNally, 1964.
Tamar, Erika. *Alphabet City Ballet*. HarperCollins, 1996.

Nonfiction

Ancona, George. *Let's Dance!* Morrow, 1998.
Dumas, Philippe. *The Lipizzaners and the Spanish Riding School of Vienna*. Prentice Hall, 1981.
Jones, Bill T., and Susan Kuklin. *Dance*. Hyperion, 1998.
Waters, Kate. *Lion Dancer: Ernie Wan's Chinese New Year*. Scholastic, 1990.

Folklore

Bryan, Ashley. *The Dancing Granny*. Atheneum, 1977.
Pollock, Penny. *The Turkey Girl: A Zuni Cinderella*. Little, Brown, 1995.
Stevenson, Sucie. *The Twelve Dancing Princesses*. Yearling, 1995.

Biographies

Garfunkel, Trudy. *Letter to the World: The Life and Dances of Martha Graham*. Little, Brown, 1995.
Glover, Savion. *Savion! My Life in Tap*. Morrow, 2000.
Pinkney, Andrea Davis. *Alvin Ailey*. Hyperion, 1993.

Poetry

McLerran, Alice. *The Ghost Dance*. Clarion, 1995.
Yolen, Jane. *Dinosaur Dances*. Putnam, 1990.

Just for Fun

Elliott, Donald. *Frogs and the Ballet*. Gambit, 1979.

Other Resources

Astaire, Fred. *Fred Astaire Top Hat: Hits from Hollywood* (sound recording). Columbia, 1994.
Bornstein, Ruth. *The Dancing Man*. Clarion, 1998.
Capon, J. *Children's All-Time Rhythm Favorites* (sound recording and guide). Educational Activities, 1994. Includes "The Hokey Pokey," "Limbo," "Bunny Hop" and others.

Christy Lane's Line Dancing (video recording). Brentwood, 1992. Includes the "Electric Slide."

Dance Party Favorites (sound recording). Turn Up the Music, 1994. Tracks: "Electric Slide," "Chicken Dance, Dance Little Bird," Hokey Pokey."

Dorian, Margery. *Ethnic Stories for Children to Dance: Rhythmic Movement, Fundamentals of Dance: A Manual for Teachers of the Primary Grades.* BBB Associates, 1978.

Drew's "Famous" Kids' Birthday Party Music (sound recording). Turn Up the Music, 1994. Includes "Simon Says," "Limbo Rock," "The Hokey Pokey," "Peppermint Twist," "Disco Duck," etc.

Disney's Dance Along (sound recording). Walt Disney Records, 1996. Track: "Tiki Tiki Tiki Room (Macarena Dance Version)."

Jones, Terry. *Terry Jones' Fantastic Stories.* Viking, 1992. See "The Dancing Horse."

Landalf, Helen, and Pamela Gerke. *Movement Stories for Young Children Ages 3–6.* Smith & Kraus, 1996.

Los Del Rio. *Macarena Nonstop* (sound recording). BMG, 1996.

Murray, Arthur. *How to Become a Good Dancer.* Simon & Schuster, 1938. Use the classic footprint diagrams in bulletin board design.

Nelson, Esther L. *Dancing Games for Children of All Ages.* Sterling, 1973. Includes "The Hokey Pokey" and others.

Rooyackers, Paul. *101 Dance Games for Children: Fun and Creativity with Movement.* Hunter House, 1996.

Rosenberg, Jane. *Dance Me a Story: Twelve Tales from the Classic Ballets.* Thames & Hudson, 1985.

San Souci, Robert D. *The Red Heels.* Dial, 1995.

Stewart, Georgiana Liccione. *Folk Dance Fun* (sound recording). Kimbo, 1984.

Let's Fly a Kite!

Kites

Bulletin Board

Start with a light blue background. At the bottom right corner, post a picture of Benjamin Franklin holding the string of a kite. Lead the string out toward the center of the bulletin board, and hang a giant, colorful kite. All around, tack up smaller pictures of people flying various types of kites. Add a few puffy white clouds in the sky.

Background Music

Make a recording of songs about flying, such as "Up, Up and Away" (The Fifth Dimension), "Fly Like an Eagle" (Steve Miller Band), and "I'm Flying" from the musical *Peter Pan*. Don't forget to include some kite songs, such as "The Kite" from *You're a Good Man, Charlie Brown*.

Opening Activity

Sing "Let's Go Fly a Kite" from *Mary Poppins* with the children.

Story

Have another librarian or a teen volunteer fold origami paper while you tell the story "Satisfaction Guaranteed" from *Folding Stories: Storytelling and Origami Together as One* by Christine Petrell Kallevig.
Materials: Origami paper.

Participation Activity

Tell the children they are going to pretend that they are kites. Have them lie on the floor. Then talk them through the motions of a kite coming up from the ground and flying. Tell the children to rise slowly off the ground, with their arms flapping like kites catching the wind. Then they can slowly stand up and stretch out their arms wide as their kites fill with air. Have them swoop and turn around as the kites blow in the wind and do loops. While they are "flying," ask each child to describe one thing that they can see from their place in the sky. For example, houses, their school, cars on the highway, famous landmarks, etc. Then talk them back down to the ground, until they are again lying flat on the floor.

Craft—Coat Hanger Kites

Materials: Bendable metal coat hanger; sheet of large newsprint paper; glue stick; markers; pencils; white string; red string; twine; cloth strips; pliers; scissors.

Procedure: Ahead of time use the pliers to bend the coat hanger into a circle. Bend the hanger hook into a closed loop. Cut a circle of newsprint about two inches wider all around than the bent-out hanger. Place a hanger on the center of the newsprint circle and trace it with a pencil. Then cut notches about two inches apart from the paper edge to the line all the way around to form tabs that will be folded later. Cut two pieces of red string 18 inches long. Cut a three foot length of white string and a three foot length of twine. Cut five strips of cloth, about three inches square.

At the program let the children decorate one side of the newsprint within the pencil line. They can draw pictures and color them in with the markers. When they are finished, turn the colored side of the paper face down, and place the coat hanger in the center. Help the children spread glue on the paper tabs and fold them over the hanger wire kite frame. Press well and make sure the paper is secured tightly onto the wire frame, without leaving any gaps. Next, turn over the kite so that the drawn side faces you, and with the loop pointed down. Using a pencil tip, carefully poke small holes next to the wire frame at the north, east and west points of the kite (there is already an opening at the south end—near the loop.) Knot one end of a piece of red string to the north wire by poking the string through the hole and the other end of string to the south end of the kite, pulling the string as tight as possible. Tie another red string to the east and west sides. Take a white string and knot one end at the point where the two red strings cross. Tell the children that when they get home, they can tie a longer piece of kite line to the free end of white string, so that they can fly their kites. Next, help the children fold five strips of cloth accordion-style and tie them onto the twine at five-inch intervals. Tie one end of the twine to the hanger loop, to give the kite a tail.

Note: This craft takes a long time to complete, so time your program accordingly. We set up different tables as stations for each step of the craft, with volunteers to help at each stage of the project. Children can move from table to table as they complete each step.

COAT-HANGER KITE

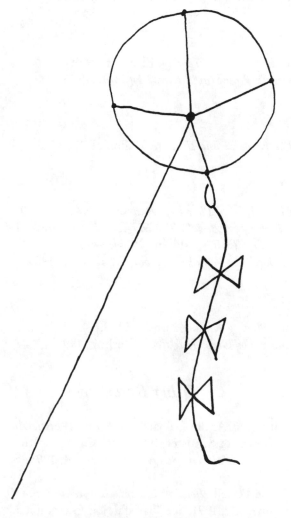

Suggested Booktalk Titles

Picture Books

Blanco, Alberto. *Angel's Kite/La Estrella de Angel*. Children's Book Press, 1994.
Haseley, Dennis. *Crosby*. Harcourt, 1996.

Kroll, Virginia L. *A Carp for Kimiko*. Charlesbridge, 1993.
Luenn, Nancy. *The Dragon Kite*. Harcourt, 1982.
Reddix, Valerie. *Dragon Kite of the Autumn Moon*. Lothrop, 1992.

Easy Books

Packard, Mary. *The Kite*. Children's Press, 1990.
Rey, Margaret. *Curious George Flies a Kite*. Houghton, 1958.

Chapter Books

Porter, Connie. *High Hopes for Addy*. Pleasant, 1999.
Schulz, Charles. *Fly, You Stupid Kite, Fly!* Holt, 1976.

Folklore

Yolen, Jane. *The Emperor and the Kite*. Philomel, 1988.

Nonfiction

Demi. *Kites: Magic Wishes That Fly Up to the Sky*. Crown, 1999.
Evans, David. *Fishing for Angels: The Magic of Kites*. Firefly, 1991.
Fowler, Allan. *Telling Tails*. Children's Press, 1998.
Gibbons, Gail. *Catch the Wind! All About Kites*. Little, 1989.

Just for Fun

Michael, David. *Making Kites*. Larousse, 1993.
Schmidt, Norman. *The Great Kite Book*. Sterling, 1998.

Other Resources

Brokaw, Meredith, and Annie Gilbar. *The Penny Whistle Any Day Is a Holiday Party Book*. Simon & Schuster, 1996. See "Go Fly a Kite."
The Great Big Book of Children's Songs. Hal Leonard, 1995. See "Let's Go Fly a Kite."
Kallevig, Christine Petrell. *Folding Stories: Storytelling and Origami Together as One*. Storytime, Ink, 1991. See "Satisfaction Guaranteed."
Mary Poppins soundtrack (sound recording). Walt Disney Educational Media, 1978. Track: "Let's Go Fly a Kite"
Sitarz, Paula Gaj. *Story Time Sampler*. Libraries Unlimited, 1997. See "Wind, Kites and Balloons."

Make a Wish

Bulletin Board

Cover this bulletin board with things that people use to make wishes: a giant wishbone made of twisted newsprint paper (or a collection of several real wishbones), a construction-paper wishing well with a coin, a birthday cake with real candles, and a foil-covered evening star. Caption this board: "If Wishes Were Horses, We'd All Be as Happy as Kings." Add tiny horses, Pegasus figures, and unicorns jumping out of the well, peeking out from behind the birthday cake, and flying around the star.

Background Music

Use "When You Wish Upon a Star" (from *Pinocchio*), "Would You Like to Swing on a Star?" (Bing Crosby), "Stardust" (various artists), "Good Morning Starshine" (*Hair* soundtrack), and other music about stars.

Opening Activity

Hold a bean bag wishing well toss.
Materials: Large plastic garbage can decorated with a trellis or roof to look like a well; bean bags.

Ask the children to think of different ways people make wishes (i.e., blowing out the candles on a birthday cake). Chant together "Star light, star bright, first star I see tonight. I wish I may, I wish I might, have the wish I wish tonight." Divide the children into two teams and instruct them to take turns tossing a bean bag into a large plastic garbage can. The team who gets the bean bag into the well the most times gets their wish.

Story

Tell "Too Many Wishes" from *Paper Stories*, by Jean Stangl.
Materials: 8½" x 11" sheet of paper; pencil; sharp scissors; a flat, hard surface to use when making folds.

This story is very similar to "The Fisherman and His Wife" except that instead of coveting more and more political power, the wife simply wants progressively bigger houses. The storyteller folds and cuts the paper and shows the paper to the children at each stage as it represents bigger and bigger houses.

Participation Activity

WISH LIST CHARADES
Developed by Lynne Perrigo

Materials: Large art pad on easel; marker.

Ask the children what they wish for most and list the wishes on the art pad. Have one child at a time stand up in front of the group and pantomime one of the wishes on the list so that the other children can guess which wish they are representing. Two or more children may want to team up to act out a wish. The only rule is that the children must choose someone else's wish, not their own, to act out.

Craft—Magic Wishing Well

Materials: One-half gallon cardboard milk or juice carton; wooden dowel about five inches long and about one-quarter inch in diameter or a sturdy plastic drinking straw; sharp pencil; yarn; pieces of colored construction paper; flowers and other shapes cut from wallpaper; glitter; sequins; glue stick; plastic coin; one cup cut from an egg carton; single-hole punch; stapler; craft knife.

Procedure: Ahead of time use the craft knife to cut a three-inch square hole on all four sides of the cardboard carton, measuring at least three inches from the bottom of the carton. Use a sharp pencil to poke two holes above the square on two opposite sides of the carton. Cut a ten-inch piece of yarn and a cardboard cup from an egg carton. Punch a single hole near the lip of the cardboard cup. If the top of the carton is open, staple it shut.

At the program have the children insert the dowel or straw through the two opposing holes so that it extends across the inside of the well. Children may then decorate the wishing wells with paper, glitter, and sequins. When they are finished, have them tie one end of the yarn around the dowel or straw and tie the other end through the hole in the egg cup to act as a bucket (see drawing). When they are done, they can make a wish and toss their coins in.

Suggested Booktalk Titles

Picture Books

Andres, Katherine. *Fish Story*. Simon & Schuster, 1993.
Carlstrom, Nancy White. *Wishing at Dawn in Summer*. Little, Brown, 1992.

MAGIC WISHING WELL

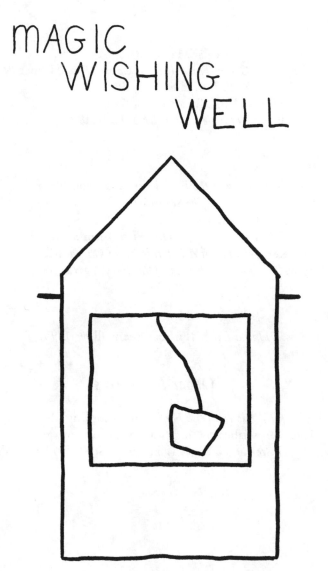

Hines, Anna Grossnickle. *Moon's Wish*. Clarion, 1992.
Hru, Dakari. *The Magic Moonberry Jump Ropes*. Dial, 1996.
Polacco, Patricia. *My Rotten Redheaded Older Brother*. Simon & Schuster, 1994.

Easy Readers

Brenner, Barbara. *Rosa & Marco and the Three Wishes*. Macmillan, 1992.
Graham, Amanda. *Picasso, the Green Tree Frog*. Gareth Stevens, 1985.
Rylant, Cynthia. *Henry and Mudge and Annie's Good Move*. Simon & Schuster, 1998.
Sato, Satoru. *I Wish I Had a Big, Big Tree*. Lothrop, 1984.

Chapter Books

Alexander, Nina. *Alison of Arabia*. Magic Attic Press, 1997.
Brittain, Bill. *The Wish Giver: Three Tales of Coven Tree*. Harper & Row, 1983.
Eager, Edward. *The Well-Wishers*. Harcourt, 1960.
Nesbit, E. *Five Children and It*. Buccaneer, 1976.
Pfeffer, Susan Beth. *The Trouble with Wishes*. Holt, 1996.

Folklore

Bruchac, Joseph. *Gluskabe and the Four Wishes*. Dutton, 1995.
Newton, Patricia Montgomery. *The Stonecutter*. Putnam, 1990. (See "Rock On" for other versions of this story.)
Wells, Rosemary. *The Fisherman and His Wife: A Brand New Version*. Dial, 1998.
Wilson, Barbara Ker. *Wishbones: A Folktale From China*. Macmillan, 1993.
Zemach, Margot. *The Three Wishes: An Old Story*. Farrar, 1986.

Biography

Stevenson, James. *I Had a Lot of Wishes*. Greenwillow, 1995.

Other Resources

Birch, Carol. *Careful What You Wish For* (sound recording). Frostfire, 1993. Includes five stories about wishes coming true with disastrous results.
Stangl, Jean. *Paper Stories*. David S. Lake, 1984. See "Too Many Wishes."

Mardi Gras

New Orleans Style

Bulletin Board

Use lots of gold, dark green, and purple, the traditional New Orleans Mardi Gras colors, for this bulletin board. Tack up a pale yellow background. Twist green and purple crepe paper streamers around the border, and crisscross streamers from end to end. Write "Welcome to Mardi Gras!" in gold letters across a purple background in the center of the bulletin board. Add a variety of decorated masks for a carnival atmosphere.

Background Music

Although Mardi Gras is celebrated in many countries around the world, the biggest party in the United States occurs in New Orleans. Zydeco music adds a festive sound to the program, but Dixieland jazz or another type of upbeat bayou music can also be used.

Opening Activity

Give the children a little background about Mardi Gras, telling its origins and other names for the day before Ash Wednesday. The article "Carnival Time!" in *Childcraft* offers a good explanation of Mardi Gras, otherwise known as Fat Tuesday, Shrove Tuesday, or Pancake Day. Then engage the children in a relay version of the traditional Pancake Race.

Materials: Two large felt circles; several shoe box tops.

Divide the children into two groups, and have them line up. Give each child a shoe box top, which will stand in for the frying pans used in the race. The first person in line gets a large felt circle to use as a pancake. Tell the children they must pass the pancake down the line using their "frying pans" and then back up to the first person. The team that finishes first wins.

Story

Tell the story *Harlequin and the Gift of Many Colors* by Remy Charlip and Burton Supree to explain why the harlequin is a traditional Mardi Gras figure.

Participation Activity

Costume parades and dancing are part of the Mardi Gras celebration. Lead the children around the room to dance the Conga.

Craft—Carnival Masks

Materials: Colorful card stock; plastic straw; small cut paper shapes, sequins, glitter, stickers of stars and butterflies, feathers, and other colorful materials for decorating the mask; scissors, stapler, glue stick.

Procedure: Ahead of time enlarge the mask pattern 200 percent on a photocopier. Trace pattern onto card stock and cut out. Also cut up the small pieces of decorative material.

At the program allow the children to decorate their masks as simply or as elaborately as they like. Then staple a straw to one side of the mask so the child can hold the mask up by the straw.

Suggested Booktalk Titles

Picture Books

Appelt, Kathi. *Bayou Lullaby*. Morrow, 1995.
Karas, G. Brian. *Home on the Bayou: A Cowboy's Story*. Simon & Schuster, 1996.
Lloyd, Errol. *Nini at Carnival*. Crowell, 1979.
Thomassie, Tynia. *Feliciana Feydra LeRoux: A Cajun Tall Tale*. Little, Brown, 1995.

Chapter Books

Duey, Kathleen. *Amelina Carrett: Bayou Grand Coeur, Louisiana, 1863 (American Diaries)*. Aladdin, 1999.
MacBride, Roger Lea. *On the Banks of the Bayou*. HarperCollins, 1998.
Moore, Elizabeth. *Mimi and Jean-Paul's Cajun Mardi Gras*. Pelican, 1996.

Folklore

Collins, Sheila Hebert. *Cendrillon: A Cajun Cinderella*. Pelican, 1998.
Doucet, Sharon Arms. *Why Lapin's Ears Are Long and Other Tales from the Louisiana Bayou*. Orchard, 1997.

MARDI GRAS MASK

enlarge 200% on photocopier

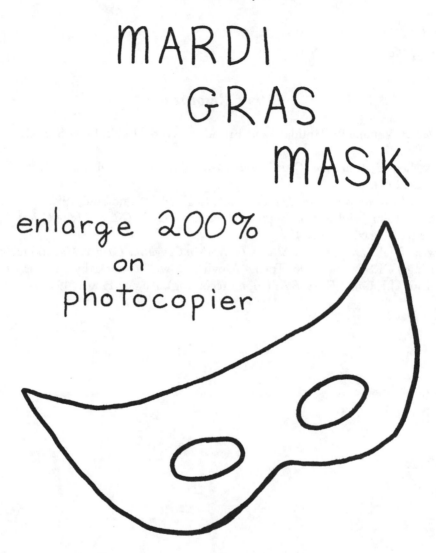

Reneaux, J.J. *Cajun Folktales*. August House, 1992.
Van Laan, Nancy. *With a Whoop and a Holler*. Atheneum, 1998.

Nonfiction

Bial, Raymond. *Cajun Home*. Houghton, 1998.
Gravelle, Karen, and Sylviane Diouf. *Growing Up in Crawfish Country: A Cajun Childhood*. Watts, 1999.
Hoyt-Goldsmith, Diane. *Mardi Gras: A Cajun Country Celebration*. Holiday, 1995.
MacMillan, Dianne M. *Mardi Gras*. Enslow, 1997.
Rice, James. *Cajun Alphabet*. Pelican, 1991.
Vidrine, Beverly Barras. *A Mardi Gras Dictionary*. Pelican, 1998.

Just for Fun
Doney, Meryl. *Masks*. Watts, 1995.

Other Resources

Childcraft Volume 9—Holidays and Birthdays. World Book, 1996. See "Carnival Time!"
Buckwheat Zydeco. *Choo Choo Boogaloo* (sound recording). Music for Little People, 1994.
Cajun & Zydeco Mardi Gras! (sound recording). Maison de Soul, 1992.
Charlip, Remy, and Burton Supree. *Harlequin and the Gift of Many Colors*. Parents Magazine Press, 1973.
Lewis, Nigel. *Dancing in the Streets: De Malibu Congaline Carnival* (sound recording). CRS Music, 1996. Track: "Movin'," as well as tracks by other artists.
Reneaux, J.J. *Cajun Fairy Tales* (sound recording). August House, 1996.

Math Mayhem

Fun with Numbers

Bulletin Board

Tack up any posters you have for counting and other math-related books. Make cutouts or computer printouts, in varying fonts and colors, of assorted math symbols and equations. Arrange these around the posters to create visual "Math Mayhem," and caption the bulletin board as such. Suspend wood blocks or other 3-D figures of numbers above the book display.

Background Music

Record a compilation of popular songs that mention numbers in the lyrics, such as "It Takes Two" (Marvin Gaye and Kim Weston), "Edge of Seventeen" (Stevie Nicks), "One" (Three Dog Night), and "25 or 6 to 4" (Chicago). Or use math-related music recorded for children's television shows such as *Multiplication Rock*.

Opening Activity

Sing a counting song such as "This Old Man," "The Ants Go Marching," or "One Was Johnny." Use props or ask the children to make up rhymes for the numbers.

Story

Tell *One Grain of Rice* by Demi.
Materials: Actual grains of rice, mounted on poster board, for the smaller amounts. For the larger amounts, make pictures of bowls, sacks, elephants carrying rice, etc., and mount them on poster board.

As the story progresses, display each amount of rice and leave it up so children can watch how the quantities of rice increase. Another good story, which you draw while telling, is "Number Story" from *The Story Vine*. Use a pad of paper and markers.

Participation Activity

Children can learn about sets and graphs with this activity.

Materials: Several sheets of graph paper, prepared ahead of time, to correspond with the following groupings (or sets).

Divide children into two groups: boys and girls. Count the number of people in each group and color in the answer on a bar graph. Then have the children move into other groups and draw the results on other graphs. Some suggestions for groups are: number of children who go to each of the local elementary schools; number of children in grades 1, 2, and 3; number of children who have pet dogs, cats, birds, and other pets.

Craft—"Numblers"

Materials: The books *Numblers* and *Puzzlers* by Suse MacDonald and Bill Oakes; plain sheets of paper; cutouts of numbers 0–9; crayons, colored pencils and markers; glue stick.

Procedure: Ahead of time cut out numbers in various sizes and colors.

At the program show children pictures from the two books, pointing out how the illustrators made shapes of animals and objects with the numbers. Show some samples that you have made. Then let children make their own number designs, or copy your examples, by gluing the cutout numbers onto plain paper and coloring to complete the pictures. When the children are done, let each child hold up his or her picture(s) and have the others guess what the pictures represent.

Suggested Booktalk Titles

Picture Books

Parker, Vic. *Bearobics: A Hip-Hop Counting Story*. Viking, 1997.
Scieszka, Jon. *Math Curse*. Viking, 1995.

Easy Reader

Cohen, Caron Lee. *How Many Fish?* HarperCollins, 1998.

Nonfiction

Clement, Rod. *Counting on Frank*. Gareth Stevens, 1991.
Haskins, James. *Count Your Way Through Russia*. Carolrhoda, 1987. (Also others in series.)

Murphy, Stuart. *Divide and Ride*. HarperCollins, 1997. Also other titles in Math-Start series.

Schwartz, David M. *G Is for Googol: A Math Alphabet Book*. Tricycle, 1998.

Schwartz, David M. *How Much Is a Million?* Lothrop, 1985.

Biographies

Lasky, Kathryn. *The Librarian Who Measured the Earth*. Joy Street, 1994.

Sis, Peter. *Starry Messenger*. Farrar, 1996.

Just for Fun

Adler, David A. *Calculator Riddles*. Holiday, 1995.

Anno, Mitsumasa. *Anno's Math Games*. Philomel, 1987.

D'Amico, Joan. *The Math Chef: Over 60 Math Activities and Recipes for Kids*. Wiley, 1997.

Keller, Charles. *Take Me to Your Liter: Science and Math Jokes*. Pippin, 1991.

Leedy, Loreen. *2 × 2 = Boo! A Set of Spooky Multiplication Stories*. Holiday, 1995.

Other Resources

Demi. *One Grain of Rice*. Scholastic, 1997.

Dorough, Bob. *Multiplication Rock: Original Soundtrack for the ABC-TV Series* (sound recording). Capitol, 1989.

Glazer, Tom. *Eye Winker, Tom Tinker, Chin Chopper: Fifty Musical Fingerplays*. Doubleday, 1973. See "This Old Man."

"Graphing All the Way." *Copycat*. Copycat Press, May/June 1997.

King, Carole. *The Broadway Cast Album of Maurice Sendak's Really Rosie* (sound recording). Caedmon, 1981. Track: "One Was Johnny."

Louis, Marcia. *Listen to Your Mama!* (sound recording). Louis Louis Productions, 1995. Track: "The Ants Go Marching."

MacDonald, Suse, and Bill Oakes. *Numblers*. Dial, 1988.

MacDonald, Suse, and Bill Oakes. *Puzzlers*. Dial, 1989. Also other books by these authors.

"Marble Math." *Copycat*. Copycat Press, March/April 1995.

"Math Flash Day." *Copycat*. Copycat Press, Sept./Oct. 1997.

"Math Mania." *Copycat*. Copycat Press, March/April 1996.

Pellowski, Anne. *The Story Vine: A Source Book of Unusual and Easy-to-Tell Stories from Around the World*. Macmillan, 1984. See "Number Story."

Raffi. *Baby Beluga* (sound recording). MCA, 1980. Track: "This Old Man."

Sendak, Maurice. *Maurice Sendak's Really Rosie: Starring the Nutshell Kids*. Harper & Row, 1975. See "One Was Johnny."

Monster Mania

Monsters

Bulletin Board

Create a "Creature Feature" that includes head shots of Frankenstein, Medusa, Dracula, a Cyclops, the Wolfman, a sea serpent, a hydra, Cerberus the three-headed dog, Grendel from *Beowulf*, the Wild Things from Maurice Sendak's book, and any other monsters that you can think of.

Background Music

Make a tape of some popular monster songs such as "Monster Mash" (Bobby Boris Pickett or the Beach Boys), "Purple People Eater" (Sheb Wooley), "Thriller" (Michael Jackson), "Scary Monsters" (David Bowie), "Werewolves of London" (Warren Zevon), "Apeman" (The Kinks), "Beauty and the Beast" (from Walt Disney's *Beauty and the Beast*), "The Munsters" (TV theme), or "The Addams Family" (TV or movie theme), or play Andrew Gold's *Halloween Howls*. For some classical pieces try Richard Wagner's "Ride of the Valkyries" or Camille Saint-Saens' "Danse Macabre."

Opening Activity

Sing "If I Was a Monster," developed by Martha Simpson.

In a large type size, print out a list of the fill-in words listed below to hold up while the children sing the song. Sing to the tune of "If I Had a Hammer."

> *If I was a <u>monster</u>, I'd <u>chase you</u> in the morning*
> *I'd <u>chase you</u> in the evening, all over this land.*
> *I'd <u>chase you</u> to be horrible, I'd <u>chase you</u> just for fun*
> *I'd <u>chase you</u> and <u>chase you</u> and scare everybody all over this land.*

Continue with other verses, substituting underlined words with types of monster and associated actions below.

172

werewolf ... howl
vampire ... bite you
giant ... stomp you
witch ... cackle
ghost ... haunt you
banshee ... shriek
zombie ... spook you

Story

Tell "Koluscap and the Water Monster" from *Keepers of the Earth: Native American Stories and Environmental Activities for Children*, by Michael J. Caduto and Joseph Bruchac.

Materials: Bullfrog puppet.

Other alternatives are "The Great Greedy Beast" from *Tales from the Enchanted World*, by Amabel Williams-Ellis, or "The Boy Who Drew Cats" from *Mysterious Tales of Japan*, by Rafe Martin (see Other Resources).

Participation Activity

Allow each child ten seconds in front of a camcorder to make their silliest faces.

Materials: Camcorder; videotape; VCR; music recorder and player.

Afterwards play the tape back with some silly monster music such as "The Monster Mash." If you don't have video equipment available, read assorted jokes from *Little Witch Presents a Monster Joke Book*, by Charles Keller and Linda Glovach.

Craft—Monster Masks

Materials: Card stock or poster board; heavy, soft yarn—such as macramé yarn—that is easy to tie and untie; construction paper in various colors; hole punch; glue stick; colored pencils, crayons or markers; scissors.

Procedure: Ahead of time enlarge the mask pattern by 200 percent on a photocopier and use the result to make a cardboard pattern to trace. Trace and cut masks from card stock. Punch holes where indicated. Cut the yarn into two 12-inch lengths. Cut the construction paper into various shapes for hair, horns, ears, etc. (see patterns).

At the program instruct the children to glue the cutouts onto the mask forms to create their own monster faces. They can cut out their own shapes or further embellish by drawing scars or other facial features. Tell them not to cover the holes that are on each side of the mask. Finished masks can be worn by tying a knot at one end of both pieces of yarn, slipping the yarn through the hole until it stops at the knot and tying the two pieces of yarn behind the child's head.

MONSTER MASKS
enlarge 200% on photocopier

→cut
flat-top head
or
split-top head

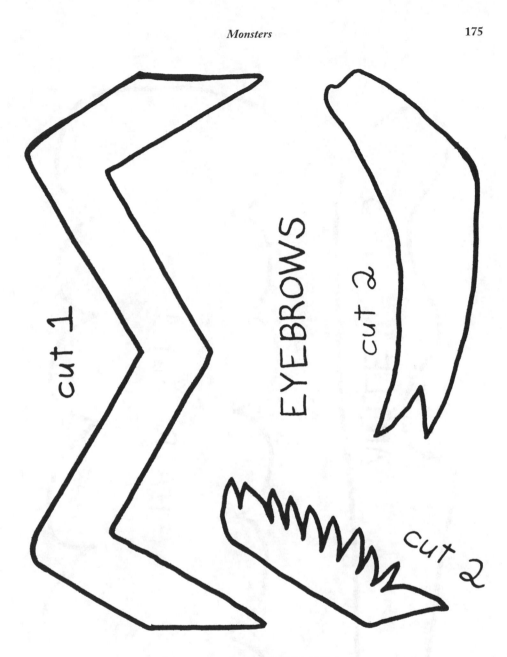

cut 1

EYEBROWS

cut 2

cut 2

Suggested Booktalk Titles

Picture Books

Adam, Addie. *Hilda and the Mad Scientist*. Dutton, 1995.
Cohen, Miriam. *The Real-Skin Rubber Monster Mask*. Greenwillow, 1990.
Emberly, Ed. *Go Away, Big Green Monster!* Little, Brown, 1982.
Gackenbach, Dick. *Harry and the Terrible Whatzit*. Houghton, 1977.
Johnston, Tony. *Goblin Walk*. Putnam, 1991.

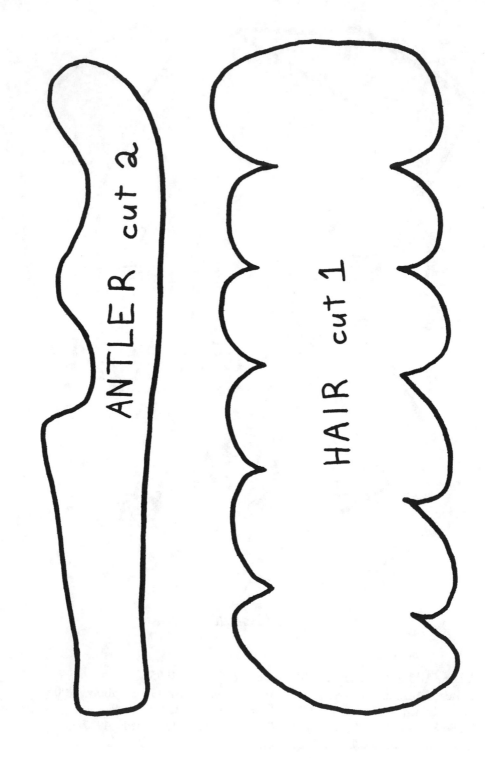

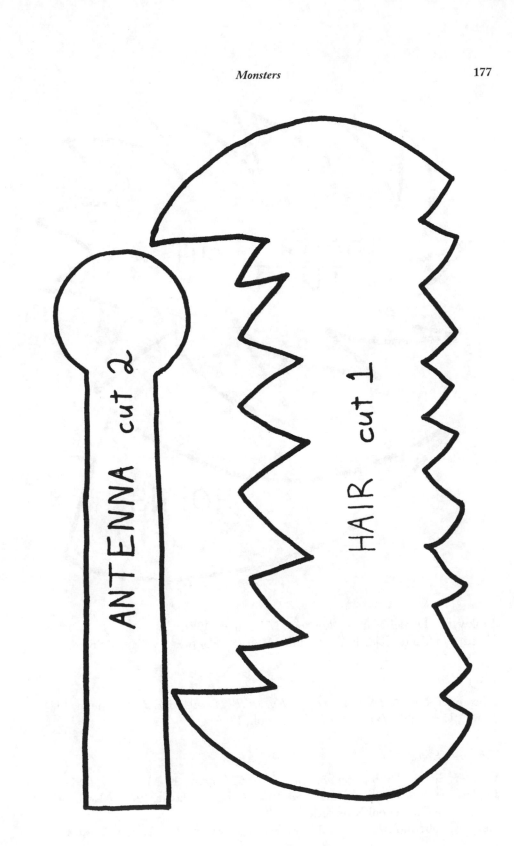

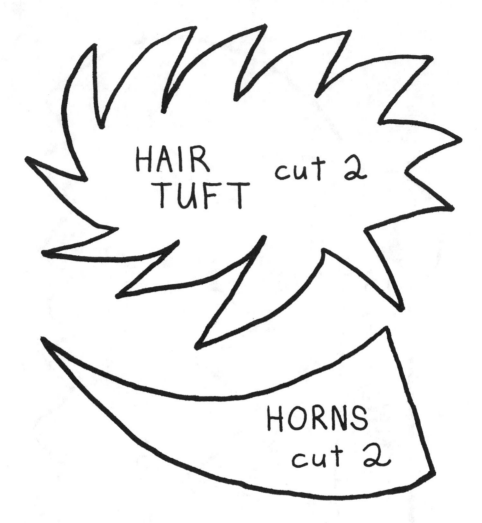

Pinkwater, Daniel Manus. *Wempires*. Macmillan, 1991.
Yolen, Jane, and Heidi E.Y. Stemple. *Meet the Monsters*. Walker, 1996.

Easy Readers

Alexander, Sue. *Witch, Goblin and Ghost in the Haunted Woods*. Pantheon, 1981.
Eaton, Deborah. *Monster Songs*. Millbrook, 1999.

Chapter Books

Cooper, Susan. *The Boggart and the Monster*. Margaret K. McEldery, 1997.
Dadey, Debbie. *Vampires Don't Wear Polka Dots*. Scholastic, 1990. Also others in the Bailey School Kids series.
Levy, Elizabeth. *Frankenstein Moved in on the Fourth Floor*. Harper & Row, 1981.

Folklore

Cabat, Ernie. *Ernie Cabat's Magical World of Monsters.* Dutton, 1992.
Carey, Valerie. *Maggie Mab and the Bogey Beast.* Arcade, 1992.
Osborne, Mary Pope. *Beauty and the Beast.* Scholastic, 1987.
Riggio, Anita. *Beware the Brindlebeast.* Boyds Mills, 1994.
Schwartz, Alvin. *Scary Stories to Tell in the Dark.* Lippincott, 1981. Also others in series.

Nonfiction

Gibbons, Gail. *Halloween.* Holiday House, 1984.
Powers, Tom. *Movie Monsters.* Lerner, 1989.

Poetry

McNaughton, Colin. *Making Friends with Frankenstein: A Book of Monstrous Poems and Pictures.* Candlewick, 1994.

Just for Fun

Ames, Lee J. *Draw 50 Beasties and Yugglies and Turnover Uglies and Things That Go Bump in the Night.* Doubleday, 1988.

Other Resources

Bauer, Caroline, ed. *Halloween: Stories and Poems.* Lippincott, 1989.
Caduto, Michael J., and Joseph Bruchac. *Keepers of the Earth: Native American Stories and Environmental Activities for Children.* Fulcrum, 1989. See: "Koluscap and the Water Monster."
Cohn, Amy L., ed. *From Sea to Shining Sea.* Scholastic, 1993. See "Scary, Creepy, Spooky Ghost Stories."
Demento, Dr. *The Greatest Novelty Records of All Time* (sound recording). Rhino, 1991. Track: "Monster Mash."
Glovach, Linda, and Charles Keller. *Little Witch Presents a Monster Joke Book.* Prentice Hall, 1976.
Gold, Andrew. *Halloween Howls* (sound recording). Music for Little People, 1996.
Martin, Rafe. *Mysterious Tales of Japan.* Putnam, 1996. See "The Boy Who Drew Cats."
Saint-Saens, Camille. *Danse Macabre* (sound recording).
Sendak, Maurice. *Where the Wild Things Are.* Harper & Row, 1963.
Sitarz, Paula Gaj. *Story Time Sampler.* Libraries Unlimited, 1997. See "Scary Tales."
Wagner, Richard. *The Ride of the Valkyries* (sound recording).
Williams-Ellis, Amabel. *Tales from the Enchanted World.* Little, Brown, 1987. See "The Great Greedy Beast."

Native American Legends
Native American Folklore

Bulletin Board

A large figure of a coyote, the famous Native American trickster, is a great centerpiece for this bulletin board. For the background, create a natural landscape scene of a desert or a forest, making sure to include a full moon in the night sky overhead.

Background Music

An abundance of Native American music is available. Try a recording by Coyote Oldman or the Native American flute music of R. Carlos Nakai.

Opening Activity

Play a recording of powwow music and show the children photographs from *Powwow*, by George Ancona. Discuss powwows, traditional costumes, dances, and music of Native Americans. You may also show pictures of totem poles and explain the principle and beliefs behind using different animals as symbols in the poles.

Story

Select one or more of the short, snappy stories from *Doctor Coyote: A Native American Aesop's Fables*, by John Bierhorst. We like the one about Coyote's encounter with White Beard, the goat. The *Keepers of...* books by Michael J. Caduto and Joseph Bruchac are a rich source for easy-to-tell versions of Native American stories.

Participation Activity

Perform a Native American Circle Dance with the children.
Materials: A small drum that can be carried; drum striker; newsprint pad and marker.

On the newsprint pad, have the children help you make a list of all the things that animals give to people. Post the list so everyone can see it and then use another sheet of paper to illustrate the spiral path that you will follow together when you dance the Circle Dance found in *Keepers of the Animals*, by Michael J. Caduto and Joseph Bruchac. With its emphasis on the kinship of all life, this simple dance is a good companion to the totem pole craft that follows. No music is necessary.

Craft—Totem Poles

Materials: Cardboard paper towel tubes; assorted colors of construction paper; patterns; white copy paper; colored markers; glue stick.

Procedure: Ahead of time cover the paper towel tubes with construction paper. Make photocopies of the totem pole patterns and cut out the pieces.

At the program have the children choose enough totem motifs to fit onto one paper towel tube. They can draw extra motifs or designs in blank totem squares (see patterns). They should color in the totem motifs and then glue them onto one side of the cardboard tubes to create their own personal totem poles.

Suggested Booktalk Titles

Picture Books

Martin, Bill, Jr. *Knots on a Counting Rope*. Holt, 1987.
Schick, Eleanor. *Navajo Wedding: A Diné Marriage Ceremony*. Marshall Cavendish, 1999.
Wisniewski, David. *The Wave of the Sea-Wolf*. Clarion, 1994.

Folklore

Bruchac, Joseph. *The First Strawberries: A Cherokee Story*. Dial, 1993.
Cohlene, Terri. *Ka-ha-si and the Loon*. Rourke, 1990.
dePaola, Tomie. *The Legend of the Bluebonnet: An Old Tale of Texas*. Putnam, 1983.
dePaola, Tomie. *The Legend of the Indian Paintbrush*. Putnam, 1988.
Goble, Paul. *Iktomi and the Ducks: A Plains Indian Story*. Orchard, 1990. Also many other titles by Goble.
Hodges, Margaret. *The Fire Bringer: A Paiute Indian Legend*. Little, Brown, 1972.
McDermott, Gerald. *Coyote: A Trickster Tale from the American Southwest*. Harcourt, 1994.
McDermott, Gerald. *Raven: A Trickster Tale from the Pacific Northwest*. Harcourt, 1993.
Rockwell, Anne F. *The Dancing Stars: An Iroquois Legend*. Crowell, 1971.

BEAR

FROG

EAGLE

Nonfiction

Erdosh, George. *Food and Recipes of the Native Americans*. Powerkids, 1997.
Hoyt-Goldsmith, Diane. *Totem Pole*. Holiday House, 1990. Also other titles by
    this author.

Biography

Bruchac, Joseph. *Crazy Horse's Vision*. Leet Low, 2000.

FISH

WOLF

OWL

Poetry

Foa, Maryclare. *Songs Are Thoughts: Poems of the Inuit*. Orchard, 1995.
Sneve, Virginia Driving Hawk. *Dancing Teepees*. Holiday House, 1989.

Just for Fun

Temko, Florence. *Traditional Crafts from Native North America*. Lerner, 1997.

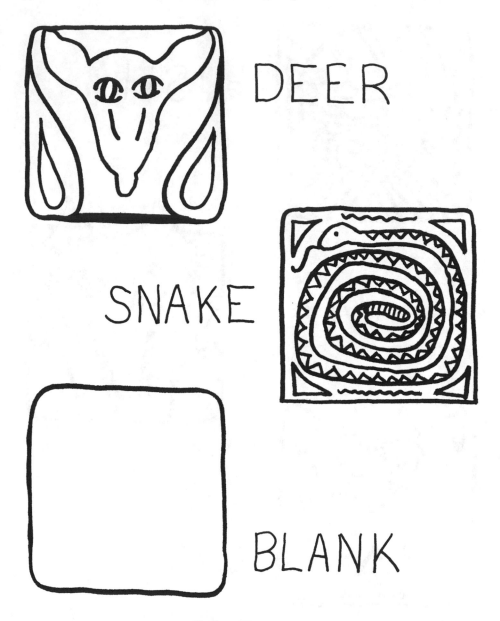

DEER

SNAKE

BLANK

Other Resources

Ancona, George. *Powwow*. Harcourt, 1993.

Bierhorst, John. *Doctor Coyote: A Native American Aesop's Fables*. Macmillan, 1987.

Caduto, Michael J., and Joseph Bruchac. *Keepers of the Animals: Native American Stories and Wildlife Activities for Children*. Fulcrum, 1991. Contains the Circle Dance.

Caduto, Michael J., and Joseph Bruchac. *Keepers of the Earth: Native American Stories and Environmental Activities for Children*. Fulcrum, 1988.

Caduto, Michael J., and Joseph Bruchac. *Keepers of Life: Discovering Plants Through Native American Stories and Earth Activities for Children*. Fulcrum, 1994.

Caduto, Michael J., and Joseph Bruchac. *Keepers of the Night: Native American Stories and Nocturnal Activities for Children*. Fulcrum, 1994.

Coyote Oldman. *Landscape* (sound recording). Xenotrope, 1988. See also other recordings by this duo.

D'Amato, Janet, and Alex D'Amato. *Native American Craft Inspirations*. Dover, 1972.

Honor the Earth Powwow: Songs of the Great Lakes Indians (sound recording). Ryko, 1991.

Nakai, R. Carlos. *Changes: Native American Flute Music* (sound recording). Canyon, 1983. See also other recordings by this artist.

"Native Americans of the Pacific Northwest." *Copycat*. Copycat Press, Nov./Dec. 1996.

Powwow Songs: Music of the Plains Indians (sound recording). New World, 1986.

Sitarz, Paula Gaj. *Story Time Sampler*. Libraries Unlimited, 1997. See "Native American Tales."

"The Story of Pocahontas." *Copycat*. Copycat Press, Nov./Dec. 1995.

Totem Poles to Cut Out and Put Together. Bellerophon, 1988.

"A Wampanaug Child's Day." *Copycat*. Copycat Press, Nov./Dec. 1994.

Naughty but Nice

Naughty Children

Bulletin Board

Caption the bulletin board "They're Naughty … But Nice." Then post pictures of some popular literary characters that get into trouble, along with their names and one book that each one appears in. For example, Max from *Where the Wild Things Are*, Rotten Ralph, Curious George, Horrible Harry, The Cut-Ups, and Goldilocks from *The Three Bears*. You may also want to add some popular trickster characters from folklore, such as Anansi and Brer Rabbit.

Background Music

In *The Sorcerer's Apprentice*, the Magician's young helper disobeys his master and gets into trouble. Play the classical music piece composed by Paul Dukas.

Opening Activity

Sing a story about a very naughty rabbit, "Little Rabbit Foo-Foo," with the children. You can also read short poems about disagreeable children, such as "Ladies First" or "Prayer of the Selfish Child" by Shel Silverstein.

Story

Tell *Tikki Tikki Tembo* by Arlene Mosel. Make a sign with Tikki Tikki Tembo's full name and teach the children how to say it. They can repeat the name with you every time it comes up in the story.

Participation Activity

Everyone knows *Where the Wild Things Are* by Maurice Sendak. Ask one boy to act out the part of Max. Everyone else can be the Wild Things. Then tell the story, letting the children dance out the wild rumpus.

Craft—"In the Dog House"

Materials: One piece of pale blue card stock, 8½" × 11"; pieces of green and white card stock; pattern pieces; white copy paper; construction paper in various colors; self-adhesive Velcro strips or buttons; colored pencils or crayons; scissors; glue stick; stapler.

Procedure: Ahead of time photocopy the dog (see pattern) onto the white card stock, making five dogs for each child you expect to come to the program. Cut out the dog pieces and a grass "pocket" from the green card stock (see pattern). Photocopy the sun and moon and the words "Naughty" and "Nice" onto the white copy paper and cut them out. Trace the dog house pieces onto construction paper and cut them out. Hold the blue card stock horizontally and draw a vertical line down the center to divide the paper in half (8½" x 5½"). If using Velcro strips, cut them into one-inch pieces—one for each dog.

At the program explain that the phrase "in the dog house" means that someone is in trouble—usually because he or she was naughty. Let children color in the happy sun, the sad moon, and the words "Naughty" and "Nice." They can also color as many dogs as there are people in their family and write the name of a family member on each dog. When all the coloring is done, instruct them to glue the dog house pieces, the moon, and "Naughty" onto the left side of the blue card stock. Then glue the sun and "Nice" onto the right side (see drawing). Help the children staple the bottom and sides of the grass to the bottom edge of the "Nice" side, making sure to leave the top open so that the grass makes a pocket. Have children take as many pieces of Velcro as they have dogs. Separate the hooked and fuzzy sides. Stick the hooked side onto the back of each dog head, and one fuzzy side inside the doorway of the dog house at about the height of a dog's head. Tell

DOG

ROOF

DOG HOUSE

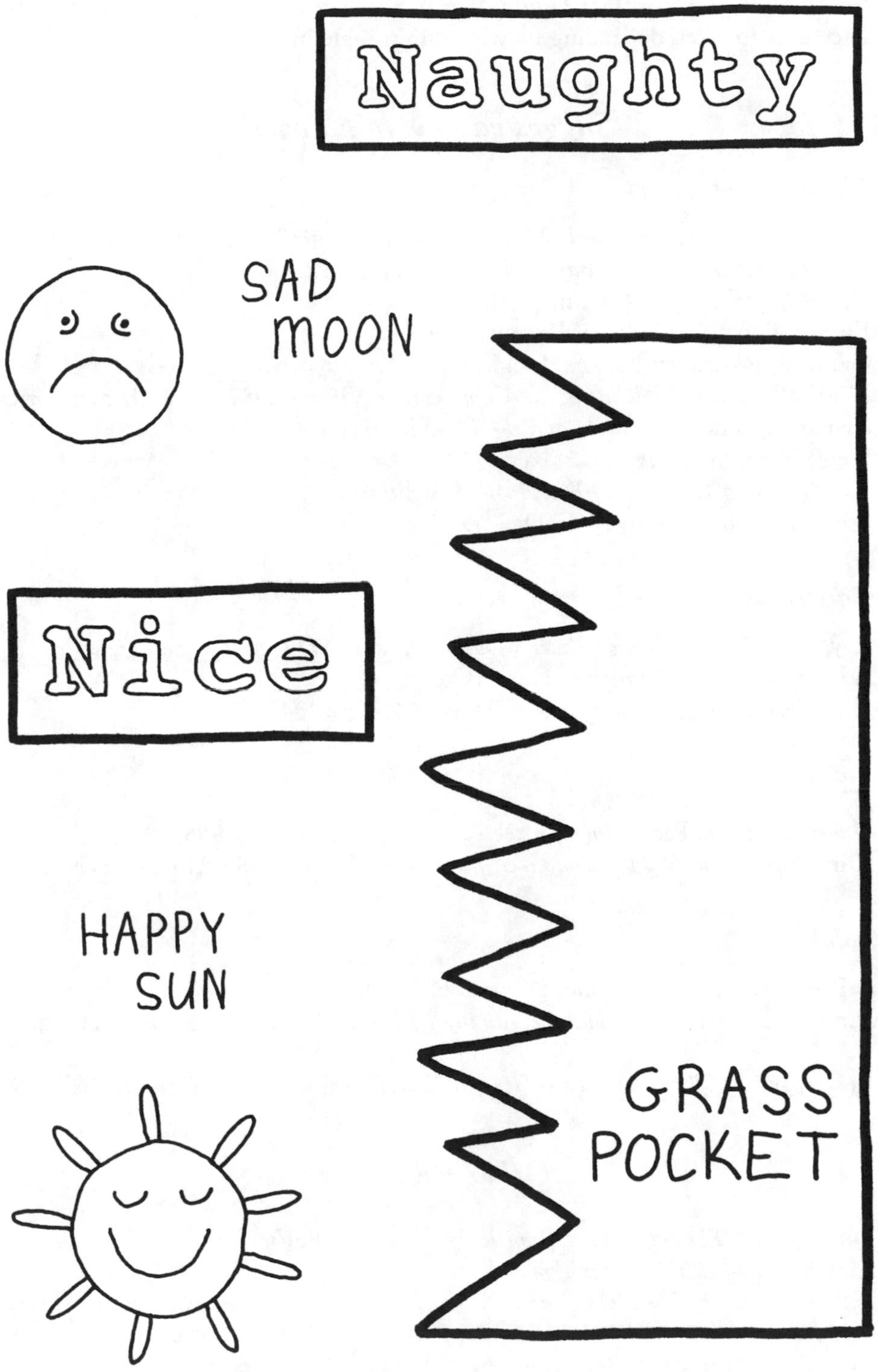

Naughty

SAD
MOON

Nice

HAPPY
SUN

GRASS
POCKET

the children to place their family dogs in either the Naughty dog house or the Nice grass pocket, depending on who is in trouble in their families.

Suggested Booktalk Books

Picture Books

Allard, Harry. *Miss Nelson Is Missing!* Houghton, 1977. Also others in series.
Bottner, Barbara. *Bootsie Barker Bites*. Putnam, 1992.
Collodi, Carlo. *Pinocchio*. Philomel, 1996.
Everitt, Betsy. *Mean Soup*. Harcourt, 1992.
Gantos, Jack. *Rotten Ralph*. Houghton, 1976. Also others in series.
Marshall, James. *The Cut-Ups at Camp Custer*. Viking, 1989. Also others in series.
Marshall, James. *Goldilocks and the Three Bears*. Dial, 1988.
Steig, William. *Spinky Sulks*. Farrar, 1988.
Van Allsburg, Chris. *Two Bad Ants*. Houghton, 1988.
Wells, Rosemary. *Noisy Nora*. Dial, 1997.

Easy Books

Rey, H.A. *Curious George Takes a Job*. Houghton, 1975. Also others in series.
Seidler, Tor. *Mean Margaret*. HarperCollins, 1997.
Slobodkina, Esphyr. *Caps for Sale*. Harper & Row, 1947.

Chapter Books

Heide, Florence Parry. *Tales for the Perfect Child*. Lothrop, 1985.
Kline, Suzy. *Horrible Harry and the Ant Invasion*. Viking, 1989. Also others in series.

Folklore

dePaola, Tomie. *Strega Nona*. Prentice Hall, 1989.
Kimmel, Eric A. *Anansi and the Talking Melon*. Holiday, 1994. Also other Anansi stories.
Lester, Julius. *The Tales of Uncle Remus: The Adventures of Brer Rabbit*. Dial, 1987.

Other Resources

Dukas, Paul. *The Sorcerer's Apprentice* (sound recording).
Mosel, Arlene. *Tikki Tikki Tembo*. Holt, 1968.
Pellowski, Anne. *The Story Vine: A Source Book of Unusual and Easy-to-Tell Stories from Around the World*. Macmillan, 1984. See "Naughty Marysia."
Rosen, Michael. *Little Rabbit Foo-Foo*. Simon & Schuster, 1990.

Sendak, Maurice. *Where the Wild Things Are*. Harper & Row, 1963.

Sharon, Lois and Bram. *Mainly Mother Goose* (sound recording). A & M Records, 1984. Track: "Little Rabbit Foo Foo."

Silverstein, Shel. *A Light in the Attic*. Harper & Row, 1974. See "Ladies First" and "Prayer of the Selfish Child."

Sitarz, Paula Gaj. *Picture Book Story Hours: From Birthdays to Bears*. Libraries Unlimited, 1987. See "Naughty Children" section.

Open Sesame!

Doors and Windows

Bulletin Board

Use large, flat cardboard boxes to make three-dimensional doors and windows that really open. Behind each box, conceal a humorous picture or poem that will be revealed when the viewer opens the door or window.

Background Music

Make a recording of songs about doors and windows: "I Hear You Knockin'" (Smiley Lewis), "Cleaning Windows" (Van Morrison), "One Less Bell to Answer" (5th Dimension), "Open the Door, Richard" (Louis Jordan), "Who Can It Be Now?" (Men at Work), "Lookin' Out My Back Door" (Creedence Clearwater Revival), "Let 'Em In" (Paul McCartney), "Knockin' on Heaven's Door" (Bob Dylan and others).

Opening Activity

You can play the game "Go In and Out the Window" or read aloud some goodies from a book of knock-knock jokes.

Story

Tell "The Squeaky Door" from *Crazy Gibberish*, by Naomi Baltuck.
Ask the children to help provide the sound effects necessary for this story.

Participation Activity

Have the children imagine that they are standing in front of a large door. Tell them that it is a magical door and it has no door knob. You may wish to describe the color and size of the door in detail or let the children describe it for you. Ask them how they are going to get the door open. Have them imagine what might lie beyond the door. Have everyone shout "Open Sesame!" and then make noises that show how they imagine the opening door would sound.

Craft—Tiffany Stained Glass Windows

Materials: Two pieces of black 9" × 12" construction paper; various colors of tissue paper; wax paper; glue stick.

Procedure: Ahead of time cut triptych window shapes into both pieces of black construction paper (see patterns). Cut a piece of wax paper to fit on the black construction paper. Rip the colored tissue paper into small pieces.

At the program have the children glue one piece of wax paper to each piece of black construction paper. Instruct them to glue the colored pieces of tissue paper into a mosaic pattern onto one of the pieces of wax paper, remaining within the translucent window spaces where there is no construction paper showing through the wax paper. When they have filled the translucent spaces to their satisfaction they should spread glue on the other piece of wax paper. Make sure both pieces of construction paper are right side up and then sandwich all four pieces of 9" × 12" paper together with the pieces of wax paper on the inside and the pieces of construction paper on the outside. The tissue paper mosaics should now be inside an envelope of wax paper framed by black construction paper on both sides.

Suggested Booktalk Titles

Picture Books

Baker, Jeannie. *Window.* Greenwillow, 1991.

Deming, Alhambra. *Who Is Tapping at My Window?* Puffin, 1988.

Hutchins, Pat. *The Doorbell Rang.* Scholastic, 1986.

Manifold, Laurie Fraser. *The Christmas Window.* Houghton, 1971.

Michaels, Tilde. *Who's That Knocking at My Door?* Barrons, 1986.

Rockwell, Anne F. *Hugo at the Window.* Macmillan, 1988.

Wong, Olive. *From My Window.* Silver Press, 1995.

Easy Readers

Matthias, Catherine. *Out the Door.* Children's Press, 1982.

Mozelle, Shirley. *Zack's Alligator.* Harper & Row, 1989.

center
WINDOW

flip this
pattern
to make
both
left &
right
windows

Sharmat, Marjorie Weinman. *Nate the Great and the Missing Key*. Coward, McCann, 1981.

Soto, Gary. *The Old Man and His Door*. Putnam, 1986.

Suen, Anastasia. *Window Music*. Viking, 1988.

Whishaw, Iona. *Henry and the Cow Problem*. Annick, 1995.

Chapter Books

De Angeli, Marguerite. *The Door in the Wall*. Doubleday, 1949.

Dixon, Franklyn. *Footprints Under the Window*. (Hardy Boys Mystery.) Grossett & Dunlap, 1993.

Folklore

Kimmel, Eric A. *The Tale of Ali Baba and the Forty Thieves*. Holiday, 1996.

Mathews, Judith, and Fay Robinson. *Nathaniel Willy, Scared Silly*. Macmillan, 1994.

SIDE
WINDOWS

Nonfiction

Rahn, Joan Elma. *Holes*. Houghton, 1984.

Biography

Stevenson, James. *Higher on the Door*. Greenwillow, 1987.

Just for Fun

Masurel, Claire. *Ten Dogs in the Window: A Countdown Book*. North-South, 1997.

Other Resources

Betting, Natalia. *Elves and Ellefolk: Tales of the Little People*. Holt, 1961. See "The Marvelous Doors—The Little People of Italy."

Disney's Children's Favorites 4 (sound recording). Walt Disney Records, 1990. Includes "Go In and Out the Window."

Fox, Don, ed. *Go In and Out the Window: An Illustrated Songbook for Young People*. Holt, 1987.

Hardendorff, Jeanne B. *Tricky Peik and Other Picture Tales*. Lippincott, 1942. See "The Servant and the Door."

Keller, Charles, and Norma Lee. *I Don't Knock on Doors: Knock, Knock Jokes*. Prentice Hall, 1983.

Kessler, Leonard. *Old Turtle's 90 Knock-Knocks, Jokes, and Riddles*. Greenwillow, 1991.

Schultz, Sam. *101 Knock-Knock Jokes: Guaranteed to Make Even a Sourpuss Smile*. Lerner, 1982.

Here are three versions of "The Squeaky Door":

Baltuck, Naomi. *Crazy Gibberish: And Other Story Hour Stretches (From a Storyteller's Bag of Tricks)*. Linnet, 1993.

Mathews, Judith, and Fay Robinson. *Nathaniel Willy, Scared Silly*. Macmillan, 1994.

Simms, Laura. *The Squeaky Door*. Crown, 1991.

Rock On

Rocks and Stones

Bulletin Board

Use wrinkled brown wrapping paper or paper bags to form cave walls. Draw some stick figures on the "walls" to look like primitive cave drawings telling a story. Use torn pieces of colored paper to make mosaic letters spelling "Rock On."

Background Music

Play a compilation of "rocky" tunes, such as "Rocky Mountain High" (John Denver), "I Am a Rock" (Simon and Garfunkel), "Rock Around the Clock" (Bill Haley and the Comets) and "Stony End" (Barbra Streisand). Or, if you prefer classical music, play *Grand Canyon Suite* by Ferde Grofé.

Opening Activity

Sing "Big Rock Candy Mountain" with the children.

Story

There are many versions of the folktale *The Stonecutter*. Choose one of these to tell the children. Or, tell one of the many versions of *Stone Soup* (see directions in "What's Cooking?").

Participation Activity

Display several different types of rocks. Read the characteristics of some rocks from a book on rocks and minerals, and let the children match the rocks you have to their descriptions. You can also let the children sample some rock candy.

Craft—Pet Rocks

Materials: Several smooth, clean fist-sized stones; assorted colors of felt and material scraps; colored markers; scissors; liquid glue; fabric scraps; googly eyes.

Procedure: Ahead of time wash the stones and let them dry. Cut felt and fabric into small circles, triangles, squares, and other geometric shapes that can be used for facial features, body parts, and clothing.

At the program let children glue pieces of felt and fabric to one or more rocks. Glue on googly eyes to make the pet rock come to life.

Suggested Booktalk Titles

Picture Books

Baylor, Bird. *Everybody Needs a Rock*. Scribner's, 1974.
Gruelle, Johnny. *Raggedy Ann's Wishing Pebble*. Bobbs-Merrill, 1990.
Lionni, Leo. *On My Beach There Are Many Pebbles*. Mulberry, 1994.
Steig, William. *Sylvester and the Magic Pebble*. Prentice, 1987.
Van Allsburg, Chris. *The Wretched Stone*. Houghton, 1994.

Chapter Book

Kline, Suzy. *Horrible Harry Moves Up to Third Grade*. Puffin, 2000.

Folklore

Crompton, Anne Eliot. *The Lifting Stone*. Holiday, 1978.

Nonfiction

Christian, Peggy. *If You Find a Rock*. Harcourt, 2000.
Complete Book of Rocks and Minerals. DK, 1995.
Fowler, Allan. *It Could Still Be a Rock*. Children's Press, 1993.
Hiscock, Bruce. *The Big Rock*. Atheneum, 1988.

Just for Fun

Blobaum, Cindy. *Geology Rocks! 50 Hands-On Activities to Explore the Earth*. Williamson, 1999.
Chapman, Gillian. *Art from Rocks and Shells*. Thomson Learning, 1995.
Gans, Roma. *Let's Go Rock Collecting*. HarperCollins, 1997.
Lohf, Sabine. *Things I Can Make with Stones*. Chronicle, 1990.

Other Resources

Cohn, Amy L., compiler. *From Sea to Shining Sea*. Scholastic, 1993. See "Big Rock Candy Mountain."

Chapin, Tom. *Family Tree* (sound recording). Sundance Music, 1988. Track: "Big Rock Candy Mountain."

Grofé, Ferde. *Grand Canyon Suite* (sound recording).

"Rock Rangers." *Copycat*. Copycat Press, Jan./Feb. 1995.

The following are versions of the same story:

Demi. *The Stonecutter* (Chinese folktale). Crown, 1995.

McDermott, Gerald. *The Stonecutter* (Japanese folktale). Viking, 1975.

Newton, Pam. *The Stonecutter* (Indian folktale). Putnam, 1990.

Stolz, Mary. *Zekmet, the Stone Carver* (Ancient Egypt folktale). Harcourt, 1988.

The following are versions of the same story:

Brown, Marcia. *Stone Soup*. Scribner, 1947.

Van Rynbach, Iris. *The Soup Stone*. Greenwillow, 1988.

Royal Rumpus

Queens, Kings, Princes, Princesses

Bulletin Board

In the center of the board, against a yellow background, place large representations of two royal playing cards—a king and a queen. The figures should be rectangular like real playing cards, but give them heads, arms and legs that project outside the rectangles (think of the card soldiers in Disney's *Alice in Wonderland*). Put crowns on their heads and have them hold hands, if you like. Use real playing cards for the border and fill in the background with black and white chess pieces. Caption the board "Royal Rumpus."

Background Music

Play "Pomp and Circumstance" and other appropriately majestic music. Remember to include "If I Were King of the Forest" from *The Wizard of Oz*.

Opening Activity

Sing "The Noble Duke of York" to the tune of "The Farmer in the Dell." Have the children march in time to the music until they reach the second verse. During the second verse everyone should reach up as high as they can or crouch down as low as they can according to the words. Sing the song several times going progressively faster each time until no one can go up and down any faster. For an even greater challenge, divide the children into two groups and try singing the song in a round.

Story

The Paper Princess, by Elisa Kleven.
Materials: A cut-out, bald paper princess decorated front and back as she is in the story; a cracker; yarn; cotton balls; a trumpet-shaped construction paper

flower blossom; a cellophane candy wrapper; a green felt-tipped pen; a bird puppet; some doll's hair (can be found in many craft shops); a paper crown; a paper elephant; a paper banjo; a red paper sweater.

Participation Activity

Play Royal Tic Tac Toe.

Materials: Chess set; marker; large art pad; easel; nine chairs or nine carpet squares large enough for a child to sit on; five "O" crowns (a strip of paper stapled into a circular crown that will fit on a child's head); five "X" crowns (a strip of paper stapled into a circular crown—staple the ends of two more strips onto the top of the circle so that they fit over the top of the head in an "X" shape).

Show the chess board and its pieces and talk about the meaning of each of the figures. Each of the pieces in the chess set represents a character or an object from a traditional European royal court. Describe how some chess clubs like to play chess on a giant board with living people as the chess pieces and explain that today we will be playing life-size Tic Tac Toe. Make sure that everyone knows how to play Tic Tac Toe by reviewing the rules of regular tic tac toe (demonstrate a game on the art pad). Set up the nine chairs or carpet squares in a square like a Tic Tac Toe board. Divide the children into two teams and have them line up on either side of the Tic Tac Toe board. Allow the teams to choose some kind of royal names for themselves so that you end up with the Dukes vs. the Earls or the Red Queens vs. the White Queens, for example. Set up a scoreboard on the art pad. Hand out crowns to the first five players on each team. Flip a coin to see which team will go first. The first player on the first team puts on the team crown and chooses a square to sit in. The first player on the other team does the same. Continue to play with each team taking turns until one team wins or the board is full. Play as many games as you wish until everyone on both teams has had a chance to sit on the board. The team that wins the most games is declared the Most High and Exalted Emperors.

Craft—Paper Princess (or Prince)

Materials: White copy paper; yarn; cotton balls; construction paper; cellophane candy wrapper; colored markers; glue stick; scissors.

Procedure: Ahead of time make enlarged photocopies of the paper princess and prince patterns and cut them out. In various colors of construction paper cut out skirts, trousers, trumpet-shaped flower blossoms, crowns, banjos, sweaters, and other accessories.

At the program have the children glue the princess or prince onto a piece of construction paper and decorate her or him with colored markers, construction paper shapes, and other items from the story.

Paper Princess
enlarge on photocopier

Suggested Booktalk Titles

Picture Books

Atwood, Margaret Eleanor. *Princess Prunella and the Purple Peanut*. Workman, 1995.
Babbitt, Natalie. *Bub, or the Very Best Thing*. HarperCollins, 1994.
Duke, Kate. *Aunt Isabel Tells a Good One*. Dutton, 1992.
Wood, Audrey. *King Bidgood's in the Bathtub*. Harcourt, 1985.
Yolen, Jane. *Piggins and the Royal Wedding*. Harcourt, 1988.

Paper Prince
enlarge on photocopier

Easy Readers

Black, Charles. *The Royal Nap*. Viking, 1995.
Lester, Helen. *Princess Penelope's Parrot*. Houghton, 1996.
Wise, William. *Perfect Pancakes, If You Please*. Dial, 1997.

Chapter Books

Coville, Bruce. *The World's Worst Fairy Godmother*. Pocket, 1996.
Paterson, Katherine. *The King's Equal*. HarperCollins, 1992.

Folklore

Andersen, Hans Christian, and Naomi Lewis, trans. *The Emperor's New Clothes*. Candlewick, 1997.

Hewitt, Kathryn. *King Midas and the Golden Touch*. Harcourt, 1987.

Matthews, Caitlyn. *The Barefoot Book of Princesses*. Barefoot, 1997.

Nonfiction

Biesty, Stephen. *Castle*. DK, 1994.

Meltzer, Milton. *Ten Queens: Portraits of Women of Power*. Dutton, 1998.

Wingate, Philippa. *The Usborne Book of Kings and Queens*. EDC, 1995.

Biographies

Guzzetti, Paula. *The Last Hawaiian Queen: Liliuokalani*. Benchmark, 1997.

Stanley, Diane. *Cleopatra*. Morrow, 1997.

Wisniewski, David. *Sundiata: Lion King of Mali*. Clarion, 1992.

Just for Fun

Hart, Avery. *Knights and Castles: 50 Hands-On Activities to Experience the Middle Ages*. Williamson, 1998.

Loehr, Mallory. *The Princess Book: Every Girl Can Be a Princess—With Princess Parties, Recipes, Costumes and More!* Random, 1996.

Other Resources

Elgar, Edward. *Pomp and Circumstance Marches* (sound recording).

Freeman, Judy. *More Books Kids Will Sit Still For: A Read-Aloud Guide*. Bowker, 1995. See "Library Tic-Tac-Toe Game."

Harris, Franklin W. *Great Games to Play with Groups: A Leader's Guide*. Fearon, 1990. See "Human Tic Tac Toe."

Kleven, Elisa. *The Paper Princess*. Dutton, 1994.

"Royals for a Day." *Copycat*. Copycat Press, May/June, 1998.

Sitarz, Paula Gaj. *Picture Book Story Hours: From Birthdays to Bears*. Libraries Unlimited, 1987. See "Your Highness: Stories About Royalty."

Yolen, Jane, editor. *The Lap-Time Song and Play Book*. Harcourt, 1989. See "The Noble Duke of York."

Sailing, Sailing

Boats and Life at Sea

Bulletin Board

Post pictures of seagoing vessels from different eras and parts of the world. Make a border of shells strung on fishing net or rope. Your armada can be supplemented by other nautical symbols, such as a ship's wheel, buoys, and flags.

Background Music

Play a recording of sea shanties and folk songs about life at sea, such as *See the Sea* by Tom and Chris Kastle or *Saturday Night at Sea* by Tom Callinan.

Opening Activity

Sing "My Bonnie Lies Over the Ocean."
The words and hand motions for this song can be found in *Juba This and Juba That* by Virginia A. Fashjian. Teach the children the hand motion for each word. Sing it with them once all the way through, using the movements. Then, sing it but take away the first word (my), using the movement only for that word. Go through the verse over and over again, each time leaving out a word, until the last round consists entirely of hand motions.

Story

There are several old sea tales you can tell. Try "With a Way, Hey, Mister Stormalong" in *From Sea to Shining Sea*, complied by Amy L. Cohn, or choose a story from *A Cavalcade of Sea Legends*, edited by Michael Brown. The first book also contains some sea shanties you can sing with the children.

Participation Activity

The story *Who Sank the Boat?* by Pamela Allen is about five animals that try to cram into a small boat. When the last and smallest animal, a mouse, jumps in, the combined weight of all the animals is enough to sink the boat. You can adapt this story to include all the children in your group. Designate an area on the floor to be the "boat." As you tell the story, assign each child the role of an animal. Start out naming large animals, such as elephants and giraffes, and name progressively smaller animals as the story unfolds. Each child sits in the "boat" on his turn. When you get to the last child, he is the mouse who finally causes the boat to sink. Have all the "animals" point to the "mouse" and say, "You sank the boat!" The mouse can take a bow while everyone applauds.

Craft—Milk Jug Ships

Materials: Plastic half-gallon milk jug; a single chopstick or dowel; empty spool; modeling dough; construction paper; patterns; card stock; stick-on dots and other shapes; string; glue; markers; scissors; craft knife; hole punch.

Procedure: Ahead of time wash the milk jugs and cut to size with the craft knife. Cut two sails and other decorations from construction paper, and an anchor from card stock (see patterns). Punch a hole at the top of the anchor and attach a six-inch piece of string. Punch a hole at the side of the plastic bottle where the anchor will be attached. Buy or make modeling dough (see Appendix I for recipe).

At the program let children decorate one side of each sail. Apply glue to the plain sides of the sails, sandwich the mast (chopstick or dowel) between them

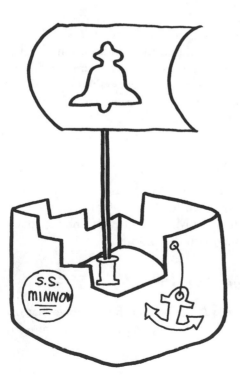

as shown in the drawing and press together. Children can decorate the outside of the boat with stickers and other shapes. Help them tie on the anchor. Then have children take a lump of dough and place it in the center of the jug. Push the spool into the dough, and insert the empty end of the chopstick or dowel in the spool's hole so the mast will stand up. If the dough seems too soft, tell the children that it will harden overnight.

Suggested Booktalk Titles

Picture Books

Borden, Louise. *The Little Ships: The Heroic Rescue at Dunkirk in World War II*. Margaret McElderry, 1997.
Calhoun, Mary. *Henry the Sailor Cat*. Morrow, 1994.

SAIL

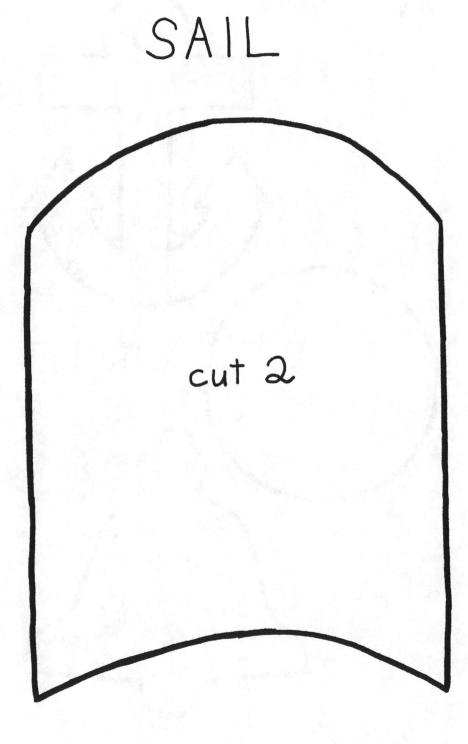

cut 2

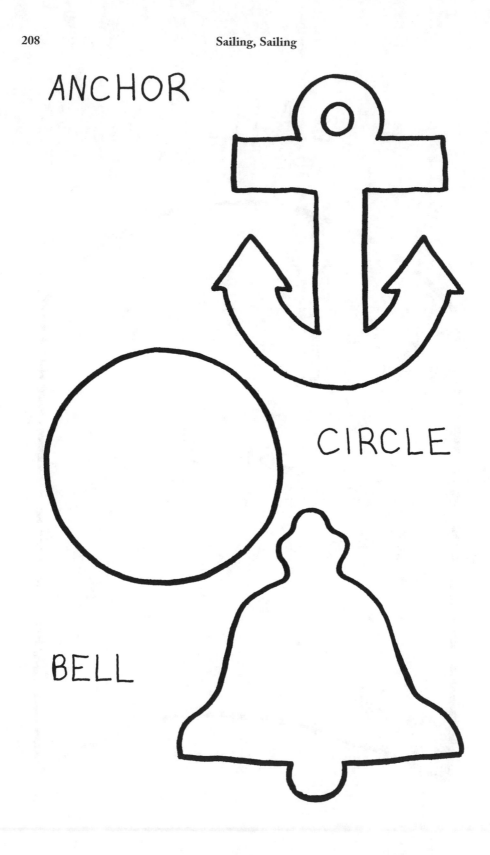

ANCHOR

CIRCLE

BELL

Rand, Gloria. *Aloha, Salty!* Holt, 1996.
Slawski, Wolfgang. *Captain Jonathan Sails the Sea*. North-South, 1997.
Williams, Vera B. *Three Days on the River in a Red Canoe*. Greenwillow, 1981.

Easy Reader

Blake, Robert J. *Spray*. Philomel, 1996.

Chapter Book

Avi. *Windcatcher*. Macmillan, 1991.

Nonfiction

Bailey, Donna. *Sailing*. Steck-Vaughn, 1991.
Flanagan, Alice K. *Riding the Ferry with Captain Cruz*. Children's Press, 1996.
Gibbons, Gail. *Boat Book*. Holiday, 1983.
Morris, Neil. *Ships*. Silver Burdett, 1998.
Paulsen, Paul. *Sailing, from Jibs to Jibing*. Messner, 1981.
Spedden, Daisy Corning Stone. *Polar the Titanic Bear*. Little, Brown, 1994.

Biography

Sis, Peter. *Follow the Dream*. Random, 1991.

Poetry

Cecil, Laura. *A Thousand Yards of Sea: A Collection of Sea Stories and Poems*. Greenwillow, 1993.

Just for Fun

Ames, Lee J. *Draw 50 Boats, Ships, Trucks & Trains*. Doubleday, 1976.
Biesty, Stephen. *Cross Sections: Man-of-War*. Houghton, 1993.
Herda, D.J. *Model Boats and Ships*. Watts, 1982.
Orii, Eiji. *Simple Science Experiments with Water*. Gareth Stevens, 1989.

Other Resources

Allen, Pamela. *Who Sank the Boat?* Coward McCann, 1990.
Brown, Michael, ed. *A Cavalcade of Sea Legends*. Henry Z. Walck, 1971.
Callinan, Tom. *Saturday Night at Sea* (sound recording). Cannu Music, 1987.
Cohn, Amy L., compiler. *From Sea to Shining Sea*. Scholastic, 1993. See "Blow, Ye

Winds, in the Morning," "With a Way, Hey, Mister Stormalong," and other selections.

Fashjian, Virginia A., ed. *Juba This and Juba That*. Little, Brown, 1995. See "My Bonnie Lies Over the Ocean."

Kastle, Tom, and Chris Kastle. *See the Sea* (sound recording). Sextant Music, 1991.

Linscott, Eloise Hubbard. *Folk Songs of Old New England*. Dover, 1993. See "Sea Chanties & Fo' Castle Songs."

Nelson, Esther L. *The Funny Songbook*. Sterling, 1984. See "A Sailor Went to Sea Sea Sea" and "The Walloping Windowblind."

"Set Sail with Books." *Copycat*. Copycat Press, Nov./Dec. 1995.

Sitarz, Paula Gaj. *More Picture Book Story Hours*. Libraries Unlimited, 1990. See "Sea and Seashore."

Shadows Know

Shadows and Silhouettes

Bulletin Board

Trace a child's body onto white butcher paper and cut out the shape. In black paper create a shorter and narrower companion shadow for the body shape and place both shapes on a pale blue background with the white shape upright and the black shape prone. Make sure their feet meet. If you don't want to use a child volunteer, try recreating Peter Pan and his shadow. You could also draw a ground-hog and his shadow. For a border use various colorful shapes of construction paper echoed in black construction paper or choose a symmetrical shape such as a flower or a butterfly and use black and white paper to make a series of "positive/negative" pictures (see Other Resources) with half of the picture in black and white and the other half reflecting all the same features oppositely in white and black.

Background Music

Make a sound recording of "Me and My Shadow" and other famous duets or you can just play Frank Sinatra's *Duets*.

Opening Activity

Make hand shadows together.
Materials: White bed sheet; small table; overhead or slide projector.
Suspend the sheet across a corner of the room. From a table in front of the sheet, aim the projector to throw light onto the sheet. Teach the children how to make some simple hand shadows. Try using the swan, etc., from *The Hand Book*, by Lassor A. Blumenthal.

Story

Tell *The Rooster's Horns*, by Ed Young.

Materials: White bed sheet; small table; overhead or slide projector; rooster puppet and dragon puppet made using the patterns in the back of Young's book; flashlight covered with red acetate; second small table or bench (optional).

Move the table with the light source so that it is between the sheet and the wall with the light source aimed through the sheet. Have three teen volunteers go behind the sheet, kneel down between the light source and the sheet, and use the puppets to portray the action while the librarian is telling the story. The puppeteers may need a second small table or bench to lean their elbows on for support while they perform.

Participation Activity

Move the table with the light source so that it is between the sheet and the wall with the light source aimed through the sheet. Allow each child to have a turn standing behind the sheet to form shadows while the other children watch. Let the audience guess what kind of creature or object the child behind the sheet is making. After each individual has had a turn, let the children work in small groups of two or more to form crazy multi-headed and multi-legged creatures. If they need some inspiration, share with them some of the ideas for Sidewalk Creatures outlined in *The Incredible Year-Round Playbook*, by Elin McCoy.

Craft—Shadow Puppets with Shoe Box Theater

Materials: Shoe box with lid; white tissue paper; colored tape; pieces of brightly colored paper; black poster board; straws or wooden chopsticks; patterns for characters (see Other Resources); scissors; glue stick; masking tape; three large paper clips (the colorful, plastic-coated kind are best).

Procedure: Ahead of time cut a large rectangular piece out of the lid of the shoe box leaving a ¾" frame around the edges. Trace outside of the lid onto a piece of white tissue paper and then cut out the paper just a bit smaller than the lid. Use the colored tape to tape the tissue paper over the outside of the shoe box lid so that it covers the rectangular hole. Cut pieces of brightly colored paper into shapes. Cut out a variety of animal and character patterns so that the children can choose two or more favorites. Totline publishes many books of silhouette patterns (see "Other Resources") or you may create your own. The children may share patterns if you like, but make sure that each child has easy access to enough patterns during the program.

At the program have the children decorate the shoe box on the outside—including the bottom—by gluing on pieces of brightly colored paper. Make sure that they keep the lid removable. For the puppets, have the children trace the characters onto black poster board, cut them out, and use masking tape to attach a straw or chopstick to the back of each figure. During a performance, the shoe box is the stage. Remove the lid and turn the shoe box on its side. The bottom of the box should be facing the audience. Use the three paper clips to attach the lid to the uppermost side—now the top—of the box so that a bright light, such as a flashlight, can be aimed to shine from behind through the tissue paper to silhouette the puppets as they perform (see drawing). The box can also be used as storage for the puppets and the paper clips.

BACKSTAGE AT THE SHOEBOX THEATER

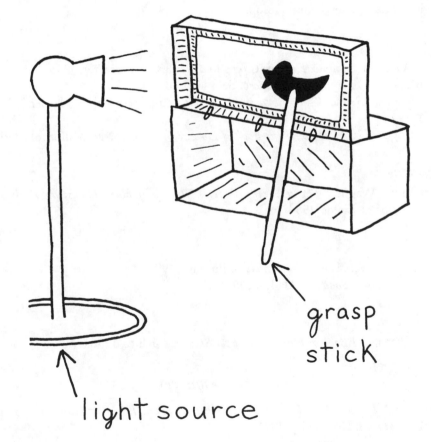

grasp stick

light source

Suggested Booktalk Titles

Picture Books

Fleischman, Paul. *Shadow Play: A Story*. Harper & Row, 1990.
Kroll, Steven. *It's Groundhog Day!* Holiday House, 1987.
Narahashi, Keiko. *I Have a Friend*. Macmillan, 1987.
Paul, Ann Whitford. *Shadows Are About*. Scholastic, 1992.
Tompert, Ann. *Nothing Sticks Like a Shadow*. Houghton Mifflin, 1984.

Easy Readers

Farber, Norma. *Return of the Shadows*. HarperCollins, 1992.
Moutran, Julia Spencer. *The Story of Punxsutawney Phil, the "Fearless Forecaster."* Literary Publications, 1987.

Folklore

Wiesner, William. *Hansel and Gretel: A Shadow Puppet Picture Book*. Seabury, 1971.
Goepfert, Paula, ed. *The Children's Treasury*. Discovery, 1987. Includes "The Dog and His Shadow" from Aesop.

Nonfiction

Bailey, Vanessa. *Shadow Theater: Games and Projects*. Gloucester, 1991.
Dorros, Arthur. *Me and My Shadow*. Scholastic, 1990.
Goor, Ron, and Nancy Goor. *Shadows: Here, There, and Everywhere*. Harper & Row, 1981.
Lade, Roger. *The Most Excellent Book of How to be a Puppeteer*. Millbrook, 1996.

Biography

Brust, Beth Wagner. *The Amazing Paper Cuttings of Hans Christian Andersen*. Ticknor & Fields, 1994.

Poetry

Stevenson, Robert Louis. *My Shadow*. Putnam, 1990.
Cendrars, Blaise. *Shadow*. Aladdin, 1986.

Just for Fun

Shadow Games: A Book of Hand & Puppet Shadows. Klutz, 1996.

Other Resources

Blumenthal, Lassor. *The Hand Book: All Kinds of Jokes, Tricks, & Games to Do with Your Hands*. Doubleday, 1976.

Blyton, Enid. *My Best Book of Enid Blyton Stories.* Award Publications, 1980. See "Susie and Her Shadow."

Bursill, Henry. *Hand Shadows to Be Thrown Upon the Wall: A Series of Novel and Amusing Figures Formed by the Hand.* Dover, 1967.

Fiarotta, Phyllis and Noel Fiarotta. *Pin It, Tack It, Hang It: The Big Book of Kids' Bulletin Board Ideas.* Workman, 1975. Contains instructions for "Positive and Negative Study."

Lewis, Shari. *One-Minute Animal Stories.* Doubleday, 1986. See "The Donkey's Shadow."

Lynch-Watson, Janet. *The Shadow Puppet Book.* Sterling, 1980.

McCoy, Elin. *The Incredible Year-Round Playbook.* Random, 1979.

Ross, Laura. *Puppet Shows Using Poems and Stories.* Lothrop, 1970.

Warren, Jean. *Animal Patterns.* Warren (Totline), 1990.

Warren, Jean. *Everyday Patterns.* Warren (Totline), 1990.

Warren, Jean. *Nature Patterns.* Warren (Totline), 1990.

Warren, Jean. *Teeny-Tiny Folktales.* (Totline), 1987.

Young, Ed. *The Rooster's Horns: A Chinese Play to Make and Perform.* Collins, 1978.

Solargraphics is a company that makes sun-sensitive paper on which objects can be placed, exposed to direct sunlight and then developed in ordinary tap water to produce shadow prints of the objects that were assembled on the paper. Look for Solargraphics products in educational toy stores or find them on the Internet through ABC Educational Supplies or Internet Education Resource Center: www.abceducation.net or www.ierc.com.

Shoe Be Do

Bulletin Board

Use the motif of the old woman who lived in a shoe as a centerpiece for this bulletin board. Post pictures of children in and around the shoe. Frame the board with a border made up of various types of footwear. Caption the board with a scroll that reads "There was an old woman who lived in a shoe...."

Background Music

Play shoe-related songs such as "Shine on Your Shoes" (Fred Astaire), "Shoeless Joe" (from *Damn Yankees*), "Blue Suede Shoes" (Carl Perkins), "Diamonds on the Soles of Her Shoes (Paul Simon), "These Boots Are Made for Walkin'" (Nancy Sinatra or Billy Ray Cyrus), "High-Heeled Sneakers" (Jerry Lee Lewis), or "Goody Two Shoes" (Adam Ant), or play the soundtrack from the film *The Red Shoes*.

Opening Activity

The children can help you sing "So Many Shoes," by Martha Simpson and Lynne Perrigo, sung to the tune of "The Green Grass Grew All Around."

Materials: Art pad; easel; marker; several types of shoes.

Bring in several types of shoes to show. Ask the children to think of other types of shoes. Write 13 of their suggestions on a large sheet of paper and have the kids vote on which one is their favorite. For the first four lines of each verse, the librarian sings a line and then the children echo it. The librarian sings line five. Everyone sings line six together.

Verse 1:
There was a man (there was a man)
Who had some shoes (who had some shoes)
So many shoes (so many shoes)
That they filled a whole room (that they filled a whole room)

He had (<u>shoes #1</u>) *and* (<u>shoes #2</u>) *and* (<u>shoes #3</u>) *and* (<u>shoes #4</u>),
But his favorite shoes were a pair of (<u>kids' choice</u>)—*and he wore them all the time.*

Verse 2:
He loved his (<u>shoes #5</u>) *(he loved his* [<u>shoes #5</u>])
He adored his (<u>shoes #6</u>) *(he adored his* [<u>shoes #6</u>])
He liked his (<u>shoes #7</u>) *(he liked his* [<u>shoes #7</u>])
And he dug his (<u>shoes #8</u>) *(and he dug his* [<u>shoes #8</u>])
He wore (<u>shoes #9</u>) *and* (<u>shoes #10</u>) *and* (<u>shoes #11</u>) *and* (<u>shoes #12</u>),
But his favorite shoes were a pair of (<u>kids' choice</u>)—*and he wore them all the time.*

Story

Tell "The Naughty Shoes" from *Movement Stories for Young Children*, by Helen Landalf and Pamela Gerke.

Materials: A pair of flamboyantly decorated shoes such as those described in the story; a musical recording suitable for vigorous freestyle dancing.

Participation Activity

Sing the call-and-response song "The Bear in Tennis Shoes" from *Crazy Gibberish: And Other Story Hour Stretches* by Naomi Baltuck, or play "Shoe Stew" from *The Incredible Indoor Games Book*, by Bob Gregson.

Craft—Shoe Decorating

Materials: Shoe pattern; white copy paper; crayons or markers; various decorative items such as pom-poms, sequins, etc.; yarn; oak tag; hole punch; liquid glue; glue stick.

Procedure: Ahead of time photocopy a shoe (see pattern) for each child. Glue each shoe onto a piece of oak tag and cut out when glue is dry. Punch holes where the laces will go. Cut yarn into one-yard lengths. Dip the yarn ends into liquid glue and let dry.

At the program have the children use the crayons and decorations to design a shoe that reflects the personality of its creator. Prompt the children to think of things that make them unique: hobbies, favorite color, pets, favorite sports, favorite words, special skills, etc. Help the children lace the yarn through the shoelace holes.

Suggested Booktalk Titles

Picture Books
Burton, Marilee. *My Best Shoes*. Tambourine, 1994.
Cannon, Annie. *The Bat in the Boot*. Orchard, 1996.

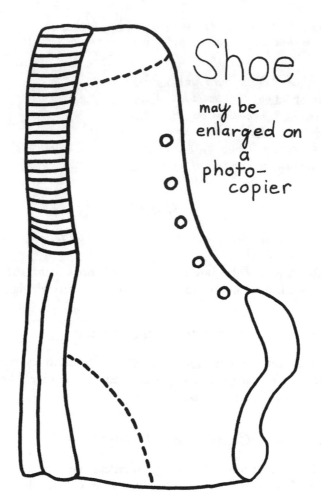

Shoe
may be
enlarged on
a
photo-
copier

Cleary, Beverly. *Growing-Up Feet*. Morrow, 1987.
Cote, Nancy. *Flip Flops*. Albert Whitman, 1998.
Dorros, Arthur. *Alligator Shoes*. Dutton, 1982.
Fox, Mem. *Shoes from Grandpa*. Orchard, 1990.
Lawston, Lisa. *A Pair of Red Sneakers*. Orchard, 1998.
Numeroff, Laura Joffe. *Dogs Don't Wear Sneakers*. Simon & Schuster, 1993.
Patrick, Denise Lewis. *Red Dancing Shoes*. Tambourine, 1993.
San Souci, Robert D. *The Red Heels*. Dial, 1995.

Easy Readers

Hurd, Edith Thacher. *Johnny Lion's Rubber Boots*. Harper & Row, 1972.
Levinson, Nancy Smiler. *Snowshoe Thompson*. HarperCollins, 1992.
Myers, Bernice. *Sidney Rella and the Glass Sneaker*. Macmillan, 1985.
Stevens, Janet. *Shoe Town*. Harcourt, 1999.

Chapter Books

Bunting, Eve. *Nasty, Stinky Sneakers*. HarperCollins, 1994.

Sobol, Donald J. *Encyclopedia Brown and the Case of the Disgusting Sneakers*. Morrow, 1990.

Streatfeild Noel, *Traveling Shoes*. Random, 1962. Also other "Shoes" books by author.

Folklore

Berson, Harold. *Kassim's Shoes*. Crown, 1977.

Lowell, Susan. *The Bootmaker and the Elves*. Orchard, 1997.

Perrault, Charles. *Cinderella*. Many different versions.

Travers, P.L. *Two Pairs of Shoes*. Viking, 1980.

Nonfiction

Fisher, Leonard Everett. *The Shoemakers*. Benchmark, 1998.

Morris, Ann. *Shoes, Shoes, Shoes*. Mulberry, 1995.

Biography

Widdemer, Mabel Cleland. *Peter Stuyvesant, Boy with Wooden Shoes*. Bobbs-Merrill, 1962.

Poetry

Grimes, Nikki. *Shoe Magic*. Orchard, 2000.

Other Resources

Baltuck, Naomi. *Crazy Gibberish: And Other Story Hour Stretchers*. Linnet, 1993. See "The Bear in Tennis Shoes."

Bomans, Godfried. *The Wily Witch: And All the Other Fairy Tales and Fables*. Stemmer, 1977. See "The Golden Slippers."

Credle, Ellis. *Tall Tales from the High Hills: And Other Stories*. Thomas Nelson, 1957. See "Janey's Shoes."

Gregson, Bob. *The Incredible Indoor Games Book: 160 Group Projects, Games, and Activities*. David Lake, 1982. See "Shoe Stew."

Landalf, Helen, and Pamela Gerke. *Movement Stories for Young Children: Ages 3–6*. Smith and Kraus, 1996. See "The Naughty Shoes."

Miller, Margaret. *Whose Shoe?* Greenwillow, 1991.

Rosenthal, Phil. *The Green Grass Grew All Around* (sound recording). American Melody, 1995.

Ross, Kathy. *Crafts for Kids Who Are Wild About Dinosaurs*. Millbrook, 1997. See "Dinosaur Feet."

"Shoe Be Do." *Copycat*. Copycat Press, March/April 1999.

Something Fishy

Sea Creatures

Bulletin Board

This makes a fun "back to school" display. Tack up a light blue background to simulate an underwater scene. Using several sheets of a contrasting color construction paper or poster board, cut out the shape of a large octopus. Tack it up in the center, with the eight arms arranged in different directions. Cut out two big eyes with eyelashes and red smiling lips, for this is a friendly lady octopus teacher. She should be facing a black chalkboard, with her nearest arm holding a piece of chalk. The octopus can hold more school-related items in her other arms, such as a box of crayons, scissors, a small book, etc. All around her, place several small groups of fish cutouts, with about five to ten in each "school" cluster, facing the chalkboard. The caption on the chalkboard can read, in white letters, "Welcome to the Library" or "Back to School."

Background Music

Sea Songs: A Celebration of Sea Creatures by Suzanne Niles Scheniman is a lively choice for kids. You could also play classical music, such as *The Blue Danube* by Strauss, or "go natural" and play a recording of whale calls or sea sounds such as waves crashing.

Opening Activity

Sing "The Three Little Fishies" by Saxie Dowell from *The New Novelty Song Book*. Children can sing the chorus and pretend to swim like the fishies.

Story

Tell *A Million Fish—More or Less* by Patricia McKissack.
As you tell the story, have children act out the alligators, racoons, birds, and cats grabbing the fish.

Participation Activity

Play this guessing game with the children: Display an assortment of large sea shells, coral, sponges, seaweed, a bottle of sand, and models or pictures of different types of fish. Then read clues, such as "You can build a castle out of me at the beach," and let the children guess the answers. Or, take children through "Life in the Bass Lane: An Undersea Adventure" from *Movement Stories for Children* by Helen Landalf and Pamela Gerke.

Craft—Sea Mobile

Materials: Two metal clothes hangers; two twist ties or masking tape; four small sea shells with a hole drilled in each; large sand dollar with a hole drilled in it; card stock in various colors; string; tape; scissors; crayons, colored pencils, markers; liquid glue; hole punch.

Procedure: Ahead of time set one hanger inside the other at a perpendicular angle. Fasten them together using tape or twist ties where they intersect at the handle and at the bottom. Also measure out string: one ten inches long, four at eight inches long, and four at six inches long. Tie the small shells to the eight-inch strings. Tie the sand dollar to the ten-inch string. Photocopy the fish pattern onto card stock to get four fish, then cut them out and punch a hole in each one as shown (see pattern).

At the program give each child a hanger set, one sand dollar on the string, four small shells on string, and four plain six-inch strings. Give them each four fish to decorate. Help the children attach the six-inch lengths of string to their fish. Then help them tie the ten-inch string and sand dollar to the bottom center intersection of the two hangers, the eight-inch strings and shells to the four outer edges of the hangers, and the six-inch strings with the paper fish halfway between the shells and sand dollar on each wire half. Adjust string lengths as needed so the mobiles will balance.

Suggested Booktalk Titles

Picture Books

Clements, Andrew. *Big Al*. Picture Book, 1988.
Frieden, Sarajo. *The Care and Feeding of Fish: A Story with Pictures*. Houghton, 1996.
Grey, Catherine. *Tammy and the Gigantic Fish*. Harper & Row, 1983.
Pfister, Marcus. *Rainbow Fish*. North-South, 1996.
Seuss, Dr. *McElligot's Pool*. Random, 1966.

SEA MOBILE FISH

punch hole

Easy Readers

Cohen, Caron Lee. *How Many Fish?* HarperCollins, 1998.
Keenan, Sheila. *The Biggest Fish*. Scholastic, 1996.
Palmer, Helen. *Fish Out of Water*. Random, 1987.

Nonfiction

Boyle, Doe. *Coral Reef Hideaway: The Story of a Clown Anemonefish*. Soundprints, 1995.
Evans, Mark. *ASPCA Pet Care Guides for Kids: Fish*. DK, 1993.
Parker, Steve. *Fish*. Knopf, 1990.

Poetry

Florian, Douglas. *In the Swim: Poems and Paintings*. Harcourt, 1997.

Just for Fun

Hall, Katy. *Fishy Riddles*. Puffin, 1993.
Ross, Kathy. *Crafts for Kids Who Are Wild About Oceans*. Millbrook, 1998.
Walton, Rick. *Something's Fishy*. Lerner, 1987.

Other Resources

"Delightful Dolphins." *Copycat*. Copycat Press, Jan./Feb. 1998.
Dowell, Saxie. *The New Novelty Song Book*. Hal Leonard, 1989. See "The Three Little Fishies."
Landalf, Helen, and Pamela Gerke. *Movement Stories for Children*. Smith & Kraus, 1996. See "Life in the Bass Lane: An Undersea Adventure."
Louis, Marcia. *Bubblegum Blues* (sound recording). Louis Louis Productions, 1991. Track: "The Three Little Fishies."
McKissack, Patricia. *A Million Fish—More or Less*. Knopf, 1992.
Scheniman, Suzanne Niles. *Sea Songs: A Celebration of Sea Creatures* (sound recording). Chroma, 1997.
"Shark School." *Copycat*. Copycat Press, May/June 1997.
"Tiptoe 'Round the Tide Pool." *Copycat*. Copycat Press, March/April 1998.

Several recordings of ocean sounds are available in the Echoes of Nature series from Delta Music, Inc., Santa Monica, CA, 90404-3061. Titles include *Ocean Dreams*, *Distant Shores*, *Ocean Voyages*, *Caribbean Shores*, and *Whales of the Pacific*.

Strike Up the Band!

Musical Instruments

Bulletin Board

On a yellow background, place a giant G clef on the left side of the bulletin board and create a free-form, wavy musical staff stretching away from it. Decorate the staff with randomly placed musical instruments made from construction paper. Above the instruments and above the staff, place brightly colored musical notes so that they appear to be rising from the instruments and floating above them. Caption the board "Tuneful Times."

Background Music

Get the program off to a spirited start by playing some John Philip Sousa music or Prokofiev's *Peter and the Wolf*.

Opening Activity

Play some water glass music for the children.
Materials: Water; water glasses; food coloring (optional).
Alex Sabbeth's *Rubber-Band Banjos and Java Jive Bass* has great directions for playing a water glass version of "Twinkle, Twinkle Little Star."

Story

Tell "The Horse-Head Fiddle" or almost any of the other musical tales from *Play Me a Story* by Adler and Cencetti. If you can borrow items from a museum collection of musical instruments, show the children whichever instruments relate to the story you tell. For "The Horse-Head Fiddle" show the children what a Mongolian fiddle looks like (there is an illustration in the book if you can't get the real thing).

Participation Activity

Divide the children into three groups. Assign Group One to be fiddles, Group Two to be trombones and Group Three to be drums. Sing or recite "The Young Musician," a German and Danish folk song from *Listen! and Help Tell the Story*, by Bernice Wells Carlson.

Craft—Pie-Pan Shake, Rattle, and Roller

Materials: Single-hole punch; two eight-inch aluminum pie pans; plastic lacing; pony beads or any large-holed beads or bells; uncooked rice or dried beans; sharpened pencil; cork.

Procedure: Ahead of time punch eight matching holes about one to two inches apart just inside the rims of the pie pans. Cut plastic lacing into two-foot lengths.

At the program explain to the children that this musical instrument is both a rattle to shake and a tambourine to bang on. For the rattle, put a small handful of rice or beans into one plate. Lower the second plate onto the first plate so that the insides face each other. Match up the rim holes. Weave the plastic lacing through the rim holes to attach the two plates together. Children can use the lacing to attach a few beads or bells while they are threading it through the holes. Children who need extra plastic lacing should tie a new piece onto the old piece and continue threading. Push a pencil into a cork to make a padded beater. Strike up some rousing marching band music, and have the children grab their pie-pan instruments and join the parade.

Suggested Booktalk Titles

Picture Books

Isadora, Rachel. *Ben's Trumpet*. Greenwillow, 1979.
Kuskin, Karla. *The Philharmonic Gets Dressed*. Harper & Row, 1982.
Moss, Lloyd. *Zin Zin Zin! A Violin!* Simon & Schuster, 1995.
Raschka, Chris. *Charlie Parker Played Be-Bop*. Orchard, 1992.
Steig, William. *Zeke Pippin*. HarperCollins, 1994.
Waddell, Martin. *The Happy Hedgehog Band*. Candlewick, 1992.

Easy Readers

Diller, Harriet. *Big Band Sound*. Boyds Mills, 1996.
Fair, David. *The Fabulous Four Skunks*. Houghton, 1996.
Isherwood, Shirley. *The Band Over the Hill*. Hutchinson, 1997.
Millman, Isaac. *Moses Goes to a Concert*. Farrar, 1998.
Nygaard, Elizabeth. *Snake Alley Band*. Doubleday, 1998.

Sharmat, Marjorie Weinman. *Nate the Great and the Musical Note*. Coward-McCann, 1990.

Chapter Books

Namioka, Lensey. *Yang the Younger and His Terrible Ear*. Joy Street, 1992.
Nichol, Barbara. *Beethoven Lives Upstairs*. Orchard, 1993. Also the video and the sound recording.

Folklore

Bartos-Hoppner, Barbara. *The Pied Piper of Hamelin*. Lippincott, 1985.
Ober, Hal. *How Music Came to the World*. Houghton, 1994.
Wilhelm, Hans. *The Bremen Town Musicians*. Scholastic, 1992.

Nonfiction

Ardley, Neil. *Music*. Knopf, 1989.
Les Chats Peles. *Long Live Music!* Harcourt, 1995.
Pfeffer, Wendy. *Sounds All Around*. HarperCollins, 1999.
Pillar, Marjorie. *Join the Band!* HarperCollins, 1992.

Biography

Greene, Carol. *John Philip Sousa: The March King*. Children's Press, 1992.
Orgill, Roxanne. *If I Only Had a Horn: Young Louis Armstrong*. Houghton, 1997.

Poetry

Strickland, Michael R., ed. *Poems That Sing to You*. Boyds Mills, 1993.

Just for Fun

Doney, Meryl. *Musical Instruments (World Crafts)*. Watts, 1995.
Drew, Helen. *My First Music Book: A Life-Size Guide to Making and Playing Simple Musical Instruments*. Dorling Kindersley, 1993.
Fiarotta, Noel, and Phyllis Fiarotta. *Music Crafts for Kids: The How-To Book of Music Discovery*. Sterling, 1993.

Other Resources

Adler, Naomi, and Greta Cencetti. *Play Me a Story: 9 Tales About Musical Instruments*. Millbrook, 1997.
Carlson, Bernice Wells. *Listen! and Help Tell the Story*. Abingdon, 1965. Contains the song "The Young Musician."

Cook, Deanna F., ed. *Disney's Family Fun Crafts*. Hyperion, 1997. Shows a paper plate tambourine with jingle bells.

Hannaford Street Silver Band. *Bring on the Brass* (sound recording). Mark Rubin, 1990.

Mattox, Cheryl Warren. *Let's Get the Rhythm of the Band* (sound recording). Warren-Mattox Productions, 1994.

Pellowski, Anne. *The Story Vine: A Source Book of Unusual and Easy-to-Tell Stories from Around the World*. Macmillan, 1984. Includes stories to tell with a thumb piano. See Other Resources in "The Big Meow" unit.

Prokofiev, Sergey. *Peter and the Wolf: Op. 67, A Musical Tale for Children* (sound recording).

Sabbeth, Alex. *Rubber-Band Banjos and Java Jive Bass: Projects and Activities on the Science of Music and Sound*. Wiley, 1997. Directions for playing a water glass version of "Twinkle, Twinkle Little Star."

Sitarz, Paula Gaj. *Picture Book Story Hours: From Birthdays to Bears*. Libraries Unlimited, 1987. See "Let's Make Music."

Sitarz, Paula Gaj. *Story Time Sampler*. Libraries Unlimited, 1997. See the "Music and Musicians" section.

Sousa, John Philip. *Stars and Stripes Forever* (sound recording). Odyssey, 1984.

Umnik, Sharon Dunn, ed. *175 Easy-to-do Everyday Crafts*. Boyds Mills, 1995. Directions for a simple pie pan tambourine.

Stuff and Nonsense

— *Silly Stories and Poems*

Bulletin Board

Use the poem "The Owl and the Pussycat" as inspiration for a wacky bulletin board. Make sure to include a pea-green boat, a honey jar, a small guitar, a pig with a ring in his nose, a turkey dressed like a minister, etc.

Background Music

Play some silly novelty songs from *The Giving Tree and Other Shel Silverstein Songs* or recordings of songs by novelty artists such as "Weird Al" Yankovic.

Opening Activity

Talk to the children about the concept of nonsense. Ask them what they think the word "nonsense" means (it describes something that makes "no sense.") Explain that nonsense songs, stories, or poems are so silly or so exaggerated that no one could possibly believe that they are true. They are also meant to make us laugh. Have the children do some nonsensical things such as bending down, looking through their legs, and making silly faces. Sing: "London Bridge Is Falling Up" from *The Fireside Book of Fun and Game Songs*, edited by Marie Winn. You could also read some humorous verses by Shel Silverstein.

Story

Tell "The Pugilist and His Wonderful Helpers" from *A World of Nonsense* by Carl Withers, *The Fool of the World and the Flying Ship* by Christopher Denise, or *The Three Sillies* by Paul Galdone.

Participation Activity

Have the children join in a dramatic recitation of the poem "Jabberwocky" by Lewis Carroll. This will work best if the presenter has the poem memorized. The children can act out the part of the devoted father, the brave son stalking the monster and the ferocious Jabberwock himself. Be sure to really ham up the sword play and the beheading of the monster.

Craft—Coat-Hanger Fool

Materials: Two metal coat hangers; construction paper; patterns; six large pom-poms; masking tape; construction paper; glue stick; pencil; scissors.

Procedure: Ahead of time for each child, cut out two construction paper circles about 4.5 inches in diameter, a fool's cap, eyes, nose, mouth, and three pairs of buttons (see patterns). Trace a pair of hands and a pair of feet onto doubled construction paper and cut them out (this should result in four hands and four feet). Tape the bottom edges of the two coat hangers together by wrapping masking tape securely around both.

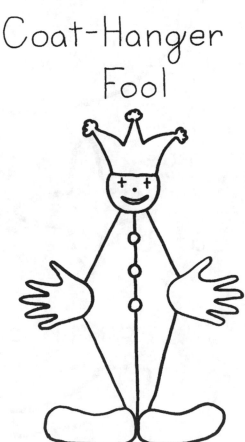

At the program construct the fool by gluing a set of cutout hands together over one of the coat hanger hooks and then doing the same with the other set of hands. Glue the two circles together for a head with one end of the hangers between them. Glue the two sets of shoes at the other end the same way. Glue facial features and a fool's cap onto the head. Glue three sandwiched pairs of buttons onto the center bar where the hangers meet.

Glue pom-poms onto the peaks of the fool's cap and onto the buttons.

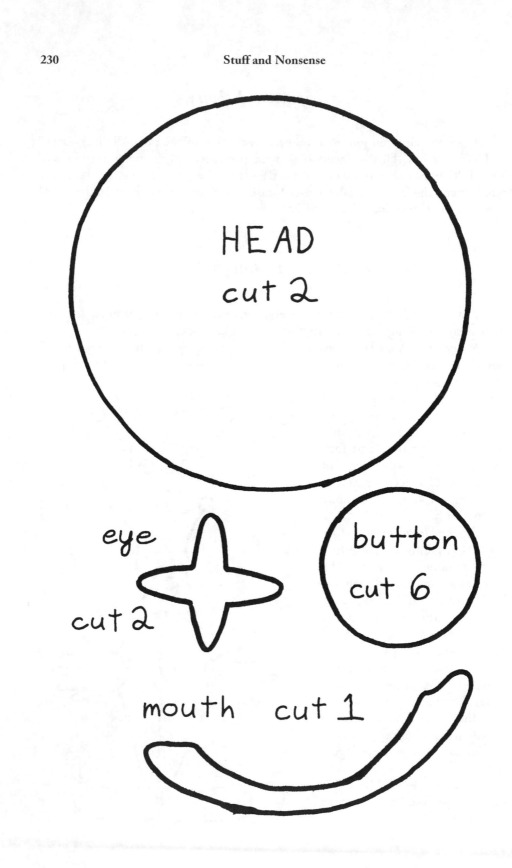

HEAD
cut 2

eye
cut 2

button
cut 6

mouth   cut 1

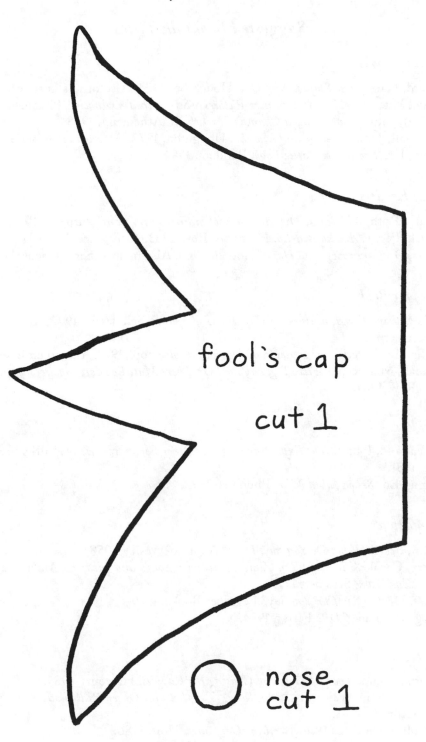

fool's cap
cut 1

nose
cut 1

Suggested Booktalk Titles

Picture Books

Allard, Harry. *The Stupids Step Out*. Houghton, 1974. Also others in series.
Anno, Mitsumasa. *Upside-Downers: Pictures to Stretch the Imagination*. Philomel, 1988.
Barrett, Judi. *Cloudy with a Chance of Meatballs*. Atheneum, 1978.
Marshall, James. *George and Martha*. Houghton, 1972. Also others in series.
Seuss, Dr. *The Butter Battle Book*. Random, 1984.

Easy Readers

Krauss, Ruth. *A Hole Is to Dig: A First Book of First Definitions*. Harper & Row, 1952.
Parish, Peggy. *Amelia Bedelia*. Harper & Row, 1963. Also others in series.
Seuss, Dr. *Green Eggs and Ham*. Random, 1960. Also many other Dr. Seuss books.

Chapter Books

Pilkey, Dav. *The Adventures of Captain Underpants*. Scholastic, 1997. Also others in series.
Sachar, Louis. *Sideways Stories from Wayside School*. Knopf, 1978. Also others in series.
Sendak, Maurice. *Higglety Pigglety Pop! Or, There Must Be More to Life*. Harper & Row, 1967.

Folklore

McFarland, John B. *The Exploding Frog and Other Fables from Aesop*. Little, Brown, 1981.
Young, Ed. *Seven Blind Mice*. Philomel, 1992.

Nonfiction

Joslin, Sesyle. *What Do You Say, Dear?* Addison-Wesley, 1958.
Korty, Carol. *Silly Soup: Ten Zany Plays, with Songs and Ideas for Making Them Your Own*. Scribner, 1977.
Seuss, Dr. *Oh Say Can You Say?* Beginner Books, 1979.
Steig, William. *CDB?* Farrar, 1984.

Poetry

Adoff, Arnold. *The Cabbages Are Chasing the Rabbits*. Harcourt, 1985.
Brewton, Sara Westbrook. *My Tang's Tungled and Other Ridiculous Situations*. Crowell, 1973.
Carroll, Lewis. *The Walrus and the Carpenter*. Holt, 1986.
Cole, William. *Oh, What Nonsense! Poems*. Viking, 1966.

Lear, Edward. *The Owl and the Pussycat*. Putnam, 1991.

Mahy, Margaret. *Nonstop Nonsense*. M.K. McElderry, 1989.

Prelutsky, Jack. *Ride a Purple Pelican*. Greenwillow, 1986. Also others by this author.

Tripp, Wallace. *A Great Big Ugly Man Came Up and Tied His Horse to Me: A Book of Nonsense Verse*. Little, Brown, 1973.

Yolen, Jane. *How Beastly! A Menagerie of Nonsense Poems*. Wordsong, 1980.

Just for Fun

Hall, Katy, and Lisa Eisenberg. *Puppy Riddles*. Dial, 1998. Also others by these authors.

Keller, Charles, ed. *Take Me to Your Liter: Science and Math Jokes*. Pippin, 1991. Also others by Keller.

Other Resources

Anderson, Celia Catlett, and Marilyn Fain Apseloff. *Nonsense Literature for Children: Aesop to Seuss*. Shoe String Press, 1989.

Betz, Adrienne, and Lucia Monfried, eds. *Diane Goode's Book of Silly Stories and Songs*. Dutton, 1992.

Carroll, Lewis. *Jabborwocky: From Through the Looking Glass*. Abrams, 1996.

Cohn, Amy L., ed. *From Sea to Shining Sea*. Scholastic, 1993. See "No-Sense Nonsense."

Cole, Joanna, and Stephanie Calmenson, eds. *The Laugh Book: A New Treasury of Humor for Children*. Doubleday, 1986.

Demento, Dr. *The Greatest Novelty Records of All Time* (sound recording). Rhino, 1991.

Denise, Christopher. *The Fool of the World and the Flying Ship*. Philomel, 1994.

Galdone, Paul. *The Three Sillies*. Clarion, 1981.

Hewitt, Kathryn. *The Three Sillies*. Harcourt, 1986.

Silverstein, Shel. *Falling Up*. HarperCollins, 1996.

Silverstein, Shel. *The Giving Tree and Other Shel Silverstein Songs* (sound recording).

Silverstein, Shel. *A Light in the Attic*. Harper & Row, 1981.

Silverstein, Shel. *Where the Sidewalk Ends*. Harper & Row, 1974.

Sitarz, Paula Gaj. *Story Time Sampler*. Libraries Unlimited, 1997. See the "Lazies, Sillies, and Fools" section.

Umnik, Sharon Dunn. *175 Easy-to-Do Everyday Crafts*. Boyds Mill, 1995. Directions for how to make Hanger People.

Winn, Marie, ed. *The Fireside Book of Fun and Game Songs*. Simon & Schuster, 1974.

Withers, Carl. *I Saw a Rocket Walk a Mile: Nonsense Tales, Chants, and Songs from Many Lands*. Holt, 1965.

Withers, Carl. *A World of Nonsense: Strange and Humorous Tales from Many Lands*. Holt, 1968. "The Ship That Sailed on Water and on Land" is another version of *The Fool of the World and the Flying Ship*.

Yankovic, Weird Al. *Dare to Be Stupid* (sound recording). Rock n' Roll Records, 1985. Other recordings by him are also fun.

Tiny Folk

Little People

Bulletin Board

In the center of the bulletin board, create a giant red and white spotted mushroom in a field of flowers. Underneath the mushroom make an elf taking a snooze. Post pictures all around of leprechauns, dwarfs, gnomes, trolls, fairies, Munchkins, and other little people from various stories and cultures.

Background Music

Make a recording of songs to evoke images of little people: "A Little Bit Me, a Little Bit You" (The Monkees), "Baby Face" (Al Jolson), "Short People—Children's Version" (Randy Newman), "I'm Glad I'm Me" (from *Barnum*). You may also wish to play selections of Munchkin songs from *The Wizard of Oz* or fairy songs from "The Nutcracker Suite."

Opening Activity

Sing "Thumbelina."
Materials: Cloth; rubber bands; felt-tip pens (optional).
Hand out small squares of cloth and tiny rubber bands—the kind that are small enough to fit around a child's thumb without doubling. Show the children how to make thumb people by putting the cloth over their thumbs and securing it with the rubber band. You may wish to hand out felt-tip pens so that the children can draw faces on their thumb people. Sing the song "Thumbelina" and teach the children to join in on the refrain while they make their thumb people dance.

Story

Tell "The Knee-High Man" from *Multicultural Folktales: Stories to Tell to Young Children*, by Judy Sierra and Robert Kaminski, or a selection from *Little Folk: Stories from Around the World*, by Paul Robert Walker.

Participation Activity

Adapt a play version of the "Tom Thumb" folktale and have the children act it out.

Materials: A construction-paper leaf for a hat; a teacup (or box) for a bathtub; puppets or costumes as needed; enough copies of the script for all the people who will participate.

There are different versions of this story—tailor yours to accommodate the number of children you plan to have at the program.

Craft—Cork People

Materials: Bottle cork; corrugated cardboard; two googly eyes; sequins; feathers; six-inch pipe cleaners or chenille stems; small pieces of colored fabric; pompoms; yarn; any other small decorative items; glue stick; scissors.

Procedure: Ahead of time cut the cardboard into small squares approximately 3" × 3". Cut the colored fabric into circles, squares, circles, rectangles, and triangles.

At the program have the children make their own little folk by decorating the corks. They can glue on the googly eyes and use yarn or pom-poms for hair. Yarn is also handy for tying scraps of cloth around the body of the cork person for clothing. Make a pair of arms by wrapping a six-inch pipe cleaner around the cork and giving it a twist or two to secure it. Anyone who would like a display stand for their cork person may glue it onto a square of cardboard.

Suggested Booktalk Titles

Picture Books

Alexander, Lloyd. *The House Gobbaleen*. Dutton, 1995.
Beneduce, Ann. *Gulliver's Adventures in Lilliput*. Philomel, 1993.
Brennan, Patricia D. *Hitchety Hatchety Up I Go!* Macmillan, 1985.
Carrick, Donald. *Morgan and the Artist*. Clarion, 1985.
Pacovska, Kveta. *The Little Flower King*. Simon & Schuster, 1991.

Easy Readers

Peterson, John Lawrence. *The Littles*. Scholastic, 1967. Also others in the series.
Seuss, Dr. *Horton Hears a Who!* Random, 1954.

Chapter Books

Banks, Lynne Reid. *The Fairy Rebel*. Avon, 1989.
Banks, Lynne Reid. *The Indian in the Cupboard*. Doubleday, 1980. Also others in the series.

Eager, Edward. *Knight's Castle*. Harcourt, 1956.
Norton, Mary. *The Borrowers*. Harcourt, 1981. Also others in the series.
Winthrop, Elizabeth. *The Castle in the Attic*. Holiday, 1985.

Folklore

Andersen, Hans Christian. *Thumbeline*. Alphabet, 1985.
Calhoun, Mary. *The Goblin Under the Stairs*. Morrow, 1968.
Fawcett, Melissa Jayne, and Joseph Bruchac. *Makiawisug: The Gift of the Little People*. Little People Pub. Co., 1997.
Galdone, Paul. *The Teeny-Tiny Woman*. Clarion, 1984.
Jarrell, Randall. *Snow-White and the Seven Dwarfs*. Farrar, 1972.
MacDonald, Margaret Read. *The Old Woman Who Lived in a Vinegar Bottle*. August House, 1995.
Sewall, Marcia. *The Wee, Wee Mannie and the Big, Big Coo: A Scottish Folk Tale*. Little, Brown, 1977.

Biography

Cross, Helen Reeder. *The Real Tom Thumb*. Four Winds, 1980.

Other Resources

Arlen, Harold. *The Wizard of Oz* (sound recording). MGM, 1956.
Betting, Natalia. *Elves and Ellefolk: Tales of the Little People*. Holt, 1961.
Goode, Diane. *Diane Goode's Book of Giants and Little People*. Dutton, 1997.
Loesser, Frank. *Danny Kaye Sings Selections from the Samuel Goldwyn Technicolor Production "Hans Christian Andersen"* (sound recording). MCA, 1973. Track: "Thumbelina."
Raffi. *Rise and Shine* (sound recording). Troubadour, 1982. Track: "Thumbelina."
Sierra, Judy, and Robert Kaminski. *Multicultural Folktales: Stories to Tell to Young Children*. Oryx, 1991. See "The Knee-High Man."
Walker, Paul Robert. *Little Folk: Stories from Around the World*. Harcourt, 1997.

Here are a few versions of the Tom Thumb folktale:
Bell, Anthea. *Tom Thumb*. Larousse, 1976.
Hoffman, Felix. *Tom Thumb: The Story by the Brothers Grimm*. Atheneum, 1973.
Watson, Richard Jesse. *Tom Thumb*. Harcourt, 1989.

Toyland

Toys and Puppets

Bulletin Board

Cut out pictures of dolls, teddy bears, rocking horses, and other toys from magazines and catalogs. Post a background on the bulletin board to resemble the inside of a toy store. Place the smaller toys on shelves and the larger toys on the floor of the shop.

Background Music

Play music from *The Nutcracker Suite, Babes in Toyland,* or the *Toy Story* sound-track.

Opening Activity

Sing "The Marvelous Toy" by Tom Paxton with the children.

Story

There are many classic stories of toys that come to life, such as *The Velveteen Rabbit* by Margery Williams, *Pinocchio* by Carlo Collodi, *Winnie the Pooh* by A.A. Milne, or the *Raggedy Anne and Andy* stories, by Johnny Gruelle. Choose a selection from your favorite to tell.

Participation Activity

Tell the children that you are a toy maker, and that they are all going to be parts in a moving toy you create. Line them up and assign each child a movement and a sound to go along with it. One child will move at a time, and his motion will cause the next child to move, and so on. For example, one child can clap his hands, them bend over to touch the person next to him. This child can spin around, saying "whee!" then tap the next child. This person can puff out his cheeks and then smack them with his hands, making the sound of escaping air. You can wind a make-believe key to set the toy machine in motion. Or, talk children through "Kids in Toyland" from *Movement Stories for Children* by Helen Landalf and Pamela Gerke.

Craft—Puppets

Materials: Toilet paper tube; construction paper; colorful fabric cut in a ten-inch circle; construction paper in assorted colors; stick-on dots; glue stick and liquid glue; scissors; markers.

Procedure: Ahead of time cut the toilet paper tube in half and cover one half with construction paper. Cut out the fabric circle. Drape the fabric on a child's hand (yours is too big) to determine where his thumb and pinkie finger (the puppet's arms) and his middle three fingers (for the toilet paper tube head) would poke through. Cut the holes for the puppet's arms (a child's thumb and pinkie), being careful to not make them too big. Also cut geometric paper shapes in various sizes that the children can glue onto the tube for the puppets' eyes, nose, mouth, ears, and hair. Cut out a half-circle (see the pattern in "Blast Off!") of construction paper. Fold and glue it into a cone that will fit onto the tube as the puppet's hat.

At the program let the children decorate the toilet paper tube heads. Glue on the hats by dipping one edge of the toilet paper tube into liquid glue and pressing the cone onto it. Show the children how to drape the fabric on their hands and place the puppet heads over their middle fingers.

Suggested Booktalk Titles

Picture Books

Freeman, Don. *Corduroy*. Puffin, 1976.
Lionni, Leo. *Alexander and the Wind-up Mouse*. Pantheon, 1969.
Ogburn, Jacqueline K. *The Magic Nesting Doll*. Dial, 2000.
Polacco, Patricia. *Babushka's Doll*. Simon & Schuster, 1990.

Chapter Books

Ahlberg, Janet. *The Bear Nobody Wanted*. Viking, 1992.
Banks, Lynne Reid. *The Indian in the Cupboard*. Doubleday, 1980.
Hoban, Russell. *The Mouse and His Child*. Dell, 1990.
Thurber, James. *The Great Quillow*. Harcourt, 1975.
Winthrop, Elizabeth. *The Castle in the Attic*. Holiday, 1985.

Folklore

Andersen, Hans Christian. *The Steadfast Tin Soldier*. Putnam, 1996.

Nonfiction

McNiven, Helen. *Toys and Games*. Thomson Learning, 1995.
Prince, Pamela. *Toyland: Classic Illustrations of Children and Their Toys*. Harmony, 1990.

Biography

Greene, Carol. *Margarete Steiff: Toy Maker*. Children's Press, 1993.

Just for Fun

Bingham, Carol, and Karen Foster, eds. *Crafts for Play*. Millbrook, 1993.
Churchill, E. Richard. *Paper Toys That Fly, Soar, Zoom & Whistle*. Sterling, 1989.
Hancock, Jill. *The Grolier Kidscrafts Toy Book*. Grolier, 1997.
Wallace, Mary. *I Can Make Puppets*. Penworthy, 1994.

Other Resources

Collodi, Carlo. *Pinocchio*. Philomel, 1996.
Gruelle, Johnny. *Raggedy Ann and Andy's Sunny Stories*. Bobbs-Merrill, 1935.
Herbert, Victor. *Babes in Toyland* (sound recording).
Landalf, Helen, and Pamela Gerke. *Movement Stories for Children*. Smith & Kraus, 1996. See "Kids in Toyland."
Milne, A.A. *Winnie the Pooh*. Dutton, 1974.
Newman, Randy. *Toy Story* (sound recording). Walt Disney, 1995.
Paxton, Tom. *The Marvelous Toy*. Morrow, 1996.
Peter, Paul, and Mary. *Peter, Paul and Mommy* (sound recording). Warner, 1990. Track: "The Marvelous Toy."
Tchaikovsky, Peter Ilich. *Nutcracker Suite* (sound recording).
Williams, Margery. *The Velveteen Rabbit*. Knopf, 1984.

Wacky Inventors

Inventions and Inventing

Bulletin Board

Create a colorful maze from cardboard tubes covered with paper and taped together with colored tape. Leave space within the maze for pictures of famous inventors such as Ben Franklin, Thomas Edison, Madam C.J. Walker, the Wright brothers, etc. Show examples of some of the more interesting inventions.

Background Music

Play the soundtrack of a film about an inventor, such as *Chitty Chitty Bang Bang*, or Disney's *Flubber*.

Opening Activity

Share Something Old/Something New.

Show pictures of old-fashioned and modern contraptions (Examples: player piano vs. Sony Walkman, sundial vs. clock, abacus vs. calculator, pencil and paper vs. keyboard, manual vs. electrical tools and appliances, etc.) Have the children guess which pairs of objects go together. Talk about the differences between newer and older ways of doing things.

Story

Tell *Ol' Paul the Mighty Logger; Being a True Account of the Seemingly Incredible Exploits and Inventions of the Great Paul Bunyan* by Glen Rounds, or *To Capture the Wind* by Sheila MacGill-Callahan.

Participation Activity

Invent a giant living Mouse Trap with the children.
Materials: Laundry basket; toy mouse.

Each child uses all or part of their body as a part of the mouse trap. Figure out a way to incorporate each person in to the final product. Think of the board game Mouse Trap in which various cogs, wheels, and slides all effect changes on each other in a chain reaction until finally the basket falls over the mouse. The first child might blow a puff of air which will cause the next child to spin around which will cause the next child to bend over, etc. Have the last child hold an upturned laundry basket to drop over a toy mouse. When you are finished, try it again to see if you can invent a better mouse trap.

Craft—Tissue Box Robots

Materials: Tissue box (the horizontal kind with a long hole in the top—the wider the hole the better); plastic cap from a liquid laundry detergent bottle; wire in various thicknesses and colors; patterns; construction paper; colored tape; metal nuts and bolts; decorative materials such as pom-poms and pipe cleaners; stick-on dots; liquid glue; scissors.

Procedure: Ahead of time trace and cut out pairs of robot hands and feet (see patterns). Also cut strips of construction paper for the arms and legs.

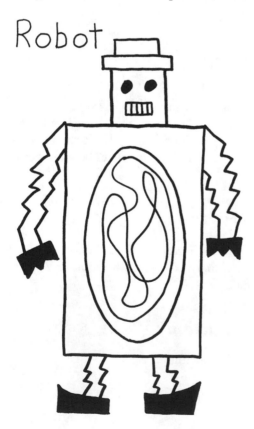

At the program encourage the children to invent their own robots using a tissue box sitting up on one end as a body and a laundry bottle cap for a head (see drawing). Dip the rim of the laundry detergent cap into liquid glue and press it onto one end of the tissue box. Children can fold the construction paper strips accordion-style to use for arms and legs. Inside the tissue box they can make a colorful tangle of wire, nuts, and bolts that will be the robot "guts" and will show through the opening in the tissue box. They can use pom-poms, stick-on dots or other decorations for facial features, etc.

Suggested Booktalk Titles

Picture Books

Christelow, Eileen. *Mr. Murphy's Marvelous Invention*. Clarion, 1983.

Robot Hand

cut 2

Robot Foot

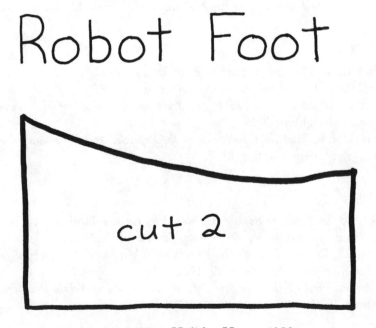

cut 2

Kroll, Steven. *The Hokey-Pokey Man*. Holiday House, 1989.
Walsh, Jill Paton. *Connie Came to Play*. Viking, 1995.
Yorinks, Arthur. *Bravo Minski*. Farrar, 1988.
Yorinks, Arthur. *Ugh*. Farrar, 1990.

Easy Readers

Himmelman, John. *The Day-Off Machine*. Silver Press, 1990.
Holland, Marion. *A Big Ball of String*. Beginner Books, 1993.
Quackenbush, Robert M. *Taxi to Intrigue: A Miss Mallard Mystery*. Prentice Hall,
    1984.
Rau, Dana Meachen. *A Box Can Be Many Things*. Children's Press, 1997.
Ziefert, Harriet. *When the TV Broke*. Puffin, 1984.

Chapter Books

Clements, Andrew. *Frindle*. Simon & Schuster, 1996.
Delany, M.C. *Deep Doo Doo*. Dutton, 1996.
Fleming, Ian. *Chitty Chitty Bang Bang*. Scholastic, 1964.
Getz, David. *Almost Famous*. Holt, 1992.
Hermes, Patricia. *Fly Away Home*. Newmarket, 1996.
Wardlow, Lee. *101 Ways to Bug Your Parents*. Dial, 1996.

Folklore

Britt, Dell. *The Emperor's Big Gift*. Prentice Hall, 1967.
Daniels, Guy. *The Peasant's Pea Patch: A Russian Folktale*. Delacorte, 1971.

Nonfiction

Erlbach, Arlene. *The Kids' Invention Book*. Lerner, 1997.
Hudson, Wade. *Five Notable Inventors*. Scholastic, 1995.
Thimmesh, Catherine. *Girls Think of Everything: Stories of Ingenious Inventions by
    Women*. Houghton, 2000.
Wulffson, Don L. *The Kid Who Invented the Popsicle: And Other Surprising Stories
    About Inventions*. Dutton, 1997.

Biographies

Adler, David A. *A Picture Book of Thomas Alva Edison*. Holiday House, 1996.
Altman, Linda Jacobs. *Women Inventors*. Facts on File, 1997.
Quackenbush, Robert M. *Watt Got You Started, Mr. Fulton? A Story of James Watt
    & Robert Fulton*. Prentice Hall, 1982.
Shea, George. *First Flight: The Story of Tom Tate and the Wright Brothers*. Harper-
    Collins, 1997.

Just for Fun

Carrow, Robert S. *Put a Fan in Your Hat! Inventions, Contraptions, and Gadgets
    Kids Can Build*. Learning Triangle, 1997.

Other Resources

Diehn, Gwen. *Science Crafts for Kids: 50 Fantastic Things to Invent & Create*. Sterling, 1994.

Disney's Flubber (sound recording). Walt Disney Records, 1997.

"Hello, Alexander Graham Bell." *Copycat*. Copycat Press, March/April 1996.

MacGill-Callahan, Sheila. *To Capture the Wind*. Dial, 1997.

Rounds, Glen. *Ol' Paul the Mighty Logger; Being a True Account of the Seemingly Incredible Exploits and Inventions of the Great Paul Bunyan*. Holiday House, 1976.

Sherman, Robert B. *Chitty Chitty Bang Bang* (sound recording). United Artists, 1968.

"Simply Marvelous Machines." *Copycat*. Copycat Press, Jan./Feb. 1999.

Walking Tall

Giants

Bulletin Board

On the left side of the board, make a colorful and cheerful giraffe. In the middle of the board, show the figure of a giant person from the hips down to the feet (you may wish to have a beanstalk winding around his or her legs). On the right side of the board make a figure of Babe, Paul Bunyan's blue ox, which is as tall as the giraffe.

Background Music

Record such hits as "Long Tall Sally" (Little Richard and others), "Tall Enough" (Big Bird—Sesame Street), "Tall in the Saddle" (Joan Armatrading), "Long, Tall Texan" (Murky Vellum), or "Giants in the Sky" (from the soundtrack of *Into the Woods*). Three other sources of giant music are *Giants!*, a sound recording by Jim Weiss, and the music-only sections of the Rabbit Ears recordings of *Jack and the Beanstalk* and *Finn McCoul*.

Opening Activity

Sing, recite, or read "Five Giants" from *Monday's Troll*, by Jack Prelutsky. Divide the children into two groups and see who can shout "Fee Fi Fo Fum" the loudest.

Story

Tell *Golem*, by David Wisniewski or *The Good Giants and the Bad Pukwudgies*, by Jean Fritz.

Participation Activity

Play a game of "Giant Steps" (also called "Mother, May I?") with the children or play the "Elephant and Giraffe" from *Great Games to Play with Groups*, by Franklin W. Harris.

Craft—Coffee Can Stilts

Materials: Two matching coffee cans with plastic lids; rope; self-adhesive stickers; a juice can opener with triangular punch at one end; a hammer; spray paint or self-adhesive contact or shelf paper; scissors.

Procedure: Ahead of time use the juice can opener to punch two opposing holes on each coffee can about one inch from the top end. Flatten all sharp edges with a hammer. Spray paint the cans a bright color or cut self-adhesive contact or shelf paper to fit around the coffee cans. Replace the plastic lids. Cut two pieces of rope at least 48 inches long (or three times the length from a child's knee to the floor).

At the program the children can string the rope through the holes in the cans and knot them inside before they decorate the cans with stickers over a layer of contact paper or spray paint. An adult should check all the knots to make sure that they are secure. To use the stilts, a child should place the cans side by side, grasp the rope handles and carefully step up onto the cans (this is best done with the help of an adult). Pull the ropes taut and walk tall.

Suggested Booktalk Titles

Picture Books

Cuneo, Mary Louise. *What Can a Giant Do?* HarperCollins, 1994.
Hasler, Eveline. *The Giantess*. Kane/Miller, 1997.
Hayes, Sarah. *Mary, Mary*. M.K. McElderry, 1990.
Heller, Nicholas. *The Giant*. Greenwillow, 1997.
Johnston, Tony. *Bigfoot Cinderella*. Putnam, 1998.
Kroll, Steven. *Big Jeremy*. Holiday House, 1989.
Seuss, Dr. *The King's Stilts*. Random, 1967.
Wilde, Oscar. *The Selfish Giant*. Alphabet, 1984.
Yorinks, Arthur. *The Miami Giant*. HarperCollins, 1995.

Easy Readers

Green, John F. *Alice and the Birthday Giant*. Scholastic, 1989.
Waddell, Martin. *Once There Were Giants*. Delacorte, 1989.
Yolen, Jane. *The Giants Go Camping*. Seabury, 1979.

Coffee-Can Stilts

Chapter Books

Dahl, Roald. *The BFG*. Farrar, 1982.
Gerstein, Mordicai. *The Giant*. Hyperion, 1995.
Morpurgo, Michael. *The Sandman and the Turtles*. Philomel, 1994.
Thurber, James. *The Great Quillow*. Harcourt, 1975.

Folklore

Compton, Kenn. *Jack the Giant Chaser: An Appalachian Tale.* Holiday House, 1993.

De la Mare, Walter. *Molly Whuppie.* Farrar, 1983.

dePaola, Tomie. *Fin M'Coul: The Giant of Knockmany Hill.* Holiday House, 1981.

dePaola, Tomie. *The Mysterious Giant of Barletta: An Italian Folktale.* Harcourt, 1984.

De Regniers, Beatrice Schenk. *Jack the Giant Killer: Jack's First and Finest Adventure.* Atheneum, 1987.

Gleeson, Brian. *Finn McCoul.* Rabbit Ears, 1995.

Isaacs, Anne. *Swamp Angel.* Dutton, 1994.

Kellogg, Steven. *Jack and the Beanstalk.* Morrow, 1991.

Kellogg, Steven. *Paul Bunyan: A Tall Tale.* Morrow, 1984.

Osborne, Mary Pope. *Kate and the Beanstalk.* Atheneum, 2000.

San Souci, Robert D. *The Brave Little Tailor.* Doubleday, 1982.

Seeger, Pete. *Abiyoyo: Based on a South African Lullaby and Folk Story.* Macmillan, 1986.

Sloat, Teri. *The Hungry Giant of the Tundra.* Dutton, 1993.

Nonfiction

Fisher, Leonard Everett. *Cyclops.* Holiday House, 1991.

Landau, Elaine. *Standing Tall: Unusually Tall People.* Watts, 1997.

Wadsworth, Ginger. *Giant Sequoia Trees.* Lerner, 1995.

Biography

Ward, Don. *Andre the Giant.* Creative Education, 1986.

Poetry

Wallace, Daisy, ed. *Giant Poems.* Holiday House, 1978.

Just for Fun

Ames, Lee J. *Draw 50 Monsters, Creeps, Superheroes, Demons, Dragons, Nerds, Dirts, Ghouls, Giants, Vampires, Zombies, and Other Curiosa...* Doubleday, 1983.

Other Resources

Cole, Joanna. *Pin the Tail on the Donkey and Other Party Games.* Morrow, 1993. Includes directions on how to play "Giant Steps."

Cook, Deanna F., ed. *Disney's Family Fun Crafts.* Hyperion, 1997. Contains directions for coffee can stilts.

Finnigan, Joan. *Look! The Land Is Growing Giants: A Very Canadian Legend.* Tundra, 1983.

Fritz, Jean. *The Good Giants and the Bad Pukwudgies*. Putman, 1982. Materials for telling this story: A map of Martha's Vineyard, Cape Cod, and Nantucket, especially if it shows the territories of the Wampanoag Indians.

Gleeson, Brain. *Finn McCoul* (sound recording). Rabbit Ears, 1991.

Goode, Diane. *Diane Goode's Book of Giants and Little People*. Dutton, 1997.

Harris, Franklin W. *Great Games to Play with Groups: A Leader's Guide*. Fearon, 1990. See "Elephant and Giraffe."

Metaxas, Eric. *Jack and the Beanstalk* (sound recording). Rabbit Ears, 1991.

Prelutsky, Jack. *Monday's Troll* (sound recording). Listening Library, 1996. Track: "Five Giants."

Silverstein, Shel. *Where the Sidewalk Ends*. Harper & Row, 1974. See "Paul Bunyan."

Sitarz, Paula Gaj. *Picture Book Story Hours: From Birthdays to Bears*. Libraries Unlimited, 1970. See "Jolly Giants" section.

Stoutenburg, Adrien. *Fee, Fi, Fo, Fum: Friendly and Funny Giants*. Viking, 1969. Stories from Irish, African, and Native American traditions, among others, are represented in this collection.

Walker, Paul Robert. *Giants! Stories from Around the World*. Harcourt, 1995.

Weiss, Jim. *Giants! A Colossal Collection of Tales & Tunes* (sound recording). Greathall, 1996.

Wisniewski, David. *Golem*. Clarion, 1996.

Western Roundup

Cowboys and Cowgirls

Bulletin Board

Mount a background of green construction paper (for grass) on the lower half of the bulletin board, and blue paper (for sky) on the upper half. Arrange a scene of cowboys and cowgirls on horses following a few head of cattle. One of the cowpokes can be on a bucking bronco. Add a border of symbols representing various cattle brands.

Background Music

Play some old cowboy standards by Gene Autry, Roy Rogers, and other folksy country and western singers.

Opening Activity

Place some twigs within a circle of stones so that it resembles a campfire. Have the children sit around the campfire and sing a few cowboy songs, such as "Home on the Range," "Happy Trails," and "I'm an Old Cowhand."

Story

There are many versions of "Pecos Bill" available. Choose one from a book of tall tales or try the humorous song rendition in *For a Cowboy Has to Sing*.

Participation Activity

Dance the "Old Virginia Reel" or a simple square dance with the children.

Craft—Cowpoke Vests

Materials: Large, plain brown paper bag; various colors of construction paper; glue stick; colored pencils, crayons and markers; scissors.

Procedure: Ahead of time cut the brown paper bags up the middle, and cut holes for the neck and arms so that the bags look like vests. You can also cut the bottom edges of the vests to add fringe. Cut out the western symbols—sheriff stars, cactus, horseshoes, diamonds, and other shapes (see patterns)—from contruction paper.

At the program let children decorate their vests by drawing cowboy scenes or gluing on cutout designs.

Suggested Booktalk Titles

Picture Books

Gerrard, Roy. *Rosie and the Rustlers*. Farrar, 1989.
Lowell, Susan. *Little Red Cowboy Hat*. Holt, 1996.
Noble, Trinka Hakes. *Meanwhile Back at the Ranch*. Dial, 1987.
Stanley, Diane. *Saving Sweetness*. Putnam, 1996.

Easy Readers

Antle, Nancy. *Sam's Wild West Show*. Dial, 1995.
Byars, Betsy Cromer. *The Golly Sisters Go West*. Harper & Row, 1989.

Folklore

Isaacs, Anne. *Swamp Angel*. Dutton, 1994.
Kellogg, Steven. *Pecos Bill*. Morrow, 1986.

Nonfiction

Gibbons, Gail. *Yippee-Yay! A Book About Cowboys & Cowgirls*. Little, Brown, 1998.

Biography

Pinkney, Andrea Davis. *Bill Pickett, Rodeo Ridin' Cowboy*. Harcourt, 1996.
Quackenbush, Robert M. *Who's That Girl with the Gun? A Story of Annie Oakley*. Prentice Hall, 1988.

Poetry

Prelutsky, Jack. *The Sheriff of Rottenshot*. Morrow, 1982.

COWPOKE VEST

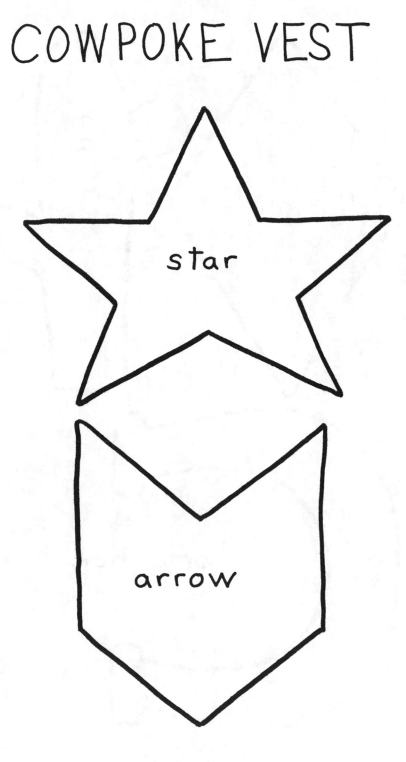

star

arrow

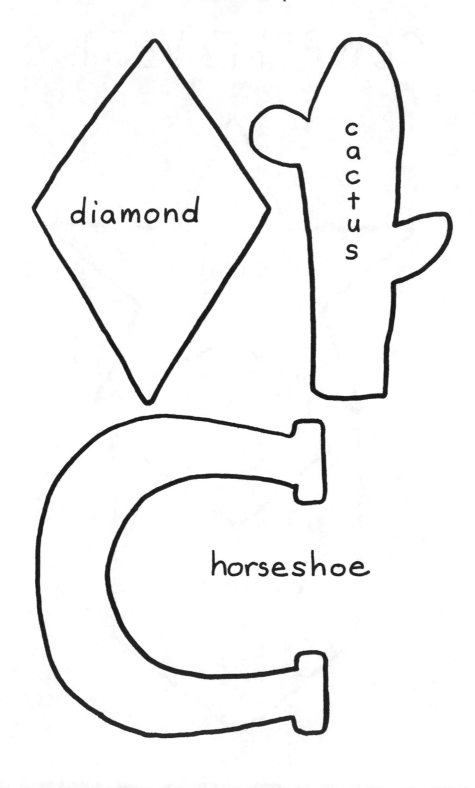

diamond

cactus

horseshoe

Just for Fun

Adler, David A. *Wild Pill Hickok and Other Old West Riddles*. Holiday, 1988.

Zaidenberg, Arthur. *How to Draw the Wild West*. Abelard, 1972.

Other Resources

Artman, John. *Cowboys: An Activity Book*. Good Apple, 1982.

Brokaw, Meredith, and Annie Gilbar. *The Penny Whistle Any Day Is a Holiday Party Book*. Simon & Schuster, 1996. See "Stampede."

Carlson, Laurie. *Westward Ho! An Activity Guide to the Wild West*. Chicago Review, 1996.

Gunzenhauzer, Margot. *The Square Dance and Contra Dance Handbook*. McFarland, 1996.

Hartford, John. *John Hartford Fiddles Wild Hog on the Red Brush and a Bunch of Others You Might Not Have Heard* (sound recording). Rounder Records, 1996. Track: "Old Virginia Reel."

McCowen, Jake. *Cowboy Crafts: Projects with a Western Flair*. Sterling, 1994.

"Recall Y'All." *Copycat*. Copycat Press, Sept./Oct. 1997.

Songs of the Wild West. Simon & Schuster, 1991.

Tinsley, Jim Bob. *For a Cowboy Has to Sing*. University of Central Florida, 1991. See "Pecos Bill."

What's Cooking?

Food Fun

Bulletin Board

Kids who have read Tomie dePaola's *Strega Nona* will recognize this scene. Cut a large cauldron out of black construction paper and place it in the center of the bulletin board. Use various colors of paper to cut out hills, trees, and buildings. Place these all around the cauldron to represent a town in the background. Use white yarn for spaghetti, and tack it up so that the spaghetti is spilling out of the pot and spreading throughout the town. Caption the bulletin board "What's Cooking?"

Background Music

Record several songs from popular music, theater, and movies that are about food. Suggestions include "Food, Glorious Food" (*Oliver*), "Chicken Soup with Rice" (*Really Rosie*), and "Cheeseburger in Paradise" (Jimmy Buffett). *Life Is Sweet* by dani-b is a recording of food songs for kids. Or, for something really goofy, play *The Food Album* by "Weird Al" Yankovic.

Opening Activity

Sing one or more food songs, such as "On Top of Spaghetti," "Found a Peanut," and "Peanut Butter."

Story

Tell the story *Stone Soup*.
Materials: Cooking pot, ladle, three large smooth stones, and several kinds of plastic vegetables. Children can place the items in the pot and stir the "soup" while you tell the story.

Participation Activity

Sing "Aiken Drum" with the children.

Materials: Two easels; two sheets from an art pad; colored markers; ladle.

Teach the children the beginning of this folk song, then invite the children to help you finish the song. Ask them to name different foods to represent the man's head, eyes, nose, ears, mouth, hair, body, arms, hands, fingers, legs, feet, and toes. As the children name the foods, draw the shapes on one sheet of paper, and list the foods on another. When all the body parts are listed, sing the song again all the way through, concluding with, "And his [body part] was made of [food]," etc.

Craft—Pasta Necklaces

Materials: A two-foot length of plastic lacing (gimp); dry pasta in an assortment of shapes (all shapes must have a hole in them wide enough for the lacing to go through); food dye and rubbing alcohol; colored construction paper; scissors; hole punch.

Procedure: Ahead of time dye the pasta in an assortment of colors using the food dye and rubbing alcohol (see instructions in Appendix I.) Cut out one-inch circles of construction paper and punch a hole in each center.

At the program children can string the pasta and paper onto the lacing to design their own necklaces. Make sure there is enough unstrung lacing to knot the ends together, and so that each necklace will fit comfortably over the child's head.

Suggested Booktalk Titles

Picture Books

Barrett, Judi. *Cloudy with a Chance of Meatballs.* Atheneum, 1978.
dePaola, Tomie. *Strega Nona.* Prentice Hall, 1975.
French, Vivian. *Oliver's Vegetables.* Orchard, 1995. Also *Oliver's Fruit Salad.*
McCloskey, Robert. *Blueberries for Sal.* Viking, 1948.

Easy Readers

Farber, Erica. *Purple Pickle Juice.* Random, 1996.
Fleischman, Sid. *McBroom's Ear.* Norton, 1969.

Chapter Books

Catling, Patrick Skene. *The Chocolate Touch.* Bantam, 1996.
Hurwitz, Johanna. *Aldo Ice Cream.* Morrow, 1981. Also others in series.

Folklore

Peck, Jan. *The Giant Carrot*. Dial, 1998.
Stevens, Janet. *Tops and Bottoms*. Harcourt, 1995.

Nonfiction

dePaola, Tomie. *The Popcorn Book*. Holiday, 1978.
Dooley, Norah. *Everybody Cooks Rice*. Carolrhoda, 1991.

Poetry

Lillegard, Dee. *The Wild Bunch*. Putnam, 1997.
Wescott, Nadine Bernard. *Never Take a Pig to Lunch: Poems About the Fun of Eating*. Orchard, 1994.

Just for Fun

Haddad, Helen R. *Potato Printing*. Crowell, 1981.
Keller, Charles. *Belly Laughs: Food Jokes & Riddles*. Simon & Schuster, 1990.
Matthews, Judith. *Oh, How Waffle! Riddles You Can Eat*. Whitman, 1993.
Ralph, Judy, and Ray Gomf. *The Peanut Butter Cookbook for Kids*. Hyperion, 1995.

Other Resources

dani-b. *Life Is Sweet* (sound recording). dani-b, 1998.
Freeman, Judy. *Hi Ho Librario! Songs, Chants and Stories to Keep Kids Humming*. Rock Hill Press, 1997. See "Alligator Pie" section.
Glazer, Tom. *"Eye Winker, Tom Tinker, Chin Chopper: Fifty Musical Fingerplays*. Doubleday, 1973. See "On Top of Spaghetti."
Nelson, Esther L. *The Funny Songbook*. Sterling, 1984. See "The Peanut Butter Song," "On Top of My Pizza," and other songs.
"Pancakes with Purpose." *Copycat*. Copycat Press, Sept./Oct. 1993.
Rosenthal, Phil. *Turkey in the Straw* (sound recording). American Melody, 1985. Track: "Aiken Drum."
Silverstein, Shel. *Where the Sidewalk Ends*. Harper & Row, 1974. See "Peanut Butter Sandwich," "Spaghetti," and "With His Mouth Full of Food."
Sitarz, Paula Gaj. *Picture Book Story Hours: From Birthdays to Bears*. Libraries Unlimited, 1987. See "Yummers: Stories About Food."
Sitarz, Paula Gaj. *Story Time Sampler*. Libraries Unlimited, 1997. See "Cooks and Cookery."
"Soupermarket" and "Dumpling Soup." *Copycat*. Copycat Press, Jan./Feb. 1995.
"Super Sandwiches ... It's in the Bag!" from *Copycat*. Copycat Press, Nov./Dec. 1996.
Yankovic, "Weird Al." *The Food Album* (sound recording). 1993.

The following are versions of the same story:
Brown, Marcia. *Stone Soup*. Scribner, 1947.
Van Rynbach, Iris. *The Soup Stone*. Greenwillow, 1988.

Appendix I—Recipes

Here are some craft recipes to use with some of the StoryCraft projects.

Modeling Dough

Materials: 2 cups flour, 1 cup salt, 4 tsp. cream of tartar, 2 TBS. cooking oil, 2 cups water, 3 quart pan, stove, plastic airtight container (optional: food dye).

Procedure: Mix ingredients in the pan. If you want, use a few drops of food dye to color the dough. Cook over medium heat until it forms a ball and pulls away from the sides. Knead the dough until it is smooth. Store in an airtight container. The clay is soft when in use, but will harden if left uncovered overnight.

Dyeing Pasta

Materials: pasta in assorted shapes—wheels, elbows, bells, etc. If you are going to string the pasta, make sure the holes in these shapes are big enough for the lacing to fit through. Also: rubbing alcohol, various colors of food dye, a deep metal or plastic bowl, rubber gloves, newspapers; plastic table cloth.

Procedure: On a table, spread a plastic tablecloth, and then a few layers of newspapers over that. Wear the rubber gloves to make cleanup easier. In a deep bowl, pour about a half cup of rubbing alcohol (this makes the pasta dry faster.) Add a few drops of food dye. Add some of the pasta, a bit at a time, and mix it around well so the coloring gets into all the pasta crevices. Then lay out the colored pasta on the newspapers to dry overnight. You can experiment with mixing food dye to get various colors. For pastels, use just a few drops of dye. Use more to get brighter colors. When you are done, wash out the bowl immediately so it doesn't stain.

Hardening String

Materials: liquid glue, string, plastic tablecloth.

Procedure: Cut the string to the lengths you want. Dip the ends of the string in liquid glue and lay it on the plastic to dry overnight. This will cause the string ends to harden, making it easier to use as lacing.

Appendix II—Resources

General

Copycat. Copycat Press. Browse through issues of this magazine to find ideas for activities, stories, and crafts.

Bulletin Boards

Fiarotta, Phyllis, and Noel Fiarotta. *Pin It, Tack It, Hang It: The Big Book of Kids' Bulletin Boards.* Workman, 1975.

Wilmes, Liz, and Vohny Moehling. *Everyday Bulletin Boards.* Building Blocks, 1988.

Craft Patterns

Warren, Jean. *Animal Patterns.* Warren (Totline), 1990.

Warren, Jean. *Everyday Patterns.* Warren (Totline), 1990.

Warren, Jean. *Nature Patterns.* Warren (Totline), 1990.

Games

Gregson, Bob. *The Incredible Indoor Games Book: 160 Group Projects, Games, and Activities.* Fearon, 1982.

Harris, Franklin W. *Great Games to Play with Groups: A Leader's Guide.* Fearon, 1990.

Nelson, Esther L. *Movement Games for Children of All Ages.* Sterling, 1975.

Music

Children's Favorite Songs (sound recording). Buena Vista, 1979–1990. Four CDs of classic children's songs performed by the Disneyland Children's Sing-Along Chorus.

Demento, Dr. *The Greatest Novelty Records of All Time* (sound recording). Rhino, 1991.

Demento, Dr. *20th Anniversary Collection* (sound recording). Rhino, 1991. A great source for novelty songs to sing with kids or to play as background music.

Flying Pigs Campfire Songbook. www.argonet.co.uk/users/flying.pigs/frames.html. A scout-sponsored website with lyrics to silly songs and links to other music-related sites.

Green, Jeff. *The Green Book of Songs by Subject: The Thematic Guide to Popular Music.* 4th ed. Professional Desk References, 1995.

The Guidezone Songbook. www.guidezone.skl.com. Another scout-sponsored musical website.

KIDiddles website at www.kididdles.com/mouseum/subject.html. Look here for more lyrics to kids' songs.

Painter, William M. *Musical Story Hours: Using Music with Storytelling and Puppetry.* Library Professional Pubs., 1989.

Reid, Rob. *Children's Jukebox: A Subject Guide to Musical Recordings and Programming Ideas for Songsters Ages One to Twelve.* ALA, 1995.

Two companies that sell lots of folk instruments are Catania Folk Instruments, www.netstuff.com/catania, and Lark in the Morning, www.larkinam.com.

Stories and Folktales

Eastman, Mary Huse, ed. *Index to Fairy Tales, Myths and Legends.* Faxon, 1926 (2nd ed.), 1937 (supp.), 1952 (2nd supp.).

Lima, Carolyn W. *A to Zoo: Subject Access to Children's Picture Books, 5th ed.* Bowker, 1998.

Sprug, Joseph W. *Index to Fairy Tales, 1987–1992, Including 310 Collections of Fairy Tales, Folktales, Myths, and Legends with Significant pre–1987 Titles not Previously Indexed.* Scarecrow, 1994. See also 1915, 1926, 1937, 1952, 1973, 1979, and 1989 editions.

Ziegler, Elsie B. *Folklore: An Annotated Bibliography and Index to Single Editions.* Faxon, 1975.

Index